P9-AOT-643

RESEARCH IN POLITICAL ECONOMY

Volume 1 · 1977

RESEARCH IN POLITICAL ECONOMY

An Annual Compilation of Research

Editor: PAUL ZAREMBKA
Department of Economics
State University of New York
at Buffalo

VOLUME 1 · 1977

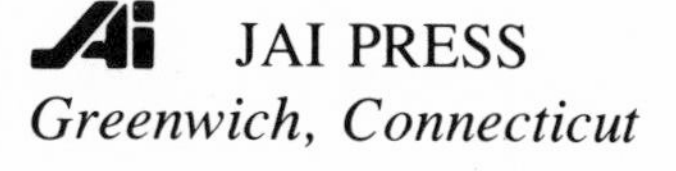

Greenwich, Connecticut

321 Greenwich Avenue
Greenwich, Connecticut 06830

ISBN: 0-89232-020-6
Manufactured in the United States of America

CONTENTS

Foreword

This series of annual volumes is founded on understanding society as a structural unity in contradiction, with political and ideological levels determined in the last instance by the economic structure. The approach, consistent with classical Marxism, thus centers on the concept of mode of production and on class struggle. With emphasis on the capitalist mode of production, some attention is also given to pre-capitalist modes and forms, as well as to socialism as a structural break from the capitalist mode. Both theoretical abstraction and case studies are included.

Ultimately, the purpose of developing theory is to aid the struggle of popular classes against their oppression and for revolutionary change. Indeed, as L. Althusser has remarked (in the supplement to his *Elements of Self-Criticism*), "without a proletarian position in theory (in philosophy), there can be no 'development' of Marxist theory, and no correct Union between the Labor Movement and Marxist Theory."

Paul Zarembka
Editor

RESEARCH IN POLITICAL ECONOMY

Volume 1 · 1977

THE CAPITALIST MODE OF PRODUCTION: ECONOMIC STRUCTURE

Paul Zarembka, STATE UNIVERSITY OF NEW YORK AT BUFFALO

A few elementary principles must guide serious efforts for understanding human society. First, study of humans begins with the same foundation as for other species—namely, the total reproduction process. In other words, how does the society reproduce itself by obtaining necessities and through forms of sexual re-creation? Second, an understanding of human society today is an understanding of human history. Yet, since human history as facts is meaningless, only history organized around the reproduction process is history with a purpose—the purpose of understanding the human society today and changing its conditions for the future. The conceptual tool for organizing understanding of this reproduction process is the *mode of production,* consisting of political and ideological levels determined in the last instance by an economic structure—that structure being the means (land and instruments of production) and social relations of production by which humans reproduce under the domination of those social relations.

In this paper the broad outlines of the economic structure of the capitalist mode of production are developed. An underlying proposition is that Marx's concept of the *accumulation of capital* is fundamentally the extension of the capital-labor social relation. As such, this concept has been very loosely used by Marxists; i.e., bourgeois ideology has penetrated through distorting the structural dominance of social relations of production on productive forces by leveling social relations with productive forces.

1. PRECAPITALIST MODES OF PRODUCTION[1] AND THEIR DEVELOPMENT OF PRODUCTIVE FORCES

In the *primitive mode of production* the producers themselves control the means of production. Any surpluses produced above subsistence needs (including needs for replacements of worn-out instruments of production) are consumed, exchanged within a community or between communities for culturally defined *equivalents,* or used for "ceremonies."[2] The society is "primitive" only in the sense that agricultural instruments are primitive relative to modern[3] and that products are used in their original form (including handicrafts); manufacturing is unknown. Human societies may have lived everywhere in this mode until the (apparent) beginnings of class society around 3500 B.C. in the Near East (and around 1000 B.C. in Middle America).[4] Sub-Sahara Africa may have been principally in the primitive agricultural mode of production right up until colonialism.[5]

The primitive society offers a concrete means of indicating that the development of productive forces of man-to-nature is socially conditioned. The purpose of remarking on the topic is that the argument of the remaining sections depends upon thoroughly understanding the extent to which the development of productive forces is indeed socially conditioned, at least beyond survival needs. In any case, Sahlins (1972, p. 13) concludes, from anthropological evidence, that:

> . . . at least as concerned nonsubsistence goods, . . . [the hunter's] wants are scarce and his means (in relation) plentiful. Consequently, he is "comparatively free of material pressures," has "no sense of possession," shows "an undeveloped sense of property," is "completely indifferent to any material pressures," manifests a "lack of interest" in developing his technological equipment.

And (Sahlins, 1972, p. 41) that in the " main run of [primitive societies], agricultural as well as preagricultural, . . . labor power is underused, technological means are not fully engaged, natural resources are left untapped." In other words, the character of primitive society is one of few needs, relatively abundant means for satisfying those needs, and (thus) considerable leisure for all—in short, an "affluent" society. Of course, the contradiction is that abundant means can give way to scarce means as population grows or climate changes (or other natural events occur).

The primitive society is structurally prepared to search for appropriate responses to changes in man's relationship to nature, but not a society based upon a *slave mode of production*. The foundation of such a society is a class of people, slaves, who are totally controlled by another class, citizens. The citizens allocate all work of production to the slaves and are totally at leisure (the image of grapes being dropped by beautiful female/male slaves into the mouths of male/female citizens lying on couches is quite illuminating once it is remembered that other slaves in turn grew the grapes, and probably built the couches). The separation of citizens from work is even so great that the managers of the slaves in the fields are usually themselves slaves, that the citizens live in cities physically separated from production, and that the citizens, as an ideology of the system, detest manual work and glorify "culture" (see Anderson, 1974a, Chapter 1). Graeco-Roman Antiquity was founded on such a slave mode of production. The decisive advantage at that time of the Mediterranean area for a slave mode of production was that the rural/urban disjuncture implies heavy transportation costs if undertaken by land, but very much less if undertaken by sea; the Mediterranean amounted to a large inland sea (see Anderson, 1974a, pp. 19–21).

Such a social system does not condition attention to the development of productive forces (even if a few developments of course do occur) since all surpluses of the only class concerned with production, the slaves, are expropriated by the citizen class and since the ideology of detesting work diverts attention. As a consequence, the social history of the Graeco-Roman period is a history of military conquest. For "military power was more closely locked to economic growth than in perhaps any other mode of production, before or since, because the main single origin of slave-labor was normally captured prisoners of war, while the raising of free urban troops for war depended on the maintenance of production at home by slaves; battlefields provided the manpower for cornfields, and, *vice-versa,* captive laborers permitted the creation of citizen armies" (Anderson, 1974a, p. 28).

The Graceo-Roman period seems to have broken down under the weight of its resistance to the development of productive forces when needed, climaxed by the Germanic invasions beginning in 406 A.D. But before turning to the resulting feudal mode of production we should remark that, historically, the slave mode of production was not free from other modes and forms of production. The point to note is that the *social formation* (see Poulantzas, 1973, pp. 15–16) was characterized by the dominance of the slave mode, while other modes and forms were preserved in it.[6]

The *feudal mode of production*[7] is founded on a rural lord-serf relation in which a lord has control over the use of a land area and the serf is allowed to work the land in return for labor services, rents in kind, or customary dues to the lord. Unlike slavery, the serf is not owned and is not bought and sold as a commodity. The lord obtains his property rights from a superior noble, in return for provision of a military in time of war, the nobles leading up in a pyramiding structure to the monarch. The geographical space between the manors can be occupied by non-feudal forms of agricultural production, as well as by independent towns of merchants and of guilds and corporations for manufacturing (often, in Western Europe, of woollen textiles). Production of the town is generally bought and sold as commodities, including to the manors, while the production of the manor is usually exchanged in kind, except the portion sent to the towns.

Relative to the slave mode of production, this mode of production does permit some development of productive forces. "For the feudal mode of production that had emerged in Western Europe generally afforded the peasantry the minimal space to increase the yield at its own disposal, within the harsh constraints of manorialism. The typical peasant had to provide labor rents on the seigneurial demesne—often up to three days a week—and numerous additional dues; he was nevertheless free to try to increase output on his own strips in the rest of the week." (Anderson, 1974a, p. 185). Furthermore, the lord is indirectly concerned with production by being directly concerned with extracting more rent, rent needed to keep up with the increasing aristocratic drive for luxury consumption.

The classic cases of the feudal mode of production are Western Europe of the Middle Ages and Japan until the events leading up to the Meiji Restoration of 1867–1868. Interpretation of the disintegration of this mode should center on dialectics of class relations. Yet, Anderson (1974a, p. 197) locates it in the increasing population which pushed production onto marginal lands, combined with the devastation wrought by the Black Death in 1348 and with the increase of money debts of the manors to the towns; Wallerstein (1974, p. 37) argues that "it is most plausible to operate on the assumption that the 'crisis of feudalism' represented a conjuncture of secular trends, an immediate cyclical crisis, and climatological decline." In any case, the lords eventually switched more and more land to wool production (implying production for commodity exchange) and the enclosure movement began, separating labor from means of production (and laying a foundation for the capitalist mode of production). In England, as early as the sixteenth century, the effect of these enclosures is "one of increasing income to [the capitalist agricultural] class as a whole including to the lesser members of it, while [involving] the beginnings of the creation of a proletariat, most of whom were still not firmly settled in the towns but rather were 'vagabonds,' seasonal wage workers with subsistence plots, and lumpenproletariat in the towns" (Wallerstein, p. 256). Indeed, by 1750 any landowning peasantry was decimated and subsistence agriculture had largely disappeared; so that "there were no major obstacles to the transfer of men from nonindustrial to industrial pursuits" (Hobsbawn, 1969, p. 38). Of course, many did not find industrial employment, and, if they could, emigrated.[8]

In much of the rest of Western Europe, in Japan, and in North America, the introduction of a simple commodity economy began the destruction of precapitalist modes of production. The feudal mode of production itself included, of course, exchange of commodities between lord and craftsman (even if the transfer of surplus from the serf to the lord was in kind—labor or subsistence goods) and the financial crisis of the manor in Western Europe during the disintegration of feudalism there often led to a shifting of the serf obligation to money rent, implying an early penetration of commodity production. While, in France, the revolution of 1789 later freed peasants from landlords, taxes stepped into the breach (taxes that become a major issue in the 1848 Revolution). Since then, large-scale capitalist agriculture has been penetrating French family farming. In Prussia, the *Bauernlegen* entailed for the peasants legal emancipation through a "compensation" (!) to the nobles in both land and cash (embodied in the agrarian reform of 1810–1816). But the effect was less a rural exodus (as in England) than to produce a large rural proletariat for the capitalist agriculture of the former manors (see Anderson, 1974b, pp. 270–271, 274).

In Japan the process of penetration by simple commodity production was considerably slower, since the 1873 agrarian settlement institutionalized a landlord/tenant private-property relationship, with heavy taxation in money on landownership included (implying increased commodization), but with the tenants generally paying landlords in kind (Halliday, 1975, pp. 42–46). The continuance of such a feudal form in agriculture was an essential factor conditioning the peculiar development of Japanese capitalism, a form only broken by the American government in their Occupation after World War II (see Halliday, 1975). As to the United States, the commodity economy penetrated the natural economy of the peasant by the introduction of heavy taxes in money after the Civil War.[9] Soon this taxation also implied that the peasant's implements were produced by and bought from manufactures (Luxemburg, 1951, pp. 400–401). Eventually, large-scale farming brought down agricultural prices and the peasant farmer into debt, then out of business (Luxemburg, pp. 396–408).

The process of the destruction of the feudal mode of production also included the separation of handicrafts from agriculture, a process that does not really begin until the eighteenth century—sixteenth-century England obtained its domination of textile production and export by simply producing coarser and cheaper wool cloth in rural areas to substitute for the finer cloth produced by the guilds in the towns (Wallerstein, 1974, pp. 220, 225–229), but with the production still for the upper classes. Thus, the penetration of handicraft production begins with technical innovations in English cotton textile production.

> . . . the technical problem which determined the nature of mechanization in the cotton industry was the imbalance between the efficiency of spinning and weaving. The spinning wheel, a much less productive device than the hand-loom (especially as speeded by the "flying shuttle" which was invented in the 1730's and spread in the 1760's), could not supply the weavers fast enough. Three familiar inventions tipped the balance: the "spinning jenny" of the 1760's, which enabled one cottage spinner to spin several threads at once; the "water frame" of 1768, which used the original idea of spinning by a combination of rollers and spindles; and the fusion of the two, the "mule" of the 1780's, to which steam power was soon applied. The last two innovations implied factory production. The cotton factories of the Industrial

> Revolution were essentially spinning-mills (and establishments for carding the cotton preparatory to spinning it).
>
> Weaving kept pace with these innovations by a multiplication of hand-looms and manual weavers. Though a power-loom had also been invented in the 1780's, this branch of manufacture was not mechanized on any scale until after the Napoleonic Wars. . . . The "mule" remained the basis of British spinning, and "ring-spinning" (invented in the 1840's and general today) was left to the foreigners (Hobsbawn, 1969, pp. 58–59).

The result is that "hand in hand with the expropriation of the self-supporting peasants, with their separation from their means of production, goes the destruction of rural domestic industry, the process of separation between manufacture and agriculture" (Marx, 1974, I, pp. 699–700). Cotton manufacture, in fact, grew so rapidly that a substantial proportion was exported from England by underpricing other exporters and by destroying domestic competition in importing countries (including political means, for example, in India).[10] Stronger countries like France, Germany and the United States were able to protect their own industrial development by protective tariffs. In Japan, the unequal treaties imposed by the Western imperial powers in the second half of the nineteenth century prevented protective tariffs there, so that English textiles flooded in to destroy Japan's handicraft textile industry (see Halliday, 1975, pp. 47, 53). Japan was, nevertheless, later able to establish a substantial textile production and export by paying very low wages. (By and large, the periphery, before the Depression, was either colonialized or not independently powerful enough to raise protective tariffs: a weakness that has permanently conditioned its development.)[11]

2. THE CAPITALIST MODE OF PRODUCTION

The separation of labor from the historically developed means of production is only possible in a sustained way when means of production have become sufficiently developed that the laboring time required to produce these means of production for most sectors is beyond the capacity of a single worker or a small group of workers. At this historical juncture laboring activity must necessarily become a cooperative undertaking of a large number of workers working in a common workplace. The historical juncture is in fact a matter of centuries and, with precapitalist forms of production still existing in the world, we are still very much involved in the process. Nevertheless, the capitalist mode of production did become articulated in the nineteenth century.

The advent of cooperative production did not, however, correspond to cooperative control of means of production, but rather to its *private* control. We may, therefore, refer to a fundamental contradiction in the capitalist mode of production between the social or cooperative nature of the production process and the private control (by capitalists) of the means of production necessary for undertaking that production process. In any case, the juridicial form by which private control over means of production is institutionalized is private ownership. While it is beyond our present purposes to give an historical analysis of the development of this institution[12] (remember that by the time of writing of constitutions like that for the United States, private property in means of production was included by men who had everything to gain by such inclusion),[13] it is useful to mention the two principal methods in which the institution is presently defended. The first method is through ideology. The child is taught by his/her parents to distinguish "his/her" property from "others"; schooling teaches the virtues of private property, points to its incorporation in a constitution or legal system, and fails to distinguish between household goods and means of production; and then the adult fears crimes against his/her possessions and in turn teaches his/her children. Even if education is the more stable defense of private property in means of production and a symptom of decay in the whole system may be "decay" in the educational process, the second defense is the repressive state apparatus—the civil administration, the juridical system, and the police and the army. If an individual or group challenges a piece of privately owned means of production, they can be physically restrained and/or imprisoned. Furthermore, if the individual or group happens to be "employed" (a concept we have yet to introduce) by the offended party, some people may find themselves suddenly without employment.

Private ownership of the means of production implies that *only* means of production are so owned, not the workers themselves, i.e., the social system is not based on a slavery. Thus, workers are "free." They are "free" to speak or not to speak, to write or not to write, to travel or not to travel, to fall in love or not to fall in love. They are even "free" to quit work. But they are *not* free of deprivation when their means of subsistence are exhausted. And in the face of deprivation they must try to return to work.[14] In other words, the *fear* of deprivation motivates work in capitalism. Thus, at the deepest level, the capitalist system is a system based on fear (as is every class society but in different ways).

Since the worker is alientated from means of production in capitalism, (s)he does not come to the workplace as a laborer—a complete human being. Rather (s)he can only bring to the workplace that which the capitalists' demand—the worker's ability to work, the worker's labor power. Thus, capitalism is a system of contracting for labor power between capitalists and laborers. The capitalist offers a wage—which the worker is free to spend as (s)he chooses; in return, the worker offers labor power—which the capitalist is free to expend as (s)he chooses. Wage-labor is then a fundamental characteristic of capitalism. On the surface this selling and buying of laboring time is a supply and demand problem in which a human's laboring ability is a commodity on a market just like any other commodity.[15] But the exchange is in fact the most important exchange in the system, as is apparent simply from recognizing that it is the worker who produces everything. In any case, if the worker has obtained a wage-labor contract with a capitalist, we may say that (s)he is employed. The concept of employment is thus a relevant category only in the capitalist mode of production.

The concept of labor power can be related to the analytic tool of "value," but only after deepening our understanding of labor power. The notion of labor power is posed at the highest level of abstraction. It is essentially the assertion that those who do not control means of production can *only* offer on the labor market their ability to satisfy the needs of capital. Since the distribution of human characteristics cannot be presumed to change over time (except perhaps over tens of thousands of years), the working ability of the workers as a whole is then proportional to the amount of hours of work performed (corrected, if necessary, for physical fatigue from long working days). Indeed, it is convenient to simply measure the amount of work performed by the number of total hours. At a more concrete level, work performed in capitalist societies undergoes constant change. Thus, Braverman (1975, pp. 403–404) describes an increasing separation in the United States of manual work from intellectual work, with two-thirds to three-quarters of the active labor force corresponding directly to a proletariat and another 15 to 20 percent corresponding to "professional" categories of engineering, technical, scientific, marketing financial, hospitals, schools, government administration, etc.[16] Nevertheless, the notion of labor power refers to the total mass of workers separated from means of production, not to how that mass is divided up through a division of labor.[17]

Since workers are the only producers and, at the highest level of abstraction, their labor power can be represented by the total number of hours worked, we may say that the workers produce *value,* measured by the total number of hours worked. We will use this value as an analytic tool for representing the mass of commodities produced by the workers in the system. The tool is particularly useful in helping remind ourselves *who* produces in the system—proletarians—; and, by its opposite, who does not produce—capitalists (which of course is not to say the capitalists are not very much concerned with the production process). And it expresses vividly that, under capital, laboring activity is abstract. But we are not in the least concerned with a labor "theory" of value in any sense of the term (e.g., a theory of relative price determination).[18]

The workers then produce a mass of value. However, their wages that were determined in the free labor market are used to consume commodities by which the workers reproduce, and the implied real wage has itself a value; i.e., the commodities consumable from expenditure of the wages themselves required a determinable number of hours of work. We may label this value of wages as variable capital (v), "variable" connoting the ability of capitalists to make hiring and firing decisions over workers as well as decisions over the intensity of work. This variable capital may be subtracted from the total mass of produced value to obtain surplus value (s). Surplus value is that portion of total produced value that is appropriated by the capitalist class. Furthermore, the rate of surplus value may be defined as the ratio of surplus value to variable capital; as such it describes the ratio of mass of value appropriated by the capitalist class to the mass of value returned to the workers.

The preceding remarks on the capitalist mode of production have only served to introduce concepts. But concepts are only useful insofar as they help illuminate the system. We, therefore, now begin to use these concepts.

It is impossible to understand the essence of the capitalist mode of production without the notion of power or control—any focus on only exchange relations, competition, or other "economic" phenomena is ultimately misleading. The essence of capitalism is control over as much living labor power as possible—i.e., extending capitalist social relations as much as possible at each historical moment. We refer to this drive as the drive for the *accumulation of capital;* it is only concerned with the extension of capitalist social relations and has nothing whatever to do conceptually with any notion of more "machines"—the latter may be an outcome but not the essence of the drive. As Marx (1974, I, pp. 575–6) says, "reproduction on a progressive scale, i.e., accumulation, reproduces the capital-relation on a progressive scale, more capitalists or larger capitalists at this pole, more wage-workers at that. . . . Accumulation of capital is, therefore, increase of the proletariat." (This increase in the proletariat is *created by destruction,* by destruction of precapitalist modes and forms of production so to separate laborers from their means of production.[19])

Since capital can only accumulate capital by enlarging the mass of means of production, capital uses surplus value to obtain more means of production. With these means themselves produced by workers, they also have a value, and we may call the total mass of value embodied in means of production constant capital (C). "Constant" connotes the fact that the value is fixed in a commodity and does not change in the production process (although that value can be "devalued," as we shall see in the next section).

Since capital needs surplus value to accumulate, the drive to accumulate capital implies a drive to maximize surplus value. This maximization has two implications. First, in the production process itself capital exploits labor as much as possible. This is primarily accomplished by production of relative surplus value, development of productive forces (technical changes) such that less labor time per given working day is devoted to satisfying needs of workers. Such a constant development of productive forces is an essential characteristic distinguishing the *effects* of capitalist social relations from precapitalist ones. Second, capital destroys alternative relationships for workers to means of subsistence (e.g., handicrafts production), most naturally accomplished by the price reductions possible through the development of productive forces. The resulting release of workers weakens the ability of the proletariat to demand higher wages. The industrial revolution in fact began with textiles because the development of productive forces there both reduces the value of labor power in the production process itself and also destroys handicraft production of textiles. This era of destroying handicrafts is also the era of "competitive" capitalism; the opportunities for extending control over labor power are so great that the system is able to sustain many independent capitalists, each of whom feels the pressure of market competition driving technical changes.[20] This era can be sustained as long as substantial handicraft production remains to be destroyed. England, particularly, was able to use colonies such as India to lengthen the process.

In order to deepen the statement that the essence of capitalism is the control over as much labor power as possible and that the system maximizes surplus value, we now introduce the concepts of relative surplus population (or industrial reserve army) and of markets. Both are essential for understanding *why* the total value produced by labor power is in fact greater than the value of labor power, or why the use value of labor power in production is greater than the exchange value of labor power, as well as *how* the difference is maximized.

The total mass of value produced by workers is, of course, determined by the total labor hours performed. But the value of labor power is determined by the labor time required to produce only the commodities consumed through the expenditure of the wages of the workers. Capital has then two focal points for devaluing labor power—(a) holding down nominal wages, or (b) keeping up market prices of wage goods. Holding down nominal wages in a free labor market is accomplished by weakening the bargaining position of the workers. In this market the workers' position is weakened by capital through constant production of relative surplus population—i.e., through constant technical changes that save labor and throw some workers out of work, at the same time that others must be drawn in through the accumulation of capital. "Relative surplus-population is therefore the pivot upon which the law of demand and supply of labor works. It confines the field of action of this law within the limits absolutely convenient to the activity of exploitation and to the domination of capital" (Marx, 1974, I. p. 598). Thus, technical changes were faster in the United States than in England in the nineteenth century because the United States had a greater labor shortage (Habakkuk, 1962).

Keeping market prices of wage goods as high as possible is achieved by making the market for the produced wage goods as large as possible, so that the supply going to workers is as small as possible. Thus, the destruction of the English and Indian handicarft textile production by English manufacturers in the nineteenth century enlarged tremendously the market for English textiles and allowed domestically retained textiles to be sold at much higher prices to English workers. The expansion of U.S. food exports in the early 1970's served the same purpose.[21] On the other hand, keeping up market prices of machinery is first a struggle of the capitalist suppliers of machinery against the capitalist buyers of machinery and, by and large, only implies a transfer of surplus value across branches or countries.

In sum, continuous production of a relative surplus population and enlarging markets of wage-goods as much as possible are indispensable components of the existence and maximization of surplus value. The limits of the relative surplus population are, of course, that proletariats that are not employed are not producing value, while the larger the total produced value, for any rate of surplus value, the larger is the mass of surplus value. Therefore, relative surplus population is bounded between the need to weaken the bargaining power of labor and the need to produce as much value and thus surplus value as possible. At this level of discussion there is consequently no tendency in the longer-run for some sort of "rising rate of unemployment." The limits of enlarging markets for wage goods are simply that the capitalist mode of production produces a larger and larger mass of commodities and the realization of produced value of wage goods is confined to proletariats or to noncapitalist regions of the country or of the world. As the noncapitalist areas contract under the pressure of capitalist accumulation, the market outside the system shrinks. As we see in Section 4, the massive structural crisis of the system in the 1930's is the result, a result probably delayed by the intercapitalist, nation-state war of 1914–1918 in which markets were maintained during the war by armament expenditures and, a decade afterward, by reconstruction.

3. DEVALUATION OF CONSTANT CAPITAL

Capital struggles in the workplace against living labor power in order to decrease the value of that labor power and increase surplus value in the cycle of capital. While this struggle implies technical change in all industries, the struggle is naturally most effective in industries producing goods consumed by workers, wage-good industries if you will. If then we label the ratio of the total constant capital to the variable capital employed with that constant capital, the *organic composition of capital* (C/v), this organic composition has a tendency to rise. For, the labor time embodied in machines lowers more slowly than for the wage-goods.

If we now let the *technical-value composition of capital*[22] k be C/(v+s), by simple algebra, the organic composition of capital C/v equals k (1 + s/v). With the rate of surplus value s/v constant (or only slowly rising), the technical-value composition is also rising. This rising technical-value composition of capital in the capitalist mode of production implies a contradiction between the capital-labor relation and the accumulating purpose of that relation. On the one hand, the rate of profit in the economy is given by s/ (C+v)[23]—i.e., $\frac{s/v}{1+C/v} = \frac{s/v}{1+k(1+s/v)}$; yet, the social relation implies rising k and, given the rate of surplus value, therefore a falling rate of profit. On the other hand, this fall in the rate of profit limits accumulation by its implied rising cost of machines. This law of the "progressive tendency of the general rate of profit to fall is, therefore, just *an expression peculiar to the capitalist mode of production* of the progressive development of the social productivity of labor" (Marx, 1974, I, p. 213, italics in original).

Various mathematical "proofs" exist that the law of the falling tendency of the rate of profit is a supposed myth. For example, Okishio (1961, p. 95) shows that "Unless the rate of real wages rises sufficiently, the technical innovations adopted by capitalists do not reduce the general rate of profit. Innovations in basic industries positively raises the general rate of profit. And innovations in nonbasic industries have no influence upon the level of the general rate of profit." Rather than disproving the law, such theorems indicate how deeply bourgeois society penetrates interpretations of Marx. For, the common characteristic of all these theorems is that the real wage rate is related to the rate of profit and the influence of technical change analysed—the Ricardian method of posing discussion. Real wages, however, are simply one expression of the *effects* on man's relation to nature of capitalism's social relationship and, as such, is never a point of departure of analysis; indeed, Marx's (1974, Volume I, Part VI) discussion of wages is primarily a discussion of the *form* taken by daily wages, not its level.

It is fully impossible to understand either the law, or the depth to which devaluation of constant capital synthesizes modern technological developments, without understanding both class struggle directly in the capitalist production process itself (as opposed, for example, to struggle over the distribution of *what* is produced) *as well as* understanding the struggle of capital against precapitalist modes of production. The former establishes the rising composition of capital. The latter establishes the contradiction between the accumulating nature of capitalism and the narrow basis of that accumulation (a point we return to in the next section). With limits to the increase in the rate of surplus value while the system is, at the same time, developing productive forces, the law *implies* that, unlike Okishio, real wages are indeed rising "sufficiently."

The law of the falling tendency of the rate of profit is then one expression of the struggle by capital against labor.[24] Capital can react to the contradiction by devaluing constant capital and, to the extent that the rate of surplus value is stable, thus raising the rate of profit. This reaction could take four forms: 1) economies of large-scale production (see Marx, 1973, pp. 765–767); 2) lowering the economy-wide average technical-value composition of capital by incorporating new, more labor-intensive industries in the cycle of capital (e.g., service industries);[25] 3) accelerating technical changes in industries producing machines (say, to the same level as the wage-goods industries); and 4) obsolescence of previously produced capital goods.

There is widespread agreement that the development of productive forces in the nineteenth century did indeed imply an ever increasing scale of operation and some devaluation of constant capital. Thus, the principal new source of power steam, the principal new material steel, the raising of the number of stages of the production process to accommodate new methods of fabrication, and the development of new transportation in the form of the railroad all implied that production processes on ever larger scale were ever more efficient. For some industries, even in the twentieth century, increasing scale still implies saving on constant capital, Thus, Hollander (1965) studied data on production costs of viscose-rayon manufacture at several Du Pont plants of the years 1929–1960. On the one hand, reduction in unit costs due only to plant expansion (i.e., exploiting of known indivisibilities) ''accounts for between 10 and 15 percent'' (p. 194) of the total unit cost reductions. On the other hand, while virtually all of the remaining sources of unit cost reductions were due to technical change (p. 118), over 80 percent of which depended upon investment, ''usually at least two-thirds, and in some cases as much as 90 percent, of the investment outlay required to implement technical change represented replacement of, or alterations to, existing equipment'' (p. 201)—i.e., another 10 to 20 percent of the total depended upon net investment (increasing scale). Therefore, taking the two observations together, about 30 percent of unit cost reductions, *at the plant level,* depended upon scale of operation.[26] Moreover, this result represents an underestimate of the importance of technical change specifically dependent upon scale of operation since ''the statements concerning the relative importance of replacement investment have been made with reference to *existing* plants; . . . we must also take into account the fact that certain plants were actually constructed either to embody cost-reducing technical change or to produce new products'' (p. 160).

Nevertheless, the U.S. Senate Subcommittee on Antitrust and Monopoly (of the Judiciary Committee) hearings on economic concentration, during the last half-decade of the 1960's, usefully sheds contrary evidence on scale economies as a source of devaluation of constant capital in the twentieth century. The Subcommittee's chief economist, J. M. Blair (1972, Chapers 5 and 6), has summarized the findings on the relation between twentieth-century technical progress and scale of operation, as well as introduced additional evidence. He concludes that the substitution of electricity for steam as a source of power, the spreading use of the multipurpose machine for the special-purpose machine, and the introduction of the truck as an alternative means of transportation, all in the first third of this century, ''initially arrested and then reversed the trend towards larger scale of operation'' (p. 114). Furthermore, the development of plastics, fiberglass, high-performance composites, prestressed concrete, fuel cells (and perhaps more efficient batteries), rotary engines, and even the computer each suggest efficient production at *smaller* scale of operation.[27] As to the invention and innovation process itself, it is a social one in which size may have substantial difficulties;[28] also, major inventions still come often from independent individuals.[29] Concerning possible economies of scale to management (so that larger size, even with multiplant operations, is more efficient than smaller), the importance in a bureaucracy of Parkinson's Law and the

Peter Principle is probably decisive and, in any case, empirical evidence is against a role for managerial efficiencies (see Blair, 1972, Chapter 8). In sum, while technical progress dependent upon continuously enlarging the scale of operation may still be relevant for particular industries such as chemicals,[30] it would be a weak theoretical posture to continue to use it to base an argument on the devaluation of constant capital.

Any devaluation of constant capital through an incorporation of new, more labor-intensive industries in the cycle of capital, through accelerating technical changes in industries producing machines, and/or through obsolescence, is less a question if such possibilities *can* be utilized than the social forces encouraging and inhibiting utilization of such possibilities. Remembering that the accumulation of capital is the incorporation in the social formation of more labor power under the domination of capital and therefore that the law of the falling tendency of the rate of profit is simply the assertion that production of relative surplus value is most effective, for such purposes of accumulation, in industries producing wage-goods (i.e., cheapening, in the first instance, goods that can be used to penetrate precapitalist modes of production, anywhere in the world),[31] devaluation of constant capital is, therefore, socially motivated when the accumulating drive of capitalism comes into contradiction with a rising relative cost of the machines produced with the labor power represented by surplus value. Yet, the development of such contradictions of capitalism can only be developed as concrete historical analysis, an analysis that would, in fact, take us too far afield from our theoretical objective here.

Devaluation of constant capital through obsolescence, in any case, deserves attention since, as we indicate in the next section, acceleration of technical change is an important method capital uses to struggle against increases in "unproductive" labor. First of all, it is essential to recognize, as Magaline (1975, p. 97) points out, that obsolescence refers to a shortening of the *actual* use value of a machine relative to the *expected* length of the use value of a machine when it was first installed. Thus, unlike bourgeois economics, it has nothing to do with the difference between the socially determined life a machine and its physical life; the physcial life is primarily determined by the materials used in construction, which, in turn, is determined by the expected life as socially determined. In other words, obsolescence refers to *unanticipated* developments of productive forces that destroy use-value of older machines. Second, developments of productive forces are indeed difficult to anticipate in capitalism because the developments are determined in the last instance by class struggle, and that class struggle is a very uneven process.[32]

At a lower level of abstraction we may add that, even though technological developments at the aggregate level may average out to be somewhat smoother, an individual firm faces considerable ignorance of developments that will be occurring in the future in its industry. This point deserves elaboration since it helps emphasize the important point that abstraction at the highest level should not lose contradictions at the level of individual capitals. Now, virtually every industry has a wide dispersion of firm size. In spite of the considerable attention to advantages of large size through control of larger markets, smaller firms have an important inherent advantage in the *dynamics* of production costs. First, remember that, with newer machines more efficient than older, a younger age distribution of machines is more efficient than an older age distribution. Furthermore, a firm that is expanding more rapidly relative to its size has a younger age distribution than those expanding less. Thus, a firm expanding more rapidly is more efficient. Second, recall that smaller firms in an industry face a higher price elasticity of their demand than larger firms. Therefore, a smaller firm expanding more rapidly has a greater ease of expanding its market, as well as competitive advantage in production costs.

The direct implication is that a smaller firm can achieve a competitive advantage over a larger firm by rapidly investing. But an indirect implication is that smaller firms should be more actively interested in *greater* technical progress than larger firms:[33] their ability to expand more rapidly implies that costs are reduced relatively more when technical progress is greater. The preferred *timing* on the part of the smaller firm of such accumulation embodying new technology is then on the occasion of a significant technical innovation, particularly given advertising advantages that larger firms often have in any case. But the timing of significant innovations in particular products is very difficult to predict: "If there is one lesson to be learned from the history of invention, it is that the course of technological progress is episodic, volatile, and unpredictable" (Blair, 1972, p. 693); or "What matters for the subject of this study is merely the essentially discontinuos character of [the innovation] process, which does not lend itself to description in terms of a theory of equilibrium" (Schumpeter, 1928, pp. 31–32).[34] In sum, much technical progress embodied in new equipment is in fact *unanticipated;* so that obsolescence is an important phenomenon of capitalism.

The significance of obsolescence is not its expression of an "economic" phenomenon, but its expression of the contradiction in capitalism between capital and capitals, between the fundamental capital-wage-labor relation and the individual nature of capitals. For, on the one hand, the very possibility of obsolescence derives from capital's struggle against the value of labor power (for the purposes of maximizing surplus value and accumulation) by the production of relative surplus value, by the continual development of productive forces that economize on labor time. On the other hand, every development of productive forces that requires investment in new fixed capital implies devaluation of that fixed capital that was produced at an earlier period and is still in place, the *form* of that devaluation being precisely *competition among capitals* which reduces the market price of the commodities produced by the labor using the new means of production. The individualistic form of capitals is very important, for every capital resists devaluation of its own existing constant capital (see Magaline, 1975, Chapter 5).

This resistance to devaluation of existing constant capital is necessarily highest in industries that have developed historically as having the highest technical value compositions of capital, since these industries would generally have the most capital that would be devalued by obsolescence. Such industries, indeed, tend to be more monopolistic, as an expression of resisting devaluation through avoiding price declines. They tend most to resist technical change that would imply obsolescence[35] (although there is such a resistance in all industries). They also tend more frequently to be industries producing means of production (investment goods industries), since such industries are generally one step removed from the penetration in the social formation of precapitalist modes of production—i.e., one step removed from the accumulation of capital.[36] Some of these industries also move into the transnational arena, thus trying to put potential losses from obsolescence on other capitals and labor in the center and/or on classes in the periphery (when not able to avoid losses through increasing the exploitation of their own labor, by, say, increasing the intensity of work or the number of shifts of work).

In the next section, we see that a consequence of the modern struggle of capital against "unproductive" labor is *increased* technical changes. Here we have seen that there is a resistance to those technical changes that are unanticipated, a resistance to obsolescence. The potential conflict can be ameliorated by trying to reduce the unanticipated component of technical changes; and the development of operations research and the increasing role of centralized research, often mediated by the state, are expressions of an attempted resolution. A second method is the development of new industries (such as electronics, today) which can , on the one hand, have higher rates of technological changes, yet, on the other hand, resist potential devaluation of constant capital by using production processes of low technical value composition of capital (and thus also implying a lowering of the aggregate technical value composition).[37] The low technical value composition often makes production in low-wage countries (such as in Southeast Asia) particularly advantageous.

As a final, if incidental, remark, the development of industries producing constant capital could never sustain the degree of competition existing in nineteenth-century textiles, for it had no destruction of handicrafts available. (As handicrafts are destroyed, even textile production becomes less able to sustain high competition—enough competition to sustain the development of productive forces but not as much as is sustainable in a period of handicraft destruction.) Some then like to refer to this development as the beginning of "monopoly capitalism." The word "monopoly" can be misleading, for capitalism still contains enough competitive pressures to enforce the development of productive forces. In fact, the role of competition cannot be defined by the number of producers for a given product, as the word "monopoly" might suggest. Thus, virtually all economists have called attention to substitutability between products (including new products), so that the development of productive forces is necessary even for dominant producers of most products. Furthermore, even concentration across several products is not sufficient to undermine the development of productive forces if there is enough development in the remainder of the economy that real wages rise and force continued technological change to prevent demand-reducing price increases.[38] (Of course, large firms may be able to convince governments to set floors on product prices or restrict wage increases; but such actions do not seem sustainable in the longer run, at least in the center.) In sum, we are not led to a theoretical support for use of the concept "monopoly capitalism."

4. SURPLUS VALUE AND UNPRODUCTIVE LABOR IN THE TWENTIETH CENTURY

Once the initial stage of capital accumulation is more or less completed, capital must squarely face the contradiction between its drive to accumulate capital and the narrow base of that accumulation, the contradiction between using surplus value for more means of production and the ultimate need to realize sale of the commodities produced with the help of those means of production. For, even though capital always seeks as wide a market as possible to overcome this contradiction, the task of penetrating remaining precapitalist modes of production becomes much more difficult and the expansion of constant capital must slow down with the slower rise of wage-labor. The scramble for colonies by European powers beginning in the latter part of the nineteenth century was one expression of the beginning of the end of the "easier" period of accumulation of capital mentioned in the previous section; the depressed business conditions, another. The spread of electricity and steel, however, devaluated constant capital associated with steam power and wood, respectively, and maintained the system for a time. Then the build-up and destruction centering around the intra-capitalist World War I (see Lenin, 1917) maintained some outlets for surplus value through the 1920's, although spawning the Bolshevik revolution.

In this light the worldwide depression of the 1930's is an outcome of a social system based upon accumulation when it comes into conflict with its possibilities of expansion. Indeed, J. M. Keynes' (1936) understanding of capitalism was vaguely related to the realization that the accumulating essence of capitalism had come into conflict with the possibilities of accumulation. (The linchpin of his system is the *expectations* of capitalists in regard to profitability of possible investments, while, for us, these expectations are nothing other than the expression to the individual capitalist of the contradiction between the accumulating essence of capitalism and its narrow basis.[39]) Thus, when surplus value can not be used for rapid accumulation, the system has no choice but to fall into a depression which lowers the rate of surplus value and thus the profit rate.

At this point nineteenth-century capitalism is truly dead, and the issue is which class takes the lead in overcoming the crisis. It cannot possibly be the capitalist class since their social function is accumulation. It can be the proletarian class as the class representing the possibility of socialist revolution. But it can also be the petit bourgeoisie as the class whose actions lead to an absorption of surplus value in *unproductive labor* (a term to be defined shortly). In fact, as Keynes well understood, unproductive labor is a way-out for capitalism for the crisis of the 1930's.

Which capitalist nation-state takes the lead? The one in which the conflict is most threatening in the sense of the proletarian class being the strongest. For in these nation-states the capitalists are most willing to make more room for unproductive labor and the petit bourgeoisie are most driven to action.[40] Since, in the Depression, these countries were precisely Italy and Germany, the petit bourgeoisie there became the vanguard in saving the world capitalist system. Capitalists everywhere were, therefore, objectively in alliance with the petit bourgeoisie of Italy and Germany.

Keynes (1936, p. 129) understood what a pointless form this unproductive labor could take from the point of view of man's relation to nature: "If the Treasury were to fill old bottles with banknotes, bury them at suitable depths in disused coalmines which are then filled up to the surface with town rubbish, and leave it to private enterprise on well-tried principles of *laissez-faire* to dig the notes up again (the right to do so being obtained, of course, by tendering for leases of the note-bearing territory), there need be no more unemployment and, with the help of the repercussions, the real income of the community, and its capital wealth also, would probably become a good deal greater than it acutally is." But this same quote also shows the weakness of Keynes' understanding of capitalism. For the *form* of unproductive labor is not pointless but is rather precisely conditioned by class struggle. In Italy and Germany, the *form* of the leadership of the petit bourgeoisie was conditioned by the circumstance there—the need for repression of the proletarian class—and implied militarism.[41] This militarism had to extend beyond the task of repressing the proletariat if surplus value was to continue to be absorbed by unproductive labor (and yet absorbed in a way consistent with the needs of the capitalist class). Defensively, but not inconsistent with their own needs for development of unproductive labor, England and the United States developed their military. The conditions for World War II resulted.

The debate over the dividing line between productive and unproductive labor can now be illuminated. In one sense all labor in capitalism is employed for the needs of maintaining the capitalist system; thus, all labor is productive for maintaining this system. But, if we are to use the productive/unproductive notion meaningfully we must use it to deepen our analysis of the development of the system. If then the essence of capitalism is accumulation, then only wage-labor that is productive of extending the capital-labor relation is *productive*—i.e., that labor which produces surplus value and works in capital-goods or wage-goods industries (services included insofar as they provide a source of expenditure out of wages and produce surplus value).[42] For, only such labor is productive of the social function of capital. The fact that the capitalist system is moving toward higher levels of unproductive labor throughout the twentieth century, and particularly since the beginning of the Great Depression, is then merely to observe the deacceleration of accumulation expressed in the labor performed in capitalism. The process is not reversable.

The lesson that the capitalist system learned from the Depression and World War II is that the system is more stable with enough development of unproductive labor to absorb the surplus value that is created at lower levels of the relative surplus population, than to allow another destabilizing Depression. The lesson, however, does not imply that the relative surplus population is no longer used to check labor. In fact, as M. Kalecki (1943)—in many ways the precursor of Keynes but in the "wrong" language (Polish)—noted, capitalists are aware that one of the great fears of individual workers is of becoming unemployed and that that fear would be considerably reduced and labor militancy increased by a government maintenance of near-full employment. Thus, capitalists first adopt an ideological posture of emphasizing "sound government financing" to discourage demand by labor for the government deficits needed to maintain near-full employment. Second, and more recently, capitalists direct attention to the inflation that has occurred with near-full employment[43] and, manifesting agreement with workers in halting inflation, call for reduced government spending and reduced wage increases.

In any case, capital accepts the need for massive amounts of unproductive labor. The main questions for capital are to limit its extent and control its form; for unproductive labor is no part of capital's social function of accumulation. One of the principal means of limiting the extent of unproductive labor is to increase the labor employed for research and development, and so also, by accelerating the rate of technical changes in the economy so that older machines become obsolete more quickly, stimulating investment-goods industries. While the growth of research and development staffs is already well-known, Mandel (1973, Chapters 7 and 8) summarizes the accéleration of technical changes and points to its implied shorter lifetime of machines.[44] (Capital, meanwhile, encourages investment tax credits.) The labor associated with this development is, of course, productive labor. A second important means of limiting the extent of unproductive labor is imperialism—all efforts to extend the sphere of the capital-labor relation in the world. To the extent that this imperialism succeeds in stimulating the accumulation of capital at the world level, the labor so employed is also productive labor.

The dividing line concerning the *form* of unproductive labor is between that employed without the intermediation of the state and that employed with its intermediation. The former includes such activities as advertising employees, sales(wo)men, and private insurance employees, while the latter includes employment in the government administration, the military and (insofar as sales are to the state) military industries, education and hospitals. Capital is more concerned about unproductive labor that is mediated through the state. For mediation always reduces control, at least to some extent, even though the state is the capitalist state. The military is well-enough integrated with capital to avoid being an independent threat and is a most important defense against socialism. While public health and government administration pose no special problems and education still remains a primary means of implanting capitalist ideology, universities have been a focus of some open antagonism to capital.

(To be concluded in Volume 2 of this yearbook by analyzing accumulation of capital in the periphery.)

FOOTNOTES

1. The characterization of ancient modes of production in Asia is under reexamination today (see, for example, Anderson, 1974b, pp. 462–549) and is left aside.
2. See Wolf (1966, pp. 7–9) for the importance of ceremony in human communities.
3. Relative to *their* needs, they may not be (see Sahlins, 1972).
4. These figures are drawn from Wolf (1966, p. 11) and are, of course, subject to new anthropological evidence.
5. ". . . primitive agriculturalists . . . comprized the vast majority of the population [in Sub-Saharan Africa until colonialism] . . ." (Saul and Woods, 1971, pp. 106–107).
6. There certainly were class forms of production preceding the Graeco-Roman Antiquity, but historical research has not resolved an understanding of it into a mode of production, for our information on that prior period is quite limited.
7. Anderson (1974a) develops it as a synthesis of the slave with the primitive forms of the Germanic invaders.
8. "Having evicted the peasant from his soil, [capital] drives him from England to the East of the United States, and from there to the West . . ." (Luxemburg, 1951, p. 410).
9. ". . . Gone were the times when the small or medium farmer required hardly any money, when he could thresh and turn into cash his wheat reserves as the need arose. Now he was chronically in need of money, a lot of money, to pay his taxes" (Luxemburg, 1951, p. 400).
10. Raw cotton was first imported from the slave plantations in the West Indies, then after the 1790's from the slave plantations in the Southern United States and in Brazil.
11. More labor power was released from agriculture than could be absorbed by textiles even with the use of textile exports to destroy handicrafts in the periphery. In England, absorption of labor power was continued from the 1840's in the development of railroads (not only in Britain but through loans abroad that were used for British material and equipment) and the associated coal, iron, and steel industries (and then the steamship industry). The railroads themselves aided the further penetration of precapitalist forms of production. And so the process deepens. And it deepens until most labor in England, France, Germany, United States and Japan today is wage-labor and the struggle against precapitalist forms is now primarily located in today's "Third World."
12. Private property in household goods is obviously of no immediate consequence here.
13. The classic work of Beard (1913) began a debate over the social forces leading to the writing of the U.S. Constitution. One conclusion of the debate is that the framers were quite clear of the dangers of the "extremism" that could develop when wage-labor would become more important, *if* they did not establish a form of government with enough layers and "checks and balances" that political change would be slow. The resulting tensions in the

United States between local, state and federal governments and branches of these governments are manifest today.

14. This is equally true of nineteenth-century capitalism as of ''welfare-state'' capitalism.

15. Neocalssical economics recognizes the commodity nature of the transaction by, for example, treating machinery and laboring time symmetrically in a production function. Hence, laboring time has a price, the wage rate, like any other commodity, and its price may be in ''equilibrium'' or ''disequilibrium.'' Neoclassical economics, however, fails to recognize the distinction, only relevant in the capitalist mode of production, between labor and labor power and fails to recognize that any use value of machines was, in turn, produced only by workers.

16. U.S. Government statistics on the increasing ''skill'' distribution of the labor force are completely misleading (see Braverman, 1975, Chapter 20).

17. The fact that the laboring class has constantly resisted capitalists' efforts to divide their labor is represented, for example, by the 1892 Homestead strike led by skilled steelworkers, a strike lost to the capitalists (see Stone, 1974). The strike was over both the threat to employment of management efforts to adopt laborsaving technical changes, as well as over the implied reduction of skills in the job content.

18. Gerstein (1976, pp. 247–261) provides a view of value that seems consistent with ours, although he refers to ''theory of value'' rather than value as an ''analytic tool.''

19. This destruction of precapitalist modes can occur through direct political means (taking of land backed by military force and oppressive taxation), or through direct economic means (''The cheap prices of its commodities are the heavy artillery with which [the bourgeoisie] batters down all Chinese walls''). Indeed, the latter has implied a great change in the last two hundred years—the vastly increased material production, the vast development of the productive forces relating man to nature. The destruction is broken into three stages by Luxemburg (1951, Chapters 27–29)—gaining possession of land and ''freeing'' some labor from this land, introducing a simple commodity economy (a market economy in products, but not in labor power), and separating rural industries from agriculture.

20. Thus, Macpherson (1962, p. 55) argues that ''The effect of competition in [the product and labor] market is to compel entrepreneurs (who must have had some capital initially, with which to hire labor) to use increasing amounts of captial as a means to more efficient production . . .'' More popularly, Fromm (1955, pp. 82–83) describes the capitalist in the nineteenth century:

> . . . The individual capitalist expands his enterprise not primarily because he wants to, but because he has to, because—as Carnegie said in his autobiography—postponement of further expansion would mean regression. Actually as a business grows, one has to continue making it bigger, whether one wants to or not. In this function of the economic law which operates behind the back of man and forces him to do things without giving him the freedom to decide, we see the beginning of a constellation which comes to its fruition only in the twentieth century.

21. See Crotty and Rapping (1975, particularly pp. 803–805). With this perspective the roots of inflation are rather easily understood.

22. This term seems to be first used by Wolfstetter (1974); Okishio (1961, p. 87) uses ''the organic composition of production'' for the same concept.

23. Gerstein (1976, pp. 262–283) develops the argument that this expression is incorrect unless the compositions of capital are the same across industries. We are in fact abstracting from differing compositons, and thus the ''transformation'' problem.

Incidentally, Morishima (1973, pp. 53–71; see also 1974) has christened as "the" Fundamental Marxian Theorem that there is a positive rate of profit in capitalism if and only if there is a positive rate of exploitation, regardless of compositions of capital. In Morishima and Catephores (1975) it is argued that Marx develops this theorem in order to compare the unequal ownership of means of production in capitalism with the *hypothetical* case of equal ownership *in capitalism*. Such a theorem is certainly an important step out of interpreting the transformation problem as a problem of price determination, but it does not motivate socially determined class *practice*—different practice according to different class position. Indeed, the theorem can be accepted by all economists (as Morishima, 1973, p. 1, would like it to be: "It is our great misfortune that economists have for a long time been divided between the 'orthodox' and Marxian camps as a result of cliquishness . . . "). Furthermore, Morishima and Catephores' interpretation of the theorem suggests a bourgeois solution to problems of capitalism—more equal ownership of means of production—and is of course idealistic in its comparison with a hypothetical case.

24. "Two things therefore worried the early-nineteenth-century businessmen and economists [in Britain]: the rate of their profits and the rate of the expansion of their markets" (Hobsbawm, 1969, p. 75).

25. Of course, discussion of this form directly requires introduction of the transformation problem (see Gerstein, 1976, particularly p. 283).

26. Incidentally, unit costs, corrected for input-price changes, declined at rates between 2.3 and 4.9 percent for the various plants through about 1952 (Hollander, p. 118).

27. Blair (1972, p. 151) is sufficiently impressed with the technological evidence to suggest that "there appears to be aborning a second industrial revolution, which, among its other features, contains within itself the seeds of destruction for concentrated industrial structures." But the question remains, what are the social origins for such a second industrial revolution?

28. A relevant study of A. C. Cooper (1964) on this point is succinctly summarized by Kamien and Schwartz (1975, pp. 9–10): "A. C. Cooper interviewed about 25 development managers with experience in both large and small companies or in rapidly expanding development organizations in either the electronics or chemical industry. He also obtained actual cost figures for a particular parallel development effort by a large company and a small company. Remarkably consistent estimates indicated a given product would cost three to ten times as much to develop by a large firm as by a small one. Larger firms, he found, seem to become enmeshed in bureaucracy and red tape, resulting in a less hospitable atmosphere for creative contributions by operating personnel. Superior technical personnel tend to be attracted to smaller companies where greater latitude may be afforded them. The larger the firm, the more difficult it may be to recognize the problems needing solution. Finally, there is evidence of greater cost consciousness in smaller firms."

29. For some examples, see Jewkes, *et al* (1969), Hamberg (1966) and Blair (1972, pp. 213–227).

30. In addition to the rayon production example, see, for chemical process plants in general, Freeman (1968).

31. In an otherwise excellent discussion, Magaline (1975, p. 93) can be misleading in commenting that "Il n' existe pas en effet de 'barrières' qui cantonneraient le développement du mode de production capitaliste et du type de développement des forces productives qui lui correspond à tel ou tel 'secteur' de la production, par example le secteur II. A contraire, le capital tend à s'emparer de toutes les sphères de la production et à provoquer partout le même type de transformations, à développer partout la 'productivité du travail' selon le mêmes modalités." It may be misleading if the point is taken to mean that the *levels* of the development of productive forces tend to be the *same* in capital-goods sectors as in

wage-goods sectors. If the levels tended to be the same, there would be no tendency for a falling rate of profit. Magaline (1975, Chapter 3), on the devaluation of labor power, does seem to recognize the particular importance of development of production forces in the wage-goods industries in the discussion of devaluation of means of subsistence.

32. "[L'] accélération du procès de dévalorisation de la force de travail [est] non prévisible dans les conditions de la production capitaliste" (Magaline, 1975, p. 97).

33. A commonly observed phenomenon that Blair (1972, Chapter 10), for example, emphasizes.

34. Schumpeter, of course, emphasizes the importance of the *new* firm (related to his "entrepreneur"), a special case of expansion by a smaller firm.

35. For the example of U.S. Steel, see Stone (1974).

36. Bourgeois economics inverts this point by supposing that investment goods industries are the heart of (their notion of) the accumulation of capital.

37. The development of new industries of lower technical value composition of capital as a resistance of devaluation of constant capital is presumably the social origin of the "second industrial revolution" perceived by Blair (see footnote 27), for him a revolution against previous advantages of large-scale production.

38. With respect to these points, we might note Earley's (1957, p. 334) observations on the modern large-scale business (quoted subsequently in Baran and Sweezy, 1966, pp. 37–38): "Competitive strength and even survival, management believes, require large innovative and substantial growth expenditures in the rapidly changing technical and market conditions of the present day. Since growth by merger is hazardous and frequently impossible, large and more-or-less continuous capital expenditures are necessary."

Baran and Sweezy (1966, pp. 36 and 39) apparently accept this observation and go on to conclude (p. 79) that "with regard to the cost discipline it imposes on its members the monopoly capitalist economy is no less severe than its competitive predecessor." Their work is primarily based on factual evidence of a rising surplus, but they fail to provide a theoretical support for their use of "monopoly capitalism."

39. Keynes (1936) also did not view investment and saving as two manifestations of the *same* process of accumulation, but rather accepted the classical distinction between investors and savers. He merely argued (p. 21) that *motives* for investment and saving are distinct—"the motives which determine the latter [decisions to provide for future consumption] are not linked in any simple way with the motives which determine the former [decisions to abstain from present consumption]."

The post-Keynesian income-expenditure model indeed often interprets this portion of Keynes' argument as his most important contribution—"The principal stress [of the modern theory of income analysis] is upon the level of total spending as determined by the interplay of the monetary forces of saving and investment. . . . The most important single fact about saving and investment activities is that in our industrial society they are generally done by *different people* and done for *different reasons*" (Samuelson, 1973, pp. 205–206, italics in original).

In fact, any separation of investors and savers is misleading. Increased unemployment can occur directly by a falling off of expectations about the profitability of investments, leading to declining expenditures on investment goods and thus declining employment in those industries. The falling employment in investment goods industries can imply that incomes and consumer spending cumulatively decline. Keynes might have been more consistent if he had integrated investment and savings; then the "separate" motives would have been a mute issue. Nevertheless, it is a major contribution or organize thought on the crises of the 1930's by directing attention toward the formation of investment expectations, even if Keynes was unclear on the sources in the social formation of "expectations."

40. The petit bourgeoisie "falls back into the abject despondency of fear as soon as the class below itself, the proletarians, attempts an independent movement" (Engels, 1969, p. 14).

41. Brazil accidentally discovered another means in its defense of coffee planters. "When in 1931 a million contos were injected into the economy for buying up and destroying coffee, purchasing power was being created that would partly counterbalance the reduction in expenditures in investors, which had been cut by some two million contos" (Furtado, 1963, p. 213).

42. Our inclusion of services accords with Wright, but not Poulantzas (see Wright, 1976). As to wage-labor in industries producing, for example, military hardware, even though this labor is used to defend and even to try to expand the capitalist system, it does not *directly* extend capitalist ownership of means of productions and variable capital. Thus, it does not produce value, and so, in contrast to Gough's (1972, p. 66) assertion (for it is only that), does not produce surplus value. This labor *uses* surplus value.

43. Why does such an inflation occur? Precisely, as we suggested at the end of Section 2, as a translation of the class struggle over the rate of surplus value into the wage-good markets. Any such inflation then sets up additional demand by labor for wage increases to meet the cost of living advance, increases to which capital would react by further inflation.

44. Baran and Sweezy (1966, p. 103) develop an argument that "under monopoly capitalism there is no necessary correlation, as there is in a competitive system, between the rate of technological progress and the volume of investment outlets." Reading for "monopoly capitalism" twentieth-century capitalism, there *is* a correlation of twentieth-century capitalism relative to nineteenth-century capitalism between the rate of technological progress and the volume of "investment outlets" (read, possibilities to penetrate precapitalist forms of production); we have seen the correlation to be inverse. In the sense that the historical movement of capitalism is not disjointed, but a continual but uneven development, the inverse correlation should also obtain within the nineteenth- and twentieth-century capitalisms separately considered. In any case, Baran and Sweezy's argument on their point (see also Baran, 1957, pp. 198–208) seems to contradict in part their own notion that cost discipline is not reduced under "monopoly capitalism" (see footnote 38).

REFERENCES

Anderson, P. (1974a), *Passages from Antiquity to Feudalism,* London: New Left Books.

Anderson, P. (1974b), *Lineages of the Absolutist State,* London: New Left Books.

Baran, P. A. (1957), *The Political Economy of Growth,* Penguin edition, Harmondsworth, England, 1973.

Baran, P. A. and Sweezy, P. M. (1966), *Monopoly Capital: An Essay on the American Economic and Social Order,* Penguin edition, Harmondsworth, England, 1968.

Beard, C. A. (1913), *An Economic Interpretation of the United States Constitution.*

Blair, J. M. (1972), *Economic Concentration: Structure, Behaviour and Public Policy,* New York: Harcourt, Brace, Jovanovich.

Braverman, H. (1974), *Labor and Monopoly Capital: The Degradation of Work in the Twentieth Century,* New York: Monthly Review Press.

Cooper, A. C. (1964), "R and D is More Efficient in Small Companies," *Harvard Business Review,* Vol. 42, pp. 75–83.

Crotty, J. R. and Rapping, L. A. (1975), "The 1975 Report of the President's Council of Economic Advisers: A Radical Critque," *American Economic Review,* Vol. 65, pp. 791–811.

Earley, J. S. (1957), "Discussion [on a paper of H.A. Simon]," *American Economic Review,* May 1957, pp. 330–335.

Engels, F. (1969), *Germany: Revolution and Counter-Revolution,* with the collaboration of K. Marx and edited by E. Marx, New York: International Publishers.

Freeman, C. (1968), "Chemical Process Plant: Innovation and the World Market," *National Institute Economic Review,* Vol. 45, pp. 29–57.

Fromm, E. (1955), *The Sane Society,* New York: Rinehart.

Furtado, C. (1963), *The Economic Growth of Brazil: A Survey from Colonial to Modern Times,* Berkeley and Los Angeles: University of California Press.

Gerstein, I. (1976), "Production, Circulation and Value: The Significance of the 'Transformation Problem' in Marx's Critique of Political Economy," *Economy and Society,* Vol. 5, pp. 243–291.

Gough, I. (1972), "Marx's Theory of Productive and Unproductive Labor," *New Left Review,* No. 76, pp. 47–72.

Habakkuk, H. J. (1962), *American and British Technology in the Nineteenth Century: The Search for Labor-Saving Inventions,* London and New York: Cambridge University Press.

Halliday, J. (1975), *A Political History of Japanese Capitalism,* New York: Pantheon.

Hamberg, D. (1966), *R and D: Essays on the Economics of Research and Development,* New York: Random House.

Hobsbawn, E. F. (1968), *Industry and Empire,* Harmondsworth, England: Penguin.

Hollander, S. (1965), *The Sources of Increased Efficiency: A Study of Du Pont Rayon Plants,* Cambridge, Massachusetts: M.I.T. Press.

Jewkes, J., Sawers, D. and Stillerman, R. (1969), *The Sources of Invention,* Second Edition, New York: Norton.

Kalecki, M. (1943), "Political Aspects of Full Employment," *Political Quarterly,* Vol. 14, pp. 322–331. Paged references to the reprint in *A Critique of Economic Theory,* edited by Hunt, E. K. and Schwartz, J. G. (1972), pp. 420–430, Baltimore, Maryland: Penguin.

Kamien, M. I. and Schwartz, N. L. (1975), "Market Structure and Innovations: A Survey," *Journal of Economic Literature, Vol. 13, pp. 1–37.*

Keynes, J. M. (1936), *The General Theory of Employment, Interest, and Money,* New York: Harcourt, Brace, and World.

Lenin, V. I. (1917), *Imperialsim, The Highest Stage of Capitalism,* Foreign Languages Press, Peking, 1969.

Luxemburg, R. (1951), *The Accumulation of Capital,* translated from German by Schwarzschild, A., with an introduction by J. Robinson, London: Routledge and Kegan Paul.

Macpherson, C. B. (1962), *The Political Theory of Possessive Individualism: Hobbes to Locke,* Oxford: Oxford Universtiy Press.

Magaline, A. D. (1975), *Lutte de classes et dévalorisation du capital: Contribution à la critique de révisionnisme,* Paris: Maspero.

Mandel, E. (1973), *Late Capitalism,* London: New Left Books.

Marx, K. (1973), *Grundrisse,* translated by M. Nicolaus, New York: Vintage.

Marx, K. (1974), *Capital: A Critique of Political Economy,* in three volumes, London: Lawrence and Wishart.

Morishima, M. (1973), *Marx's Economics: A Dual Theory of Value and Growth,* London: Cambridge University Press.

Morishima, M. (1974), "Marx in the Light of Modern Economic Theory," *Econometrica,* Vol. 42, pp. 611–632.

Morishima, M. and Catephores, G. (1975), "Is There an 'Historical Transformation Problem'"? *Economic Journal,* Vol. 85, pp. 309–328.

Okishio, N. (1961), "Technical Changes and the Rate of Profit," *Kobe University Economic Review,* Vol. 7, pp. 85–99.

Poulantzas, N. (1973), *Political Power and Social Classes,* London: New Left Books.

Sahlins, M. (1972), *Stone Age Economics,* Chicago and New York: Aldine-Atherton.

Samuelson, P. A. (1973), *Economics,* Ninth Edition, New York: McGraw-Hill.

Saul, J. S. and Woods, R. (1971), "African Peasantries," in *Peasants and Peasant Societies,* edited by Shanin, T., pp. 103–114, Harmondsworth, England: Penguin.

Schumpeter, J. (1928), "The Instability of Capitalism," *Economic Journal,* Vol. 38, pp. 361–386. Paged references to reprint in *The Economics of Technological Change,* edited by Rosenberg, N. (1971), pp. 13–42, Harmondsworth, England: Penguin.

Stone, K. (1974), "The Origin of Job Structure in the Steel Industry," *Review of Radical Political Economics,* Vol. 6, Summer, pp. 113–173.

Wallerstein, I. (1974), *The Modern World-System: Capitalist Agriculture and the Origins of the European World-Economy in the Sixteenth Century,* New York: Academic Press.

Wolf, E. R. (1966), *Peasants,* Englewood Cliffs, New Jersey: Prentice-Hall.

Wolfstetter, E. (1974), "The Law of the Falling Tendency of the Rate of Profit," Lecture Notes, Department of Economics, State University of New York at Buffalo.

Wright, E. D. (1976), "Class Boundaries in Advanced Capitalist Societies," *New Left Review,* No. 98, pp. 3–41.

THERE IS NOTHING SIMPLE ABOUT A COMMODITY*

Jesse Schwartz, ESSAYIST AND JOURNALIST

A commodity appears at first, a very trivial thing, and easily understood. Its analysis shows that it is in reality, a very queer thing, abounding in metaphysical subtleties and theological niceties.—KARL MARX.

SECTION 1

Exchange-Value Becomes Independent

Ricardo begins his *Principles* with a discussion of the peculiar form taken by the products of human labor under capitalism; he does not consider previous social forms. He starts with a commodity, the elemental social cell, the smallest unit wherein social mediations are discernible. His enquiry is exclusively concerned with a form of capitalism in which production, exchange, money, circulation and banking have fully matured; as he says, his study is directed to "such commodities only as can be increased in quantity by the exertion of human industry and on the production of which competition operates without restraint."

Now a commodity, Ricardo tells us, possesses two qualities. "The one may be called *value in use;* the other, *value in exchange.*" The first refers to the size, texture, shape, structure and so on of the commodity. These physical properties

*This paper is original in this volume, but through an oversight is reprinted in *The Subtle Anatomy of Capitalism,* J. Schwartz, ed., Goodyear, Santa Monica, California, 1977, Chapter 23, without attribution.

make it a useful object. The second, the power to exchange with other commodities is purely social. Use-value is the abode of lovers of tangible facts. Here they can appeal to the certainty of perception to assure us, say, of the texture, color or weave of a piece of cloth. This is the realm of solid fact. What indeed can vie with it in solidity? The "man of common sense" has always applauded as academic economists have sought to "measure" use-value and fill textbooks with an unceasing rumination over utility, tastes and indifference curves.

The other category, "exchange-value," has proven somewhat less amenable. Indeed, the power of one commodity to exchange for others has long been a subject of speculation. Aristotle pondered it as did scholars during the Middle Ages and, much later, William Petty and Benjamin Franklin. In previous social forms exchange occurred mainly on the periphery or boundaries of communities, while the production and distribution of useful objects within them was settled according to custom or decree. Only after a very gradual process, in the late Middle Ages, do we see exchange seizing hold of relations within communities. Perhaps, at first in Italian and Hanseatic maritime republics as Engels (1870) tells us, labor began to be sold as a commodity replacing earlier forms of bondage, indenture and serfdom. By the nineteenth century exchange had reached a level of universality, so that the general and abstract qualities of a commodity could be discerned in theory. This was accomplished by Karl Marx.

The Theory of Value

Marx's theory represents the fullest and most complete statement of the notion of value. Let's outline it and view Ricardo's work from its perspective.

Any commodity, no matter how humble, can exchange for an unlimited variety of other commodities. Potatoes in sufficient quantity can exchange for a watch, a house or gold. Consider the expression

$$\text{(1)} \quad \text{A potatoes} = \text{B watches} = \text{C houses} = \text{D gold}$$

where a quantity of potatoes is expressed in terms of watches, houses and innumerable other commodities. How is it that things so different can exchange as equivalents?

Here the voice of common sense might say that it is their "price" that brings them into equality. This is simply repeating our question. True, we can express the watch, house or airplane in terms of potatoes and thus arrive at "potato prices," if you will. This is but an expression for the exchange-value of watches, houses and airplanes in terms of one particular use-value, namely, potatoes. The point is that the potatoes can be compared with the watch or the house only because they are qualitatively identical, homogeneous magnitudes. The potatoes, watch and house exist as values, as things which are equal and different from their existence as potatoes, watches, etc. The potatoes here are full-fledged citizens of the world of commodities with the inalienable right to exchange, in sufficient quantity, with watches, houses, gold, etc. These mirror the value of the potatoes.

Let us try to understand something more of value.

The man of common sense looking at the exchange

1 watch = 50 lbs potatoes

sees only the value of the watch as expressed in so many potatoes and the value of the watch is nothing apart from this. Apart from its "potato price," no meaning can be given to the "value" of the watch.[1] "Hear! Hear!" exclaims the man of common sense. If, the next day, a watch should exchange for 60 lbs potatoes or 40 lbs potatoes, well then, that is its value.

This is another way of saying that value denotes *nothing* (Marx, 1968, Part III, p. 141.) If 1 watch = 50 lbs potatoes, what is the value of 1 watch? Fifty lbs of potatoes. Of 50 lbs of potatoes? One watch. Since 1 watch equals 50 lbs of potatoes and 50 lbs of potatoes equals 1 watch, it follows that the value of 1 watch is equal to 1 watch, and by the same reasoning the value of 50 lbs of potatoes is equal to 50 lbs of potatoes.

(Very sound. You know where you're at with a theory like that.) This paralysis of the ability to abstract, this narrowing of reality to factual immediacy, reduces economics either to a cataloging of each and every of the myriad million exchanges occurring daily or to an equally empty conjecture that "everything depends on everything."

Furthermore, if we are restricted to saying that value is whatever has occurred in exchange, how then is it possible to express the price of a palace in terms of potatoes, or a milling machine in terms of a house? We can indeed do this, though the exchanges in question have never occurred. This would not be possible unless there is a substance common to both palaces and potatoes.

It is not with the mere fact of exchange that we are dealing. Watches have no intrinsic property that make them exchange with a certain quantity of potatoes. Only because the watches and potatoes are values can the value of one be expressed in the other. The watch must have a value independent of potatoes and must be equal to a third thing. "What," we may ask, "is the difference between a nail in one's boot and Pushkin?" Unless the watch and potatoes can be subsumed in a common space of commodities, we have as much chance of comparing them! Their existence as commodities is a purely social creation. Their separate existences as things is brought into unity by the social substance common to each (Marx, 1968, Part III, p. 143.) This can only be social labor. Now considering expression (1) representing exchange in general, we see that it is a purely quantitative relation and abstracts from the specific qualities of commodities. In exchange, the particular qualities of commodities are subsumed and only the quantitative relation, the proportion in which the commodities exchange has any importance. Now various concrete labors of farming, watchmaking, carpentry, and so on have produced the commodities. With the reduction of useful things to values, concrete labor is subsumed into universal abstract labor. The qualities of the commodities disappear when they are considered as values; the labor that has produced them also has no particular quality—it is abstract, universal social labor brought about by the universal alienation of labor.

As humanity in the West is totally immersed in commodity production, an individual understandably finds it hard to gaze with wonderment at the historical specificity of a mode of production where every commodity is something different from its own physical make-up. That a commodity is exchangeable for any other commodity—i.e., so many potatoes for a palace, so much cloth for gold—this universal exchangeability demonstrates that exchange-value has become independent, separate from the mundane properties of potatoes or cloth. This universal exchangeability shows that all act as social labor and can be exchanged for other commodities in proportion to the amount of social labor they contain.

This remarkable independence of exchange-value from use-value finds its fullest expression in money. Here one commodity is set aside and the others are measured in terms of the use-value of this one; i.e., so many ounces of gold for so many potatoes or watches. We can rewrite (1) as

$$1 \text{ potato} = x \text{ gold};\ 1 \text{ watch} = y \text{ gold};\ 1 \text{ house} = z \text{ gold}.$$

In this way we arrive at money prices of potatoes, watches and houses.

Indeed, the concept of value first arose from a consideration of the properties of money. In money, commodities acquire a definite *measure* of their value in terms of the use-value of some particular commodity. Indeed, when a commodity is sold, transformed into money, we see clearly its exchange-value acquiring an independent existence. But note our path of reasoning from the nature of a commodity as a value to money to price, a progress from the essence to the phenomenological form. Consider:

COMMODITY	MONEY
Labor of private individuals transformed into abstract social labor.	Universal exchangeability; different magnitudes measured in terms of one exclusive use-value.
Individual labor represented as social labor.	Individual price related to total price.
Exchange-value becomes independent from use-value.	Price separate from use-value.

This underlines that the power of one commodity to exchange with any other (potatoes for a palace) reflects how the labor of private individuals must be a proportionate part of the labor of society. That the price of a commodity is separate from its use-value and is related to the prices of all other commodities reflects that exchange-value is independent of use-value and that commodities are but different expressions of the same substance.

Had we followed the Samuel Bailey's of this world (who insist as designating as "real" that which can only be counted on ten fingers) by starting with price and not value, we would be doing violence to a world of understanding. Only by seeing the inner structure which prices hide can we speak of them meaningfully; otherwise we are limited to repeating "a price . . . is a price . . . is a price."

> Labor-time is the measure of both gold and commodities, and gold becomes the measure of value only because all commodities are measured in terms of gold; it is consequently merely an illusion created by the circulation process to suppose that money makes commodities commensurable. On the contrary, it is only the commensurability of commodities as materialized labor-time which converts gold into money. (Marx, 1971, pp. 67–68.)

Money then is an intimation of the secret language of commodities.

"One beaver should naturally exchange for, or be worth two deer."

With the rudiments of the theory of value, we can discusss Ricardo's achievement. First of all, we see that when Ricardo speaks of labor, not the particular labor in potato growing, watchmaking or house building, it is of abstract social labor that he talks. He contents himself with presupposing it and considers only the quantity or *magnitude* of this abstract labor contained in different commodities.

Taking this abstract labor as "the foundation of the exchangeable value of all things," without reflecting upon it, was bound to encumber his doctrine. For example, he invokes Adam Smith's "rude and early state" as justification for his theory of value. Recall Smith's famous example of a society of hunters—if it took twice as long to kill a beaver as a deer, then one beaver should "naturally" exchange for two deer. Smith's example does not answer altogether to Ricardo's purpose. In this mythical economy, trade consists of the exchange of the labor of one sort, beaver hunting, for another sort, deer hunting. Now these are specific types of labor and we are not told what has brought them into equality.

Why is the expenditure of the sort of labor in beaver hunting a measure of that in deer hunting or vice versa? There is no natural property of beaver that permits it to exchange for two deer. Exchange here would be settled by custom, or chance or even whim. Only where specific labor has been reduced to a common standard or measure is exchange governed by general laws. This occurs only with commodity production seizing all sectors and labor itself becoming a commodity. Unfortunately Ricardo rests his theory for capitalism on such a primitive basis.

But this example does show, strikingly enough, that the rate at which commodities exchange does not determine their value; rather, their value determines the rate of which they exchange. That is, *value is prior to exchange*. The labor materialized in beaver or deer hunting determines that they exchange 1:2. If we could not ascertain value except where an exchange had occurred, how could we estimate the value of a house or airplane in terms of potatoes?

Adam Smith Tries to Speak the Language of Commodities

Ricardo's theory of value is a further development and critique of Smith's view. Indeed, much of his chapter on "Value" is an ongoing argument with Smith. Let us consider, for a moment, some of Smith's ideas.

As we have seen, he took labor to be the source of exchange value in his "rude and early state." Here the whole product of labor goes to the laborer. At this level of abstraction, commodities exchange for equivalents, as values. This, according to Smith, requires that part of the labor of the worker must pay his wages and another part must be due for profits. But then this bucolic social order of small artisans gives way to one in which instruments, raw materials, machinery and land are appropriated by one class as capital confronting a mass of humanity who live by selling their labor-power.

At first Smith maintained that here part of the labor of the worker goes to pay his wages and another part goes for profit. That is, with the separation of materialized labor (machinery, equipment, raw materials and so forth) from living labor, the worker no longer receives the full value of what he produces. In a remarkable anticipation of Marx's theory of surplus value, Smith sees profit and rent as coming from that portion of the product of labor remaining after wages. In other words, Smith clearly sees how the profit of the capitalist is an appropriation of the unpaid labor of others (see Smith, 1950, p. 41). Then he does a remarkable reversal. In one sentence he says,

> As the price or exchange value of every particular commodity taken separately resolves itself into some one or other or all of these three parts so that of all the commodities which compose the whole annual labor of every country, taken complexly, must resolve itself into the same three parts, and be parceled out among different inhabitants of the country, either as wages or their labor, the profits of their stock or the rent of their land.

He clearly resolves here, the value of either an individual commodity or the total annual product into profit, rent and wages. But two sentences later, "Wages, profit and rent are the three original sources of all revenue as well as all exchangeable value." (Smith, 1950, pp. 58–59.) Now he declares wages, profit and rent to be independent elements which are added up to form exchange value. He goes on to say that there exist average or ordinary rates of rent, of profit and wages, independently determined. The natural price of a commodity, he goes on to tell us, is equal to the sum of these three components when at their natural levels. Instead of having their source in value created by labor-wages, profit and rent become the source of value. This is merely a recitation of how an individual capitalist sees things—so much for wages, so much for profit, so much for rent.

It puts the question of exchange value at one remove. Rather than the value of the commodity itself, we must consider its components and are still at a loss as to how to find them. There is also a logical error here in that it assumes that the total social product is resolvable into only wages, profit and rent, thereby neglecting constant capital. Smith had to assume what he did or he would have had to convince us not only of "natural" rates of wages, profits and rent but of machinery, buildings, raw materials and semifinished goods as well. He had to omit these elements of constant capital—"For otherwise he would have to say: The value of a commodity consists of wages, profit, rent and that part of the value of the commodity which does not consist of wages, profit, rent." (Marx, 1968, Part II, p. 219.)

There is nothing simple about a commodity.

His Confusion of Tongues—Materialized and Living Labor

Ricardo everywhere contested Smith's second conception. He felt that not merely in Smith's "rude and early state" but even in circumstances of full-blown capitalism, even then Smith's first conception was true. As we have said, this requires, on the one hand, a mass of instruments and means of production appropriated by a small number of people and a mass of humanity on the other hand who have only one commodity, their life energy, to sell. This they exchange for wages with which they replenish their muscles, nerves and tissues. Viewing this as a process, we can say that only a part of the labor of the workers materialized in their product is returned to them. The rest becomes the property of another who blithely gives the worker chits or claims on each round, to a fraction of their product. Thus the labor materialized in wage goods exchanges for a greater quantity of labor than itself.

Ricardo accepts this as the way things are under capitalism. He felt that not merely in Smith's "rude and early state" where the whole product of labor goes to the laborer but even in circumstances of full-fledged capitalism where only part goes to the worker and the rest goes to capitalists and landlords, even then Smith's first conception was true. Regardless of how the product is distributed—no matter how much goes to A or B—this does not affect its value. Value is created in production and unaffected regardless of whether the mass of commodities is owned by A or B or both.

Regardless of how much or little of their product is received by the workers, he held that if the quantity of labor regulated exchange when *all* was received by the workers, it should continue to do so when only a part is received by them. Now if only a part of the value of the product goes to the laborer, it follows that the materialized labor in wages commands a greater quantity of labor than it contains.

But the exchange of living for materialized labor is not done on the basis of equivalents. This is not a mere exchange between commodities but between commodities acting as capital on the one hand and labor power on the other.

Imagine a society where individual workers produce and sell their commodities. Each worker expends a quantity of labor in producing some commodity which he exchanges for an equal value of the other commodities. Therefore, each worker receives the full value of his product in the form of use-values produced by other workers. In effect, each worker exchanges his living labor for an equivalent quantity of the materialized labor of others. Here a definite quantity of materialized labor always commands an equal quantity of living labor. We are, formally speaking, indifferent as to whether we take labor commanded or materialized, "value of labor" or "quantity of labor" as our measure. When Smith finds that under capitalism a quantity of materialized labor commands a greater quantity of living labor, he should have realized that "value of labor" and "quantity of labor" are no longer identical. As Ricardo says forthrightly,

> . . . if the reward of the laborer were always in proportion to what he produced, the quantity of labor bestowed on a commodity, and the quantity of labor which that commodity would purchase, would be equal, . . . but they are not equal. (Ricardo, 1970, Vol. I, p. 14.)

This peculiar exchange between capital and labor-power so impressed Smith that he no longer maintained his first conception, as we have seen. Rather, he felt that value could be "added up" from "natural" rates of wages, profits and rent. Furthermore, he drops his first conception of the determination of the value of commodities by the labor required for their production and takes as his measure the quantity of living labor that a definite quantity of commodities can command, or—which is the same thing—the quantity of commodities that a definite quantity of labor can command. In other words, he takes wages to be a measure. But as Marx comments,

> The value of labor, or rather of labor-power, changes like that of any other commodity and is in no way specifically different from the value of other commodities. Here value is made the measuring rod and the basis for the explanation of value—so we have a vicious circle. (Marx, 1968, Part I, p. 71.)

Ricardo believed that Adam Smith was guilty of the rather obtuse error of taking "as two equivalent expressions the labor materialized in a commodity and that which it could command." But Smith nowhere asserts that "these were two equivalent expressions." On the contrary, he argues,

> Because in capitalist production, the wage of the worker is *no* longer equal to his product, therefore, the quantity of labor which a commodity costs and the quantity of

> commodities that a worker can purchase with this labor are two differnt things—*for this very reason* the relative quantity of labor contained in commodities ceases to determine their value, which is now determined rather by *value of labor,* by the quantity that I can purchase, or command with a given amount of commodities. Thus the value of labor (or the compensation paid for labor) becomes the measure of value. (Marx, 1968, Part II, p. 396.)

Ricardo does not understand the causes for Smith's abandoning the theory of value when dealing with capitalism. As he says,

> Adam Smith thought, that as in the early stages of society, all of the produce of labor belonged to the laborer, and after stock was accumulated, a part went to profits, that accumulation, necessarily, without any regard to the different degrees of durability of capital, or any other circumstance whatever, raised the prices or exchangeable value of commodities, and consequently that their value was no longer regulated by the quantity of labor necessary to their production. In opposition to him, I maintain that it is not because capital accumulates, that exchangeable value varies, but it is in all stages of society, owing only to two causes: one the more or less quantity of labor required, the other the greater or less durability of capital—that the former is never superseded by the latter, but is only modified by it. (Ricardo, 1970, Vol. VII, p. 377.)

Ricardo thinks that it was only because labor no longer obtains its entire product—that is, because a part goes to the owner of "stock"—that Smith no longer held his first conception. Thus he reads into Smith his own overriding concern with distribution.

But Smith's difficulty arises from the inner essence of capitalism. As Marx points out,

> Adam Smith feels the difficulty of deducing the exchange between capital and labor from the law that determines the exchange of commodities, since the former apparently rests on quite opposite and contradictory principles. And indeed the contradiction could not be solved so long as capital was set directly against labor instead of labor-power. Adam Smith was well aware that the labor-time expended on the reproduction and maintenance of labor-power is very different from the labor, which it [i.e., labor-power] itself can perform. (Marx, 1968, Part I, p. 73.)

Therefore Smith is "startled," as Marx says, (Marx, 1968, Part I, p. 74) to find that the general law that commodities exchange according to the labor materialized in them ceases to apply in the exchange between capital and wage-labor, materialized and living labor.

There is another reason why he drops the general law. We have seen when a commodity functions as capital it can command or exert power over more of the labor of others than it itself contains. When Smith adopts as his standard, labor commanded, he brings this into relief.

Smith's labor commanded measure, while not scientifically correct, nonetheless reflected a poignant truth—the unequal exchange between capital and wage labor. Indeed, "commanded" bespeaks coersion; it hints of something very different from a mere exchange of commodities among free, equal, and independent sellers and buyers of commodities, which ideologists have tried so hard to demonstrate as an eternal law of nature and reason. The essence of capital is its power to appropriate labor without exchange, without an equivalent. It is not merely that capital commands labor, it is the command over *unpaid* labor.

"Something is happening here, but you don't know what it is, do you Mr. Smith?"!

"There is nothing simple about a commodity." (Dunayevskaya, 1971, p. 99.)

The Necessity for a Standard of Value

There is still a *hidden reason,* as Marx[2] tells us, for Smith's view that as soon as capital and wage-labor intervene it is the labor commanded, not materialized, in a commodity that regulates its value. It is that labor has a *permanent* relative value with respect to corn. Smith, taking corn to denote food in general, reasoned that as long as labor is sold at its "natural price," it will exchange for a certain quantity of corn or a given quantity of corn will always exchange for the same amount of labor. The one will always command the same use-value of the other. For this reason, we can take either the corn or labor that a commodity could purchase as a measure of its value.

Suppose that the labor expended per bushel of corn falls by half. A bushel of corn, would by Smith's assumption, purchase a week's labor as before. Smith would say that the value of corn is unchanged as it commands the same amount of labor; he would also have to say that its value has fallen, as it can command a lesser quantity of other commodities. How then can we find out whether the value of the corn has changed? Let us return to our discussion of exchange for a moment.

Suppose that we observe a quantity of potatoes to exchange for wrist watches in the proportions

$$50 \text{ lbs potatoes} = 2 \text{ watches.}$$

Then suppose that one day we find

$$50 \text{ lbs potatoes} = 1 \text{ watch.}$$

We are at a loss to say whether a greater quantity of labor has been expended in making watches or a lesser quantity in making potatoes, or a greater quantity in making both though proportionately more in watches or a lesser quantity in both, though lesser still in potatoes.

Suppose we know for certain that the value of potatoes has remained unchanged, then we can say with confidence that the value of a watch has risen. We can call potatoes an *external measure* of value. It is a commodity in terms of which we can measure the values of the other commodities. We can contrast this to an *imminent measure*.

Suppose the labor materialized in the potatoes and watches doubled. We would still have

50 lbs potatoes = 2 watches.

The value of watches in terms of our external measure, potatoes, remains unchanged.

Only with an imminent measure can we ascertain that the absolute value of watches has changed, that more labor has been expended. We can also see that relative value cannot change without a change in absolute value but the converse is not true.

As we have argued, the rate at which potatoes and watches exchange does not determine their value, but their value detemines the rate at which they exchange. (If there were no imminent measure common to both, the value of potatoes could not be expressed in terms of watches before it had been exchanged against watches.)

We can thus distinguish between *external* and *imminent* measures of value. As the former must be a commodity, its value must be variable and subject to the same fluctuations as any commodity.

We have tried to show that the very nature of value necessitates that one commodity be taken as the measure of value of the rest. Such a commodity, gold, for instance, serves as money, allowing the relative values of other commodities to be measured in terms of it. If the value of gold changes, it does so to an equal degree with respect to all commodities. The money price of a commodity, therefore, is a relative measure of its value.

Before watches, however, can be expressed in potatoes or gold, the watches and the rest must be represented as equivalents, as expressions of the same substance. How the potatoes have been made qualitatively equal to watches so that the measurement can occur is left unanswered by Ricardo.

An imminent measure of value, on the other hand, cannot be another commodity, another value, and consequently cannot be subject to the same variations in value as other commodities. It is the common substance rendering physical objects qualitatively equal so that they differ only quantitatively. This is labor time, in its unique form as abstract social labor which is found only under capitalism. It should not be thought that labor time is the answer to Ricardo's puzzle of an invariable standard in the same way as corn, gold, wages or silver, have been proposed at various times. The latter can play a role only in finding the magnitude of value, wherein they serve as a form of money, presupposing value. Labor time, on the other hand, qualitatively transforms useful objects into values and is their substance as values.

This is not to deny the historic meaning and validity of the search for a standard of value. Ostensibly it rose from a need to compare the value of commodities in different times. It could be used, for example, to find whether the rise in the price of corn sold in the eighteenth century was due to the circumstances of its production or to the medium in which it was measured. If we knew that the value of gold remained the same during this time, then by observing the proportions in which corn exchanges with gold we can ascertain the variations in the value of corn, knowing for certain that our measurements are not obfuscated by changes in our standard. But such a rather academic concern concealed, as Marx tells us, a profound question, that of the nature of value itself. (Marx, 1968, Part III, p. 133–135.) The mazy entanglements of the Classicals in their effort to define value in terms of some particular value were inevitable stages in the inquiry. It culminated in the discovery that abstract social labor is the substance of value. ''A quantity of labor has no value, is not a commodity, but is that which transforms commodities into values, it is their common substance.'' (Marx, 1968, Part III, p. 135.)

Scholars have assiduously rummaged the lumberyard of commodities for an ''invariable standard.'' Scattered in the archaelogical museum of bygone doctrine we find corn, gold, wages or ''silver picked up on the seashore in a day.'' Of late there has been an ingenious attempt by Piero Sraffa to construct, artificially, a ''standard commodity'' from a mass of commodities. All of these can only measure with respect to themselves. If the value of corn, gold, wages, etc. changes, it does so with respect to all commodities. Hence the relative values remain unchanged. Rather than go through the cumbersome and tedious task of expressing values in silver or corn, it is just as well to simply read them from a price list—to express them in money. One external measure is as good as another. In so far as Ricardo sought his ''invariable measure'' in terms of some commodity, he might just as well have chosen money. Hence Marx concludes, ''The problem of finding an 'invariable measure of value' is thereby eliminated.'' (Marx, 1968, Part III, p. 133.)

SECTION 2

Ricardo Progresses from Value to Capital

Just before, Ricardo was seeking to establish a general law of exchange with an image of individual commodity producers in mind. Now, he tries to apply it to the realm of wage labor and capital. That is, past labor materialized in machinery and raw materials is concentrated in a few hands and confronts living labor. Here we have not only an independent expression of value, as in money, but dynamic value, value in the process of expansion.

Ricardo begins by considering the relation of the value of raw materials, semifinished products and machines to the finished product. These simply transfer their value to the product though their use-values undergo the most varied changes. The entire value of cotton cloth is transferred to the shirt whereas only a small part of the value of the weaving machine is also given up; the more durable an instrument, the less value it transfers to the product. The value of a commodity is simply the sum of the materialized and living labor expended on it. The formal difference between the two sorts of labor does not affect its value. Marx stops and asks at this point, "If this difference is of no significance in the determination of the value of commodities, why does it assume such decisive importance when past labor (capital) is exchanged against living labor?" (Marx, 1968, Part II, p. 399.) How is it that the exchange of past for living labor is not on the basis of equivalents, that the one commands a greater quantity of the other? (If only Ricardo had inquired further!)

Ricardo continues his discussion of capital in Section 4 by classifying it as "circulating" or "fixed" according to its period of turnover. (Smith, by the way, had no need to make such a distinction because, in his time, means of production of relatively long life were rare.)

He Bypasses Mediations to Confound Value and Price

With this, Ricardo leaps in with a uniform rate of profit. How he jumps from exchange value to profit and, what is more, a general rate of profit, is difficult to understand. Instead of presupposing a general rate of profit, he should have tried to explain it. In order to scientifically discuss these matters, it seems that at the very least we must go from value to money, to the nature of prices and then to the creation and functioning of capital. But Ricardo, in bypassing these questions, encumbers his doctrine and his followers imitate him, even to this day.

The question that he faces and that he struggled with all his days can be briefly put by looking at one of his examples:

Suppose that a farmer employs 100 men at a wage of £50 per year, and a cotton manufacturer likewise employs 100 men at £50 to construct a machine. Each employs a capital of £5000 and since, as Ricardo tells us, profits are 10%, the "value" of the machine and the corn at the end of the first year must be £5500. In the second year, the farmer again employs 100 men, advances a capital of £5000 and sells his corn for £5500. The manufacturer also employs 100 men, to use the newly created machine in weaving cloth. The manufacturer, to be on a par with the farmer, must not only obtain £5500 but must receive in addition £550, the profit on the £5500. Hence the cloth must sell at £6050.[3]

Ricardo concludes, "Here then are capitalists employing precisely the same quantity of labor annually on the production of their commodities, and yet the goods they produce differ in value on account on the different quantities of fixed capital, or accumulated labor.'' He gives a number of examples, in essence, the same, which show that in the following circumstances the value of commodities will differ from their relative prices:

a) differing degrees of durability of fixed capital;
b) differing periods of durability of circulating capital;
c) differing proportions in which materialized and living labor are combined; and
d) differing times required to bring commodities to market.

He has proven in fact with his examples that the establishment of a general rate of profit brings into being prices which are determined and regulated by it and are quite different from the values of commodities. *Indeed, the cause of the variation of prices from values is the general rate of profit.*

But does Ricardo see things in this light? Not at all.

Just a few pages before, Ricardo tells us that there is ''another cause, besides the greater or less quantity of labor necessary to produce commodities, for the variations in their relative value—this cause is the rise or fall in the value of labor, i.e., changes in the wage rate.'' But he does not vary the wage in three of the four examples he gives. Yet ''relative values'' or prices differ from values. This he takes to be an exception or modification to his general rule, ''The quantity of labor bestowed on the production of commodities regulates their relative value,'' and he ascribes this variation *solely* to changes in wages.

I maintain that all the elements of a correct solution to this problem have been provided by Marx. Its essence is that capitals, regardless of their compositions, regardless of the proportion of machinery and raw materials to wages, must yield the same return. This can come about only if there is a permanent deviation of prices from values, ''permanent'' because it occurs with the wage rate remaining the same. (We will call it the ''Marx effect''; it is very different from the ''Ricardo effect,'' the change in relative prices consequent upon a change in the wage, which we will consider later on.)[4]

Now a capital consisting of £5000 of machinery and raw materials and £5000 in labor must yield the same profit as a capital of £7500 in machinery and £2500 in labor. It is only the variable capital that sets in motion living labor productive of surplus value. The proportion of constant to variable capital is accordingly most significant, and Marx calls it the ''organic composition.'' It is 1:1 in the first case and 3:1 in the second. He shows how surplus value regardless of where it originates can be thought of as going into a kind of pool from which it is redistributed back to each capital in proportion to its size. The resulting prices deviate from values, but total price is equal to total value and total profit is equal to total surplus value. Marx's solution is a wondrous description of industrial competition.

How then would Marx have solved the problem that Ricardo proposes? This is not hard to guess, as he discusses several problems of the same sort in the third volume of *Capital*. (Marx, 1970, Vol. III, Chapter IX.) Let's try to work it out:

During the first year both the manufacturer and farmer employ only variable capital of £5000. The total value of machines and corn at the end of the year is £5500, and as Ricardo has not considered raw materials or depreciation of the machines used in the production process, the augmentation of £500 in the value of the corn and machines is due solely to living labor. From this we can conclude that the rate of surplus value S/V is 500/5000 or 10%. That is, it is equal to the rate of profit that Ricardo assumed.

To help our discussion of the second year we can set up a table of much the same sort that Marx used:

	Capitals	Surplus Value S	Rate of Profit	Value of Commodities C+V+S	Cost-Price C+V
Manufacturer	5500C+5000V	500	4.75%	5500	5000
Farmer	5000V	500	10.00%	5500	5000

The manufacturer employs the newly constructed machine of value £5500 and also outlays £5000 in wages as does the farmer. With a rate of surplus value of 10% each produces a mass of surplus value of £500. As Ricardo assumes that the machine does not depreciate, the value of the cloth is £5500 as is the value of the corn. Marx calls "cost-price" the cost of materials and labor and as only labor is considered, the cost-price of both the cloth and corn is £5000. The rate of profit of the manufacturer, the proportion of surplus value to his total capital, S/C+V is 4.75% while that of the farmer is 10%.

Now both capitals must yield the same rate of return. This can only occur if they sell at prices different from their values. Let's construct another table to show how this can come about:

		Surplus Value	Value of Comod-ities	Cost-price of Commodities	Price of Commodities	Rate of Profit	Deviation of Price from Value
Manufacturer	5500C+5000V	500	5500	5000	5677	6.45%	+ 177
Farmer	5000V	500	5500	5000	5323	6.45	− 177
Total	5500C+10000V	1000	11000	10000	11000		

The total mass of surplus value is 1000; dividing this by total capital, 5500C + 10000V we have an overall rate of profit S/C+V = 1000/15500 = 6.45%.

Reckoning this rate on the capital of the manufacturer and farmer, respectively, and adding the resulting mass of profit to the cost-price, we have the prices of production of the two commodities. The price of the cloth is above its value by + 177 and that of the corn is below its value by the same amount. What has occurred is that the mass of surplus value has been redistributed so as to equalize the profit rate on both capitals. The selling price of each commodity is no longer equal to its value, but total price is equal to total value and total profit is equal to total surplus value.

In summary, the capital of the manufacturer and the farmer set in motion the same amount of labor and produce the same amount of surplus value. But as the total capital of the manufacturer is greater than that of the farmer, their rates of profit are originally very different. These different rates are equalized by competition into a single uniform rate. The profit accruing to each capital depends only upon its magnitude, not upon its organic composition. The price of production of each commodity is equal to its cost-price plus the profit reckoned on the total capital.

We see that the manufacturer secures not merely the £500 surplus value that he has produced but an additional £177. The farmer, on the other hand, produced £500 in surplus but secures only £323 of this. We may think of the capital of the manufacturer, £10,500, and the farmer, £5000, regardless of its composition, as drawing an amount of surplus value from the total pool of £1000 in proportion to their magnitudes.

> So far as profits are concerned, the various capitalists are just so many stockholders in a stock company in which the shares of profit are uniformly divided per 100, so that profits differ in the case of the individual capitalists only in accordance with the amount of capital invested by each in the aggregate enterprise, i.e., according to his investment in social production as a whole, according to the number of his shares. (Marx, 1970, Vol. III, p. 158.)

We have sketched the steps from values to the derivation of a uniform rate of profit and prices of production. When a capitalist sells at these prices, he recovers the cost-price of his commodities and a profit in proportion to his capital advanced as a part of the total social capital. We have shown how a uniform rate of profit is derived.[5] By leaping in with his uniform rate of profit, Ricardo ignores a world of understanding right in front of his nose. Instead of showing that a uniform rate of profit necessitates that prices of production be different from values, he forcibly asserts their identity and talks only of changes in prices consequent upon changes in wages.

To fix this in our minds, let us recall that the divergence of cost of production from value is the "Marx effect." Changes in prices of production consequent upon a change in the wage rate, the "Ricardo effect," we will next consider.

There is nothing simple about a commodity.

"Another cause, besides the greater or less quantity of labor necessary to produce commodities, for the variations in their relative value—this cause is the rise and fall in the value of labor." (Ricardo, Vol. I, p. 30.)

In the example cited above, Ricardo has proven, although he does not know it, that a general rate of profit implies prices will differ from values. Following this, he considers the effect of a change in the wage rate. Suppose that in the previous example wages rise so that the profit rate falls from 10% to 9% . . . "instead of adding £550 to the common price of their goods (to £5500) for the profits on their fixed capital, the manufacturers would add only 9% on that sum, or £495; consequently, the price would be £5995 instead of £6050. As corn would continue to sell for £5500, the manufactured goods in which more fixed capital was employed would fall relatively to corn." This is a striking result. In general, a rise in wages will cause some prices to fall, namely, of commodities with higher organic composition than average; the rest will rise. It demolishes both Smith's view that a rise in wages would cause all prices to rise as well as the flim-flam of "supply and demand."

The value of the mass of "corn" (Ricardo, Vol. I, p. 35) equal to £5500 does not change when wages rise. Before, £5000 went to the workers as their wages and £500 to the farmer so as to yield 10% on his capital. Now the farmer must lay out £5045.9 in wages and his profit is 454.1 to yield him $\frac{454.1}{5045.9} = 9\%$ on his capital. The manufacturer, like the farmer, sets in motion the same quantity of labor as before. It produces a product equal to £5500 in value. As with the farmer, £5045.9 goes in wages and £454.1 to profits. However, instead of earning £500 on his machine built last year, the manufacturer earns only 9% or £495. Hence his selling price is £495 + £5500 = £5995; it has fallen by £55 from its previous level of £6050, whereas the price of corn remains unchanged. Note that by presupposing a rate of profit of first 10% (and later 9%), this necessitates prices differing from values at each respective rate. But Ricardo considers only *changes* in prices consequent upon *changes* in the wage-rate. He has not told us how the general rate of profit came into being. As Marx notes, "This illustration has nothing to do with the essential question of the *transformation of values into cost-prices*."[6]

To Leave a Legacy of Confusion

By confounding value and cost of production, Ricardo has left for his followers, old and new, a legacy of confusion. He criticized relentlessly Smith's confounding of labor materialized in a commodity and labor commanded by it, but was guilty of the same with value and cost of production.

Consider this: "Mr. Malthus appears to think that it is a part of my doctrine, that the cost and value of a thing should be the same—it is, if he means by cost, 'cost of production' including profits" (Ricardo, Vol. I. p. 47); and, "consequently a tax upon income, whilst money continued unaltered in value, would alter the relative *prices* and *value* [our italics] of commodities." (Ricardo, Vol. I, p. 208.)

Marx refers to the first passage several times to show how Ricardo consciously identifies value with cost of production. Thanks to Piero Sraffa's profound scholarship we can see, perhaps more clearly, what he meant. Ricardo wrote detailed notes on Malthus' *Principles of Political Economy*, which appeared in 1820. Only in 1919 were these discovered and were not published until 1928.

> If by cost Mr. Malthus means the wages paid for labor, I do not confound cost and value, because I do not say that a commodity the labor on which cost £1000, will therefore sell for £1000: it may sell for £1100, £1200 or £1500—but I say it will sell for the same as another commodity the labor on which also cost £1000; that commodities will be valuable in proportion to the quantity of labor expened on them.
>
> If by cost Mr. Malthus means cost of production, he must include profits, as well as labor; he must mean what Adam Smith calls natural price, which in synonymous with value.
>
> A commodity is at its natural value, when it repays by its price, all the expenses that have been bestowed, from first to last to produce it and bring it to market. If then my expression conveys the same meaning as cost of production, it is nearly what I wish it to do. (Ricardo, Vol. II, pp. 34–36.)

Ricardo is telling us that his theory of value is not that vulgar conception that wages regulate prices (presumably for some such reason as wages are a large portion of a capitalist's expenses). However, he does say that the wage can serve as an *index*, an indicator of the quantity of labor expended though only the latter determines value. (Needless to say, this index depends on there being a uniform working day and wage rate.)

But after all this, he unsays his high language by taking value to be the same as Smith's natural price. Let us remember that Adam Smith's natural price of a commodity is compounded from separate and independently determined rates of wages, profit and rent. These are taken to be "natural rates" which commonly prevail; aside from this, we are not told whence they are found. (See Section 1, "Adam Smith tries to speak . . .) Ricardo sees well enough through Smith's "adding up" theory of price as an inconsistency. Adam Smith, however, succeeded in ensnaring him again with his natural price.

His Theory Further Encumbered by Lack of Distinction between Surplus Value and Profit

Ricardo constructed categories, "fixed" and "circulating" capital, according to its durability and period of turnover. This tells us something of the observable nature of capital though nothing of its role in value creation. Marx's categories reflect that process. His "constant" capital denotes the materials, semifinished products, wear and tear of machinery that simply transfer their value to the product. His "variable" capital is that portion of capital that exchanges for living labor; it is self-expansive capital, the mother of surplus value. Ricardo's categories are phenomenological, Marx's are etiological. Ricardo's analysis is thus narrowly limited from the onset.

Ricardo's concept of capital is related closely to his view of profit. Marx maintained that a telling inconsistency of his system was his failure to distinguish between the ratio of surplus value and the ratio of profit. The one is the ratio of surplus value to the variable part of capital, the other is the ratio of surplus value to the *total* capital advanced. A capital of £500C may consist of £400C of constant capital and £100V of variable capital and produce a surplus value of £100S. Then the rate of profit would be $S/C+V = 20\%$ and the rate of surplus value $S/V = 100\%$. Evidently any number of rates of profit can correspond to one particular rate of surplus value, and to any one rate of profit there can be any number of rates of surplus value. We see then that the rate of profit is quite different from the rate of surplus value and may depend on many circumstances that do not affect the latter. Even though it is not reflected in his categories and he talks only of "profit," yet Ricardo gives views on surplus value quite distinct from profit. The two are identical only when the capital advanced goes entirely for wages.

> In his observations on profit and wages, Ricardo . . . abstracts from the constant part of capital, which is not laid out on wages. He treats the matter as though the entire capital were laid out directly in wages. *To this extent,* therefore, he considers *surplus value* and *not profit,* hence it is possible to speak of his theory of surplus value. (Marx, 1968, Part II, p. 373.)

For example, throughout his *Essay on Profit* he maintains that only a fall in wages can increase profits, utterly neglecting constant capital.[7]

Ricardo was an acute observer. He crystallized into language several facets of capitalism that had only just developed in his day. He introduced the category of fixed capital to underline the importance of machinery that was, at that time, just becoming prominent. Indeed, he startled his contemporaries with his notorious Chapter XXXI, "On Machinery," wherein he gives his opinion as to its effects on the working class. Why then did he omit, by and large, any consideration of constant capital in his discussion of the rate of profit?

This is well explained, in my view, by Marx:

> It is so much in the nature of the subject-matter that surplus-value can only be considered in relation to the variable capital, i.e., capital laid out directly in

wages—and without an understanding of surplus-value no theory of profits is possible—that Ricardo treats the entire capital as variable capital and *abstracts* form constant capital, although he occasionally mentions it in the form of advances. (Marx, 1968, Part II, p. 374.)

It seems then that Ricardo's neglect of constant capital in determining the profit rate is no mere slip—rather, an intimation of genius. A glimpse just beyond recognition, that somehow variable capital, the component of capital that exchanges with living labor, is solely productive of surplus value, the stuff of profits.

In our example, Ricardo, by neglecting the constant capital C, would say that the rate of profit was 100%. Suppose he had considered it. If for some reason the value of the constant capital employed fell from £400 to £300, the rate of profit would rise from 20% to 25%, yet the same quantity of labor would be employed. It would seem as if the mass of capital too, played some essential role as regards profit. His intuition indicated, it seems, that it was labor alone. He never succeeded in working out the intermediate steps (see Section 1) from this recognition to profit and so he omitted constant capital; he did this, it appears, instinctively. Hence his laws of profit are really of surplus value.

Perhaps Ricardo comes closest to the notion of surplus value when he tells us that profit depends on the "proportion of the annual labor of the country . . . devoted to the support of the laborers" and "in all countries, and all times, profit depends on the quantity of labor requisite to provide necessaries for the laborers." (Ricardo, Vol. I, pp. 49, 126.) Consider also, "Although a greater *value* is produced, a greater proportion of what *remains of that value,* after paying rent, is consumed by the producers, and it is this, and this alone, which regulates profits [our italics]." (Ricardo, Vol. I. p. 125.)

After rent is deducted, then the mass of profit (read surplus-value) is equal to the excess of the value of the commodities minus the value of the labor-power. By "producers," Ricardo means the workers. This is an exact description of surplus value as the value created by the actual producers which the capitalist appropriates. (Ricardo though, is not correct in maintaining that after rent is deducted, what remains goes entirely to workers and capitalists, as he neglects constant capital—see Section 2, "Ricardo Progresses from Value to Capital.")

He accepts as a fact, though, that the value of the product is greater than that of the wages. The nature of capital as a coercive social relation in which the laborer must perform surplus-labor is neglected. Here Adam Smith is to the point,

> The value which the workmen add to the materials, therefore, resolves itself in this case [with the advent of capitalism] into two parts, of which the one pays their wages, the other the profits of their employer upon the whole stock of materials and wages which he advanced.

and

> In this state of things, the whole produce of labor does not always belong to the laborer. He must in most cases share it with the owner of the stock which employes him. Neither is the quantity of labor commonly employed in acquiring or producing any commondity, the only circumstance which can regulate the quantity it ought commonly to purchase, command, or exchange for. An additional quantity, it is evident, must be due for the profits of the stock which advanced the wages and furnished the materials of the labor. (Smith, 1950, pp. 54, 55.)

This statement is perhaps the most explicit before Marx of the origin of surplus value.

Ricardo's inability to distinguish between surplus value and profit gets him into difficulties. Consider his well-known doctrine that a rise in the wage rate would cause a lowering of the rate of profit (and vice versa) with the overall price level remaining unchanged. It is possible in fact for the wage rate and the profit rate to move in the same direction. As he neglects constant capital—as usual—what this refers to is the wage rate and the rate of surplus value. Suppose that the wage rate rises so that the rate surplus value falls; but, if more workers at the same time are being employed, the mass of surplus value and hence profit may increase. Hence the wage rate and the profit rate may both rise. The same will occur if as the wage rate rises, with the same number of workers, the length of the working day is extended, the labor process is intensified or there is a marked cheapening in the elements of constant capital.[8] His inability to explicate the causal relation of labor to surplus value removes all of this from his field of vision and we are left with a narrowly restricted theorem that does not tell much of the underlying process.[9]

Ricardo, alas, steadfastly maintained that the rate of profit could be influenced only by changes in the wage rate. But consider the following:

> I must again observe, that the rate of profits would fall much more rapidly than I have estimated in my calculation: for the value of the produce being what I have stated it under the circumstances supposed, the value of the farmer's stock would be greatly increased from its necessarily consisting of many of the commodities which had risen in value. Before corn could rise from £4 to £12 his capital would probably be doubled in exchangeable value, and be worth £6000 instead of £3000. If then his profit were £180, or 6 percent, on his original capital, profits would not at that time be really at a higher rate than 3 percent; for £6000 at 3 percent gives £180; and on these terms only could a new farmer with £6000 money in his pocket enter into the farming business. (Ricardo, Vol. I, p. 122.)

Ricardo is dealing here with the consequences of an increase in the price of necessaries. (Note his talk of "absolute profit," still another anticipation of surplus value.) He speaks of a further fall in the rate of profit due to a rise in the value of the capital stock. As Marx comments, "He throws overboard his identification of profit with surplus-value and [admits] that the rate of profit can be affected by a variation in the value of constant capital independently of the value of labor.'' (Marx, 1968, Part II, p. 431.) This is quite by way of exception however.

SECTION 3

His Paper on "Absolute Value and Exchangeable Value"

Ricardo's final vision, written in his last few weeks, is a worthly sequel to a life dedicated to truth. He bequeaths to humanity riches painstakingly gleaned. Sometimes those beings in harmony with the spirit of their age have such final prophetic visions as did the poet Shelly in *Triumph of Life*.

The paper is, sad to say, unfinished. It is a record of intellectual struggle. Amidst the whirls and eddies of images, some beyond those in his previous writings, others vexingly the same, there are glimpses of sunlight. Needless disputation could have been avoided had this been known long before its fateful discovery in a little tin box in 1943. Marx would have clapped his hands had he read of the rudiments of ideas he was to evolve, laboriously, thirty-five years later.

Malthus' *Measure of Value* had just appeared. He argued that the value of a given quantity of labor, or the wage rate, should be the measure of value. (A suggestion not conspicuous by its originality.) Ricardo had no trouble in showing its pitfalls as this, after all, is what Smith had said. Further, Ricardo clearly sees the true nature of the conflict between capital and labor. Consider, ''If all commodities were produced by labor employed only for one day there could be no such thing as profits for there would be no capital employed, beyond that of which every laborer is in possession before he commences to work.'' (Ricardo, Vol. IV, p. 365.)

In other words, profit arises where the means of production are concentrated in a few hands and the mass of people sell their labor-power. This cannot occur in a society of self-employed artisans. This is an advance over his *Principles,* where there is not much discussion of the social organization of capitalism.

He goes on to paint a charming vista,

> One class gives its labor only to assist toward the production of the commodity and must be paid out of its value the compensation to which it is entitled; the other class makes the advances required in the shape of capital and must receive remuneration from the same source. Before a man can work for a year, a stock of food and clothing and other necessaries must be provided for him. This stock is not his property but is the property of the man who sets him to work. Out of the finished commodity they are in fact both paid—for the master who sets him to work and who had advanced him his wages must have those wages returned with a profit or he would have no motive to employ him, and the laborer is compensated by the food, clothing and necessaries with which he is furnished, or which is the same thing which his wages enable him to purchase. (Ricardo, Vol. IV, pp. 365–366.)

In no other writing of Ricardo is the spirit of capitalism so lucidly portrayed.

Compare this with Marx,

> What flows back to the laborer in the shape of wages is a portion of the product that is continuously reproduced by him. The capitalist, it is true, pays him in money, but this money is merely the transmitted form of the product of his labor. While he is converting a portion of the means of production into products, a portion of his former product is being turned into money. It is his labor of last week, or of last year, that pays for his labor-power this week or this year. The illusion begotten by the intervention of money vanishes immediately, if, instead of taking a single capitalist and a single laborer, we take the class of capitalists and the class of laborers as a whole. The capitalist class is constantly giving to the laboring class order-notes, in the form of money, on a portion of the commodities produced by the latter and appropriated by the former. The laborers give these order-notes back just as constantly to the capitalist class, and in this way get their share of their own product. The transaction is veiled by the commodity-form of the product and the money-form of the commodity. (Marx, 1970, Vol. I. pp. 567, 568.)

Ricardo goes on to say of profits,

> It greatly depends then on the proportion of the finished work which the master is obliged to give in exchange to replace the food and clothing expended on his workman what shall be his profits. It not only depends on the relative value of the finished commodity to the necessaries of the laborer, which must always be replaced, to put the master in the same condition as when he commenced his yearly business but it depends also on the state of the market for labor . . . for if labor be scarce the workman will be able to demand and obtain a greater quantity of necessaries and consequently a greater quantity of the finished commodity must be devoted to the payment of wages and of course a less quantity remains as profit for the master. (Ricardo, Vol. IV, pp. 365–366.)

Ricardo still resolves the finished product into wages and profit, neglecting the replacement of machines, equipment and raw material; hence when he speaks of the profit rate here, it is the rate of surplus value. He rightly sees that it is the value of the finished product to the value of the wages on which depends surplus value (what he calls profits). Here once more he considers only commodities already produced, with *given* values determined by labor. If only Ricardo had followed Mr. Moneybags through the factory gates (as did Marx), instead of remaining outside and observing the outflows of finished products and inflows of wage-goods. For it would have been but a small step to have said that as the value of the product is created by labor and the mass of profit is equal to the remaining or surplus value after wages are deducted, then this surplus value is the unpaid labor or *surplus labor* which the worker is forced to perform for the capitalist.

Socialists were not slow to see the connection between profit and surplus labor.

Indeed, the first jump in understanding appears to have occurred in an anonymous pamphlet, *The Source and Remedy of the National Difficulties: A Letter to Lord John Russell* (London, 1821). It appeared during Ricardo's lifetime but apparently never came to his notice.[10]

In the sentences following the above passage, Ricardo returns to his old problem of the effects on "relative value" of a change in the wage rate as not only the labor materialized in commodities but the rise and fall of wages "does affect the value of commodities," he tells us. If only he had distinguished between price and value! Rather he pursues the academic subject of a measure of value, "In this then consists the difficulty of the subject that the circumstances of time for which advances are made so various that it is impossible to find any one commodity, which will be unexceptional measure."

Against Malthus' proposal of a wages measure, Ricardo argues as he did with Smith, that wage-goods are commodities like any other and so are subject to as much variability. Even if one supposes that a given quantity of corn will purchase the same amount of labor, (the permanent relative value of labor notion cited earlier) whether double or half the quantity of labor is required to produce corn, its value in this measure will always be the same. Ricardo remarks, "But still Mr. M. says it would not fall in absolute value, because it did not vary in his measure." (Ricardo, Vol. IV, p. 373.) What would happen is that all things would rise with respect to corn or wages; and gold, too, the standard of money, would rise. But he goes on, "In Mr. Ricardo's measure everything to which such improvements were applied would fall in value and *price and value would be synonymous* while gold, the standard of money, cost the same expenditure of capital and labor to produce it [our italics]."

Following his thinking from the reference to absolute value, two sentences before, the improvements would cause the "absolute" value to diminish of those commodities to which they were applied, *both* their prices and their values would fall (provided the value of gold were unchanged) whereas with Malthus' corn or wages standard their prices would remain the same but they would have fallen in value. Here at last is a recognition that price and value need not be synonymous—indeed, that they can move in different directions.

As an archaeologist succeeds in recreating a lost civilization from broken bits of pottery so Marx pouring over Ricardo's texts had speculated, "Ricardo . . . doubtlessly realized that his prices of production deviated from the value of commodities." (Marx, 1970, Vol. III. p. 179.)

But shortly after in discussing James Mill's thoughts on value, Ricardo takes up the venerable example of wine and cloth. The same quantity of labor has been bestowed on both but the wine is brought to market years after the cloth. Rather then saying that the values of both are the same but their prices different, he confounds value and price nicely by telling us that if the wage rate falls the "wine would alter in relative value to the cloth." Then he discusses an example of

McCulloch's showing the "Marx effect"—the permanent deviation of prices from values without any change in the wage rate and closes the section by again considering effects of a change in the wage rate. Here we have "Ricardo effect," Marx effect" and "Ricardo effect" all confounded by identifying price and value as the same. No wonder that Ricardo is puzzled—"The subject is a very difficult one, for with the same quantity of labor employed a commodity may be worth £100 or £35 of a money always produced under the same circumstances and always requiring the same quantity of labor." (Ricardo, Vol. IV, p. 378.) Then as if by way of collecting his thoughts and affirming his doctrine he sets out 12 basic principles: The first is:

> 1. All commodities having value are the result either of immediate labor, or of immediate and accumulated labor united.

And the third is:

> 3. That part of the value of a commodity which is required to compensate the laborer for the labor he has bestowed on it is called wages, the remaining part of its value is retained by the master and is called profit. It is a remuneration for the accumulated labor which it was necessary for him to advance, in order that the commodity might be produced. (Ricardo, Vol. IV, p. 380.)

Once again we see that he starts with given values of commodities. Though he sees clearly enough that labor creates a larger value than the share it receives as wages, by ignoring production he cannot relate this to necessary and surplus labor. Instead he talks legalistically of the distribution of the product—a part goes to "compensate" the laborer, another part to "remuneration" for the "master." (The part that must go to replace raw materials, semifinished goods, and wear and tear is neglected.)

But then he returns to the puzzle over a measure of value. He is in agreement with Marx that the relative value of all commodities can be found with respect to any commodity[12] but he wishes to go further and seek an absolute measure of value. (Ricardo, Vol. IV, p. 381.) Such a measure could be used "to ascertain the variations in the values of commodities for one year, for two years, or for any distant portions of time."

Here he considers for a moment using labor materialized in a commodity,

> All then we have to do it is said to ascertain whether the value of commodity be now of the same value as a commodity produced 20 years ago is to find out what quantity of labor for the same length of time was necessary to produce the commodity 20 years ago and what quantity is necessary to produce it now.

With such a measure we would be enabled to know the *absolute* value of a commodity, he goes on to say. But then he gives this up by saying, "A commodity that requires the labor of 100 men for one year is not precisely double the value of a commodity that requires the labor of 100 men for 6 months." (Ricardo, Vol. IV, p. 382.) Again confounding, alas, price and value!

His examples of wine and cloth led him to regard differences in time of production as the core of the difficulty. "This then seems to hold universally true that the commodity valued must be reduced to circumstances precisely similar (with respect to time of production) to those of the commodity in which the valuation is made." This leads him to choose gold or cloth as his measure, reasoning rather dubiously that most commodities are produced under the same circumstances.

In considering one of Malthus' arguments he returns to the example of wine. This he rightly sees will exchange for more labor than it cost. It will, Ricardo sees, exchange for say the labor of 1000 men while it cost that of 200 men. Therefore, "the value of labor of 800 men will constitute the profit and the whole value of the wine is divided into fifths, one fifth of which is the value of the wages and four fifths the value of the profits." Recall our example of the cloth manufacturer and the farmer. We saw that a surplus value of £177 accrues to the cloth manufacturer above what his laborers produce, as its selling price is above its value. The same occurs with the wine. Ricardo sees, though as if looking through the wrong end of a telescope, an essential of Marx's solution to the "transformation problem."

He ends reaffirming his principle:

> That the greater or less quantity of labor worked up in commodities can be the only cause of their alteration in value is completely made out as soon as we are agreed that all commodities are the produce of labor and would have no value but for the labor expended upon them. Though this is true it is still exceedingly difficult to discover or even to imagine any commodity which shall be [a] perfect general measure of value. (Ricardo, Vol. IV, p. 397.)

It appears from this that the measure of value is not a secondary enquiry; rather, it is organically related to his theory of value. The examples of wine, cloth and so forth refute it, *prima facie,* and his search for a measure was really an attempt to establish his great principle in a full generality.

Ricardo's Faulty Architectonics

Ricardo relying on the certainty of immediate perception regards capitalism as a mode of production eternal, reasonable and natural. Hence he was not under any necessity to scrutinize the nature of value and the *differentia specifica* that sets a commodity producing society apart from the multitude of other historical, social forms in which useful things are merely useful things. Had he done so, he would have caught the dim shape of futurity amidst the fog of fetishism.

Rather, immersing himself at the onset in a sea of commodities, he concerns himself, understandably enough, with the magnitude of value. His surmise that this was determined by labor-time was an advance. But he posited at the onset a mass of commodities of given value, a crystallized quantity of human labor and asked only what part goes to the worker as his wages and what is appropriated by capital. By concerning himself with the distribution of commodities already produced he cannot enquire into the creation of value. Futhermore, the unequal exchange between capital and labor seems to contradict his general law that value is determined by labor time. This was to lead eventually to the shipwreck of the Ricardian school. (Decades later Marx solved the problem with the distinction between labor and labor-power, rightly calling it the ''fulcrum upon which Political Economy turns.'')

Instead he takes the difference between the value that labor produces and what it receives as matter-of-fact as an apple falling from a tree. By not asking why the exchange between living and materialized labor should be different from the exchange between the immense mass of commodities containing only materialized labor, he could not discover the source of surplus value.

Other, apparently contradictory, phenomena present themselves. In the face of these, Ricardo instinctively maintained his law, vindicating it by a violent abstraction. Thus he confounded values and prices. By leaping in with his general rate of profit, by accepting the rate of profit as something preexistent, he was unable to consider how through the competition of capitals, a general rate of profit is established and how this necessitates that values are transformed into prices of production.

His struggle with the apparently arid, academic question of an ''invariable standard'' is really an attempt to reconcile his premises with things that at first sight apparently contradict it.

If only Ricardo had paid less attention to a dead mass of things and more as to how they came into being! Although he steadfastly maintained that only living labor was productive of value, he does not progress from this understanding to seeing profit and rent as manifestations of surplus value created by unpaid labor.

Later on others would turn Ricardo's vision of capitalism into a reification of a stock market where capital and labor receive dividends or shares in the total product. (Marx, 1973, p. 553.) His followers would drop that part of his doctrine dealing with value as materialized labor and put in its place a mechano-mystical view of the value of commodities as originating in dead matter; ''economic science'' would come to be a ceaseless meditation on the ''allocation'' or ''distribution'' of a mass of things. Marx, on the other hand, saw in the exchange between *living* and *dead* labor a clue to the subtle anatomy of capitalism.

FOOTNOTES

1. This is how Samuel Bailey argued against Ricardo's theory. See Marx's brilliant discussion (Marx, 1968, Part III, pp. 142–143).

2. The author cannot but marvel at the image of a mighty intellect traversing many valleys, snow-clad mountain tops and chilly plateaus—such is Karl Marx in his quest in *Theories of Surplus Value*. This essay is but a pale reflection of the truth therein.

3. One peculiarity here is that neither the farmer nor the manufacturer expend capital on raw materials and equipment; they only purchase labor. We will see the significance of this omission later on.

4. These terms were suggested by Frank Roosevelt.

5. By following Marx in deriving prices of production from values, we may meet with the same objections raised so long ago by Bohm-Bawerk and L. von Borkiewicz. Though we have "transformed" the value of the output of each Department to a price of production, we have left the inputs unchanged, thereby saying in effect that though the price of production of each item of output deviates from its value, the price of production of each input item is equal to its value. We are guilty of the same error as Marx but we maintain that our solution shows the essence of what any solution must be. Qualitatively our solution correctly shows the production and redistribution of surplus value in accordance with the total value of the capital stock in each sector. While an approximation, Marx's solution explicates causal relations and is further along the path to totality than the "exact" one proposed by L. von Bortkiewicz.

6. Marx (1968, Part II, pp. 191–192). The author would like to express his thanks to Professor Tsuyoshi Sakurai for his helpful comments on the above example.

7. It was vital for British capitalism to import cheap raw materials, thereby cheapening constant capital. But Ricardo myopically maintained that foreign trade could only increase profits to the extent that cheap food was imported. Marx notices one instance where Ricardo takes a different position. (See Marx, *ibid.*, p. 431.)

8. That Ricardo nowhere considers the consequences of an extension of the working day underlines his failure to explicate the causal relation of labor to profit.

9. With the Ricardian vogue, Ricardo's "law" has come to the fore again. We should always bear in mind how severely limited it is. Ricardo did make a singular contribution here in considering wages with respect to profits—that is, by speaking of relative wages. By focusing on the amount of wages relative to the total product, the social relation of workers to capital is underlined. The dynamics of class struggle depends more on relative shares than abolute quantities.

10. See Frederick Engels discussion (Marx, 1970, Vol. II, pp. 12–13).

11. *Ibid.*, p. 36. Compare our quote (our italics) with the quote on p. 36 where he says, "natural price . . . is synonymous with value."

12. "We are possessed then of plenty of measures of value" (Ricardo, Vol. IV, p. 381).

REFERENCES

Dunayevskaya, Raya (1971), *Marxism and Freedom,* p. 99, London: Pluto Press.

Engels, Frederick (1971), *Supplement to Capital,* Vol. III, Moscow: Progress Publishers.

Marx, Karl (1968), *Theories of Surplus Value,* Part I, pp. 71, 73, 74; Part II, pp. 191, 192, 219, 373, 374, 396, 399, 431; Part III, pp. 133, 134, 135, 141, 142, 143; Moscow: Progress Publishers.

Marx, Karl (1970), *Capital,* Vol. I, pp. 567, 568; Vol. II, pp. 12, 13; Vol. III, Chapter 9, pp. 158, 179; Moscow: Progress Publishers.
Marx, Karl (1971), *A Contribution to the Critique of Political Economy,* pp. 67, 68, London: Lawrence and Wishart.
Marx, Karl (1973), *Grundrisse: Foundations of the Critique of Political Economy,* p. 553, Harmondsworth: Penquin Books.
Ricardo, David (1970), *The Works and Correspondence of David Ricardo,* edited by Sraffa, Piero, Vol. I, pp. 14, 30, 35, 47, 49, 122, 125, 126, 208; Vol. II, pp. 34, 35; Vol. IV, pp. 365, 366, 373, 378, 380, 381, 382, 397; Vol. VII, p. 377; Cambridge: Cambridge University Press.
Smith, Adam (1950), *Wealth of Nations,* edited by Canaan, E., Vol. I, pp. 54, 55, 58, 59, London: Methuen.

THE POLITICAL ECONOMY OF U.S. STEEL PRICES IN THE POSTWAR PERIOD

Edward Greer, ROOSEVELT UNIVERSITY

INTRODUCTION

For most of the twentieth century the United States was the world's leading steel producer. As late as 1950 it produced as much steel as the combination of Western Europe, the Soviet Union and Japan. But its share of world steel production has been steadily declining ever since. In 1974, a boom year for American steel, both the European Economic Community and the U.S.S.R. outproduced the United States, and Japan produced virtually as much. (*Citibank,* April 1976, pp. 12–13.)

This essay attemps to summarize the underlying reasons for this relative decline in the steel industry of the United States. While not entirely discounting the reasons conventionally advanced (bad management, overpaid and slothful workers, product substitution in a "post-industrial society"), emphasis is placed upon other institutional factors, both domestically and internationally, which are largely responsible. In particular, attention is focused on the price policy of the American steel industry adopted by its oligopolistic leadership and how that policy has both been shaped by and in turn altered the character of the industry.

Throughout the twentieth century the American economy has rested on its manufacturing base, at the core of which has been the steel industry. (Estall, 1972, p. 252, Table 15; U.S. Bureau of Economic Analysis, 1973, pp. 72–74, 81;

Hogan, 1971, Vol. V., pp. 1850–1999). During the first half of the century, the industry grew apace with the economy (Broude, 1963, p. 32). But after World War II, steel began to lag. While the overall growth of manufacturing productivity has averaged 2.9 percent annually, that of steel has been only 1.7 percent annually. (Hogan, 1972, p. 79; U.S. Bureau of Economic Analysis, 1973, pp. 82–87.) Both the relative size of the major American firms and their profitability compared to manufacturing firms generally have also dropped.[1]

In the immediate aftermath of the devastation of World War II, it was not surprising that American production reached three-fifths of the world total; nor that by the mid-fifties (consequent to the reconstruction of the steel industries of the other major powers), it had fallen to two-fifths. (Wittman et Thouvenot, 1972, p. 57). During the initial post-War decade, world demand constantly surpassed supply, and the American industry kept expanding: from 1947 to 1957 American capacity was increased by almost half (Ullman, June 1958, pp. 424–425; McDonald, December, 1967, p. 135).

The fundamental change occurred in the following decade. After 1955 absolute American steel production declined and was not surpassed until 1964. Worldwide, capacity continued to expand rapidly and actually surpassed effective demand by the early 1960's. During this period the American economy was relatively stagnant, and the major users of steel products such as construction and automobiles reduced their orders (McDonald, December 1960, p. 135; Adelman, February 1961, pp. 24–30; Silberman, December 1960, pp. 123–127; Manners, 1974, pp. 117–122; Wittman et Thouvenot, 1972, p. 55; Parker, 1969, p. 57; McConnell, 1963, pp. 28–29).

More decisively, the United States lost its foreign market to the newly competitive overseas manufacturers. In the early 1950's, American steel manufacturers enjoyed a sixth of the entire international steel trade. Over the period form 1953 to 1968, American steel exports fell off at an average rate of 4.5 percent each year—so that by 1968 the U.S. held only 2 percent of the world total (Adelman, February, 1961, p. 31; Friden, 1972, p. 91).[2] As late as 1957, the United States exported four million tons more steel than it imported, for an $800 million trade surplus. By 1959, the physical balance of steel had shifted, and by 1961 the balance-of-payments effect was also negative (Adelman, February, 1961, p. 31; McConnell, 1963, p. 65; Weiss, 1967, p. 181; Kefauver, 1965, p. 107). This swift reversal shocked American governmental leaders and played a major role in precipitating the Kennedy steel confrontation of 1962 (McConnell, December 1960, p. 65; Schlesinger, Jr., 1965, p. 634; Sorenson, 1965, p. 444). Throughout the 1960's, even after President Nixon imposed steel import quotas in 1969, imports substantially exceeded exports, and the steel trade deficit reached as much as $2 billion a year (*The New York Times,* May 21, 1972, January 5, 1975; Manufacturers Hanover Trust, June, 1973; *Business Week,* June 4, 1966, p. 60; Blair, 1972, p. 515).

Reduced steel output—itself a cause of lagging domestic economic growth—has led to some peculiar explanations of its cause. The most prominent is to allege that the industry suffers from "technological backwardness." It is buttressed by a simple statistic: the American steel industry spends only about a quarter the proportion devoted by all American manufacturing to research and development (*Business Week,* June 4, 1966, p. 101; MacPhee, 1974, p. 13).[3] However, this is misleading. With the exception of a handful of industries (whose high investments in R&D are directly consequential to military-oriented federal subsidies), the steel industry's investment pattern for research and development approximates the American manufacturing average.[4] Thus, if American steel tends not to be an innovator in new technique, it is a result not of some peculiarity of that industry's management policies, but due to a general weakness in American manufacturing's research activities (Bell, 1973, p. 259).[5] Moreover, the evidence is very impressive that while there might have been some temporary lag in the introduction of new techniques in the 1950's, by the 1960's the industry was fully abreast of and equivalent to its foreign competitors technologically (Ault, March 1973, pp. 89–97; Hiestand, 1974, p. 17).

Actually, the relative decline of American steel production is in keeping with larger structural trends in American manufacturing. Currently, manufacturing exports are concentrated among a few industrial groups, which, while they account for only two-fifths of all manufacturing sales, engross three-quarters of all manufacturing exports (Gruber, Mehta and Vernon, February 1967, p. 25). These industries—transport, machinery, chemicals, instruments—are not necessarily the most capital-intensive, but those which systematically export new products. The larger and wealthier American market stimulates new product development, especially in those areas subsidized by federal military-oriented research. But this initial advantage erodes as other industrialized nations come to mass-produce the same products (Keesing, February 1967, p. 45; Gruber, Mehta and Vernon, February 1967, pp. 20–37). The relative secular decline of American steel on the world stage comports with this large structural tendency.

The second most popular explanation of lagging American steel production, that of "product substitution," also seems to be true only to a limited degree. It is true that some product substitution has taken place in the post-War period. With steel prices rising in the decade following 1947 at two-and-a-half times the rate of concrete, it would have been surprising if the substitution of prestressed concrete for steel did not occur to some degree (Blair, 1972, p. 114; Silberman, December 1960, pp. 249–250).[6] That this substitution turned in large measure on relative prices—and not some generalized economic transformation of the economy in which steel was gradually phased out of use—is clear from the excellent recovery American steel production made in the mid-1960's when demand rose due to the Vietnam War boom, and the surplus capacity problem was overcome (Manners, 1974, pp. 117–122).

In short, it appears that both imports and substitution effects in the steel industry turn on the price structure of American steel. And thus to explain post-War developments in the industry, the closest possible scrutiny should be given to the problem of steel price trends.

An analysis of steel prices must begin with an effort to determine the cost of production. Because the private property system permits the steel companies to keep their cost figures secret, the best that is possible is a rough estimate. For the purposes of this discussion, costs are divided into the categories of raw materials, wages, and capital investments and taxes. The different between these costs and the selling price represents the profits of the steel companies.

RAW MATERIALS

Contrary to the popular view encouraged by the industry, labor costs are not the main component of steel prices. Over half of the cost of producing steel is accounted for by the cost of purchasing and transporting to the steel mill the required raw materials (Manners, 1974, pp. 10–12; *The Wall Street Journal,* May 30, 1974; Thorn, December 1968, p. 377). The main raw materials used in steelmaking are coal and iron ore. Currently it takes one ton of coal and two tons of iron ore to produce a ton of steel. In addition, limestone and trace materials such as chromium and manganese are necessary, as is a substantial amount of water which makes waterside manufacturing sites obligatory (*Economic Priorities Report,* June–July 1973, pp. 3–4, Jones and Darkenwald, 1965, pp. 562–563, 567; L. King *et al.,* July 1971, p. 403; *The New York Times,* November 16, 1973, November 17, 1973; O.E.C.D., 1973, p. 59).

Coal

In 1970 American coal production was 600 million tons, of which the steel industry consumed 95 million tons. Despite the tremendous increase in steel production since World War II the industry's demand for coal has remained virtually constant (McAteer, 1973, p. 3; *The New York Times,* October 21, 1974; Warren, 1973, p. 249). The reason is simple. The quantity of coal needed to produce a ton of steel has, consequent to technological progress, fallen almost in half (Warren, 1973, pp. 253–254; Wittman et Thouvenot, 1972, p. 16, Boylan, Jr., 1975, pp. 190–191). Consequently, the location of coal supplies has—in contrast to access to iron ore and markets for steel products—come to play an ever decreasing role in determining where steel capacity shall be added.

Not only has the quantity of coal needed per ton of steel dropped, but so too have the costs of coal transport. The cost of rail transport of coal has fallen in the post-World War II period by as much as 50 percent (Manners, 1974, pp. 217–218; Warren, 1973, p. 311; Boylan, Jr., 1975, p. 205). It is likely that these trends have more than overbalanced the increases in coal production costs, among which are coalminers wages.[7]

It is impossible to determine the actual costs of coal to the steel companies, because two-thirds of all the coal used by them is produced in mines which they themselves own—the so-called "captive mines." These mines produce a full eighth of the nation's coal (Klein and Gordon, 1971, p. 11; U. S. Bureau of Labor Statistics, 1966, p. 7.). With respect to their ore, Gerald Manners concludes:

> Much of this captive ore is transported to the blast furances over railways and in vessels owned by the iron and steel producers. Any prices charged in such circumstances are in large measure a matter of internal company accountancy, and strongly influenced by the structure of taxation and depreciation allowances . . . (Manners, 1974, p. 258).[8]

The 10 percent depletion allowance of coal is one of the factors leading to low steel company federal tax rates, and this makes the "bookkeeping" price of coal even more suspect.[9] A similar problem occurs with inferences based upon state coal taxes. Thus, for instance, in West Virginia, U.S. Steel's 38,000 acres of coal land (whose true value probably exceeds $1 billion) was taxed on an assessment of $1.5 million (McAteer, 1973, pp. 140–177; Ridgeway, 1973, pp. 34–36). Under these circumstances it is only an educated guess to conclude that, in the post-War period, coal costs for the companies have declined on a per-ton-of-steel basis.

Iron Ore

It is clear that iron ore prices per ton of steel have declined since World War II. As with coal, iron ore mining is carried out by subsidiaries of the steel companies. Until the 1890's, American iron ore was produced competitively by a large number of companies, but as production came to be concentrated in the Mesabi range, so too did cartel-like price setting. In the late 1890's the iron ore industry was transformed as the steel companies—especially the Carnegie interests which later provided the core of United States Steel—bought up the iron ore companies. When the U.S. Steel Corporation was formed in 1901 it controlled over half the Mesabi reserves. Indeed, these ore reserves "were worth twice as much as its manufacturing plant and represented almost half of the value of all its properties" (quote from Warren, 1973, p. 127) (Manke, July 1972, pp. 220–222; Temin, 1964, p. 189; Schroeder, 1953, pp. 38, 125–126).

Despite its continuing decline in its share of American steel production, the Corporation was still producing almost half of all Mesabi ore throughout the post-World War II period. In 1963 it still controlled three-fifths of the region's reserves (Hines, September 1951, pp. 650–652; Lippert, 1950, p. 2; Martin, 1967, p. 126). This U.S. Steel hegemony over the main desposits of domestic ore has had a substantial effect on the character of the industry. In the early years of the century, its commanding position in the iron ore market "facilitated the maintenance of high ore prices," which in turn helped lead to oligopolistic price control of steel products (Temin, 1964, pp. 198–199). Second, over the years this control of ore reserves has made entry into the industry by new competitors extremely difficult (Weiss, 1967, pp. 198–199; Martin, 1967, p. 121).[10]

Third, U.S. Steel's unique position among the major steel producers of consistently producing a surplus beyond its own requirements—which surplus has been sold to its competitors—helps explain its historic role as "leader of the industry" (Martin, 1967, pp. 120–130; Adam, 1961, pp. 154–156).[11] Since World War II, the Corporation has been a consistent seller of iron ore. In the period 1939 to 1950 it sold over 50 million tons of ore. And since then, despite the radically changing patterns of ore production discussed below, it has continued to sell a quarter or more of its annual production on the open market (Lippert, 1950, p. 2; Martin, 1967, pp. 119–120; Ridgeway, 1973, p. 322; U.S. Steel *Annual Reports, 1952, 1972).*

The period since 1950 has seen a true revolution in the role of iron ore in American steel production, and it is this revolution which is responsible for declining iron ore costs. In 1950, almost all the ore was domestic in its origins, and the steel industry was spending almost nothing on the development of new ore sources.[12] But the high quality Mesabi reserves were rapidly being depleted. American ore production peaked in 1953 and has been declining since. The difference has been met by imports which have already reached one-third of the total annual consumption (Wittman et Thouvenot, 1972, pp. 89–91; Hogan, 1971, Vol. 4, pp. 1439, 1485; Klein and Gordon, 1971, p. 6).

It must be added, however, that the Mesabi range has scarcely become obsolete, notwithstanding the revolutionary shift toward foreign ores. As a consequence of technological advances, lower grade taconite ores can be processed and concentrated. The American steel companies have made a substantial investment in such processing plants, and as a result Mesabi ores are still competitive, especially in the Midwest (Warren, 1973, pp. 249–250; Martin, 1967, pp. 122–124).[13]

In additon to this continuing use of American ore, the industry also recycles huge amounts of steel scrap obtained domestically. Due to the shift to the basic-oxygen process (which uses far less scrap), the absolute quantity of scrap used by the industry declined slightly in the late 1950's and early 1960's; and did not fully rebound even in the late 1960's—with the result that there "was a near collapse in scrap prices for a number of years" (Manners, 1974, p. 253).[14]

Only half of the discarded ferrous scrap is recycled. If it all were, consumption of new ore would be reduced by a full quarter. Such recycling would be of inestimable ecological benefit. But because of the structure of the industry and tax benefits of using new ore as opposed to recycling scrap, this method—despite its advantages to society in general—is unlikely to be adopted on a wider scale than the current one (*Economic Priorties Report,* June–July, 1973, pp. 3–14).

Internationalization

Despite the continuing reliance on American ore and domestic scrap, on balance the steel industry has come to rely upon foreign iron ore as an integral and essential part of its functioning. All of the major steel producers—with the notable exception of the Soviet Union—have come to rely upon foreign iron ore, largely supplied by new sources in the Third World.[15] In the fifteen-year period beginning in 1950, the proportion of all iron ore in the world entering into international trade doubled to reach two-fifths of the total. Thus, while in 1950 thirty million tons of iron ore were carried by ocean transport, in 1965 one hundred fifty million tons were (Whittman et Thouvenot, 1972, pp. 173, 269).

This reliance upon imports has been matched by a transformation of maritime shipping. Due to advances in shipping technology, long-distance ocean transportation of ore became increasingly economical throughout the 1950's and 1960's. The key factor in this development has been the creation of a substantial number of ore transport ships whose average size has been progressively increasing. A large proportion of these new ships are designed so that they can also transport petroleum, the other main item of ocean trade.

The net result of this technological advance has been a sustantial reduction in the cost of shipping iron ore (Wittman et Thouvenot, 1972, pp. 94–106).[16] Between 1950 and 1965, the raw materials transportation costs for an American steel mill with a seaboard location fell by a third (Manners, 1974, p. 253; Rosegger; January 1974, pp. 185–190).

This ongoing massive shift to foreign ore is exemplified by the United States Steel Corporation. After World War II, it began iron ore explorations throughout the Caribbean which were capped with fantastic success in Cerro Bolivar, Venezuela. A literal mountain of high grade ore, with reserves of one billion tons, was developed by a subsidiary formed in 1949. In January, 1954, after mammoth engineering work, the first shipments began. In 1955, the Orinoco Mining Company shipped five millions tons of ore; a decade later production reached 14 million tons (Lippert, 1950, pp. 11–14; U. S. Steel *Annual Reports, 1953, 1955, 1966).*

Iron ore became Venezuela's second largest export after oil, with the bulk of it going to the United States and a smaller portion to Western Europe (Gomez, 1971, pp. 313, 337; *The New York Times,* November 28, 1974). On January 1, 1975, the Venezuelan government nationalized the Orinoco Company, agreeing to pay U.S. Steel $84 million in compensation over a ten-year period. The Corporation is "expected to stay on during the transition period as operators in exchange for a continuing supply of ore" (*The New York Times,* November 28, 1974, December 2, 1974, January 2, 1975). After nationalization, the Venezuelan government successfully raised the selling price of the ore by 68 percent—which indicates how advantageous were the terms under which the Corporation had been exploiting this foreign resource (*The New York Times,* January 4, 1976).

The Corporation is now beginning a similar process of iron ore exploitation at a magnificent new find in Brazil, with a 49 percent interest and a far more sympathetic political regime (*The New York Times,* July 24, 1976; Mikesell, 1971, pp. 345–364). A similar course of development has been pursued by U.S. Steel in Canada. In 1957, it set up the Quebec Cartier Company which began constructing facilities in 1958, including a 193-mile railway to transport its ore.[17] By 1964, the mine was shipping 9 million tons of concentrate annually to Corporation mills. (U.S. Steel *Annual Reports, 1957, 1958, 1964*).[18]

These developments have led careful students of the steel industry to the conclusion that while it has not fully followed the course of most large manufacturing oligopolies in becoming a "multi-national industry," it has in recent years become substantially internationalized in its sources of raw materials (Segre, December 1972, pp. 125–127; Hogan, 1972, p. 6).

In a recent interview with *Forbes* Magazine, U.S. Steel Chairman Edgar B. Speer candidly spoke of this development:

> When foreign steel flooded our market and . . . we couldn't compete, spending for additional finishing capacity didn't seem too attractive economically. But we wanted a piece of the growth we saw in world steel. So we decided the way would be to become a supplier of raw materials (*Forbes,* January 15, 1975).

Sales of iron ore, coal, cement, and the sale of transport services from the Corporation's trains and ships now constitute a full fifth of its revenues and a substantially larger and growing share of its profits (U.S.Steel *Annual Reports, 1971; Burcke,* January 1956, p. 92).

The internationalization of the American steel industry by means of its increasing involvement with foreign raw materials is evidenced by manganese as well. All the manganese used by American steel manufacturers is produced by foreign subsidiaries of U.S. Steel and Bethlehem Steel. The main manganese producer in Brazil is Bethlehem Steel; U.S. Steel has a small operation there. The other main source of manganese is a joint French-U.S. Steel venture in Gabon, Africa (in which the Corporation owns a 44 percent share). It provides a third of America's manganese supply. And the United States Steel Corporation also obtains manganese from the Republic of South Africa (Klein and Gordon, 1971, p. 11; Mikesell, 1971, pp. 365–367; Hogan, 1971, Vol. 4, pp. 1660, 2077; *The Elements,* November 1975, pp. 4–5).

Despite is efforts to keep a low profile, the American steel industry has become heavily involved in South African mining and refining. The mining editor of the South African *Rand Daily Mail* asserts that: "American companies maintain a stony silence on their work . . . principally because the State Department prefers no publicity on American involvement in South Africa" (*The New York Times,* September 4, 1972).

The U.S. Steel Corporation, for instance, bought a 31 percent interest in two

South African firms engaged in the production and refining of chromium in 1968 for $8.4 million.[19] Over the following few years it also acquired an interest in African Triangle, a South African firm producing copper and zinc; and a 46 percent share of Prieska Copper Mines Ltd (U.S. Steel *Annual Reports, 1970, 1972; New York Times,* September 4, 1972). The Corporation also revealed to its stockholders that "the company in conjunction with others is exploring large areas in South-West Africa" (U.S. Steel, *Annual Reports, 1969;* Rogers, 1976, p. 197).[20] The leading analyst of American investment in the Republic of South Africa, Barbara Rogers, asserts that the Corporation:

> has numerous and increasing investments in South African mining and is involved in developing the ferro-chrome industry, using Rhodesian chrome ore, through Ferro-alloys. U.S. Steel has been among the companies lobbying in the U.S. Congress for the continued importation of chome and ferrochrome originating in southern Rhodesia in violation of international commitments (Rogers, 1976, p. 144).

Given its racially discriminatory employment policies at home, there is nothing surprising about U.S. Steel participation in the South African *apartheid* regime's exploitative methods.[21] The rate of return on South African mining investments exceeds 20 percent a year (*The New York Times,* January 11, 1976).

Location Effects

The combination of the sharp reduction in coal requirements and the recent advances in seagoing iron ore transport have combined to strongly influence the location of steel production. In turn, these location changes have influenced final costs.

Of course the location of steel plants tends to shift at a glacial rate—partially because of the infrequency of new plant construction, and partially because of factors of inertia which rest on economic advantages to oligopolies in maintaining existing investments. Thus, the actual pattern of plant location does not correspond to one which would be derived from an abstract analysis of the most economically rational location (Rodgers, January 1952, p. 61; Stocking, 1954; Alexandersson, April 1961, pp. 95–114; Stigler, December 1949, pp. 1143–1159). Moreover, as the case of the U.S. Steel Duluth Works suggests, political factors also enter into location decisions of manufacturing oligopolies.[22]

American steelmaking emerged from World War II overhelmingly located in the middle-sized cities of the "manufacturing belt" (Alexandersson, 1956, pp. 38–39; Stocking, 1954, p. 33; Berry and Horton, 1970, pp. 133, 138). In theory, the effect of the attraction of markets for steel products should have been the largest single factor in determining location decisions since the end of the War (Manners, 1974, p. 21; Rogers, January 1952, p. 58; Yeates and Garner, 1971, pp. 150–151). But in practice, the attraction of an ocean site where long-distance iron ore shipments can be directly utilized without any "break of bulk" seems to have proven the most powerful factor (Wittman et Thouvenot, 1972, pp. 111–123; Kimble, January 1952, pp. 44–53).

Only two major new plants have been constructed in the United States in the post-War period: Bethlehem's Burns Harbor mill on Lake Michigan near Gary, and U.S. Steel's Fairless Works on the Delaware River. Consequently, "changes in the location pattern were caused almost entirely by differences in growth rates among existing steel plants" (Alexandersson, April, 1961, pp. 100–104). But since the post-War ore transport revolution the majority of new steel mills elsewhere in the world (at least where the country in question has substantial ocean frontage) have been built on the oceans. This has also been advantageous for their steel export trade (Wittman et Thouvenot, 1972, pp. 111, 117). While inland locations have often increased their capacity substantially, new foreign mills are invariably located on the coasts. Thus, for example, between 1953 and 1966 the proportion of European Common Market steel produced on the coasts rose from 3 to 14 percent and has continued to rise since (Parker, 1969, pp. 62–68; *The New York Times,* June, 1974).

The Chairman of the Board of Directors of U.S. Steel at the time the Fairless Works were built explicitly credited the Orinoco ore development as being the basis for that ocean site. And its location near major east-coast markets to which the Corporation had had only limited prior access also played a role (Fairless, 1956, pp. 36–37). Chairman Fairless tactfully omitted from his explanation of the Corporation's decision that Congress simultaneously passed an accelerated depreciation allowance on new industrial capacity (to encourage manufacturing expansion for the Korean War); and that the site "was free of high urban taxes and regulation" (quote from Boorman, 1951) (Warren, 1973, pp. 260, 303, 321–323; Jones and Darkenwald, 1965, p. 571).

It thus seems fair to conclude that when all factors are taken into account the raw materials and transport costs of steel production actually declined from the end of World War II through the early 1960's.

WAGES

In the United States, as throughout the world, the historic wage level of production workers in steel substantially exceeded those of manufacturing generally. From the turn of the century until the depths of the Depression, American steelworkers enjoyed a wage differential about a fifth greater than the average proletarian (Howe, 1973, pp. 6–7; Weiss, 1967, pp. 189–191; Rees, June 1951, pp. 389–404; Ullman, June 1958, pp. 408–425; Means, 1962).

This differential was earned, however, by the extremely arduous character of the work. The popular description of a pre-World War I steelworker's life was "old age at forty" (U.S. Senate, 1913, Vol. III, pp. 96–98; Walker, 1922, p. 44;

Garraty, Winter 1960, p. 5.) While a third of all immigrants returned to Europe, almost half of all immigrant steelworkers left America—a mute testimony to mill labor conditions. Part of the arduousness was the result of extremely long hours of toil. While in the pre-War period the average work week was 60 hours, in the steel industry it was a killing 72 hours. And in the 1920's, when the work week in manufacturing was reduced to 55 hours, that of unskilled steelworkers (even after the famed 1923 shift from a 12-hour to an 8-hour day) remained 60 hours (Brody, 1960; Rees, 1961; Gulick, 1924; Bernstein, 1966).

Despite the wage differential, the economic conditions of the unskilled workers approximated subsistence levels. The skilled craftsmen were earning double the wages of unskilled workers up until the Depression. And these craftsmen could manage a decent life. They "could rent or own a six-room house distant from the smoke and din of the mill. There was money enough for a healthy, varied diet; for furniture, clothes, and small pleasures; and for insurance and some savings" (Brody, 1960). But for the majority, plagued by frequent layoffs, wages were so low that they could not even affort to feed their families adequantely. As late as 1919, after substantial wartime wage increases, two-thirds of the children of the black and foreign-born workers in the steel center of Gary, Indiana, had no milk, fruit or eggs in their diet. Over half had no vegetables, and a third lacked any meat. This situation reflected itself in far higher rates of infant disease and mortality. This pattern continued into the 1920's and, given the impact of the Depression, there is good reason to believe that it prevailed until the onset of World War II (Bernstein, 1966; Gulick, 1924; *School and Society,* October 20, 1923, pp. 460–461; Murray, December 1951, p. 449; Quillen, 1942, p. 425).

Moreover, steel employment was quite dangerous. The safety movement led by U.S. Steel had halved the industry's accident rate by 1920—at which time it was still double that of American manufacturing. Accident rates continued to decline during the 1920's and reached a new low in 1930. In that year only 142 men were killed and another 1,200 permantely disabled (Gulick, 1924, pp. 35, 148; Bernstein, 1966, p. 178; Davis, 1933, p. 36). Thus it seems fair to conclude that rather than wage differential reflecting affluence for the steelworkers, it was indicative of the particularly harsh conditions of work of the majority of employees in the industry. These wage differentials continued into the Depression but were of small consolation under circumstance of widespread unemployment and across-the-board pay reductions.

The big breakthrough for the steelworkers came with the organization of the CIO. In this period their wages made a veritable leap forward, with the result that by 1939 they were enjoying a differential a full third over the proletarian average. Moreover, these benefits were greatest for the poorest steelworkers, in accord with the radical egalitarian thrust of the CIO in its formative period. A key indicator of this policy of redistribution—in which the lower paid workers gained relatively larger raises than the most skilled—was the situation of the black steelworkers, historically consigned to the "more unpleasant" and least well-paid jobs. Between 1935 and 1938 the relative pay of black as opposed to white steelworkers advanced from 79 percent of the average to 85 percent (Greer, September–October 1976).[23]

In the period from the outset of World War II through the Korean War, steel wages rose less rapidly than those of manufacturing wages in general. As a result, by 1953 the steelworkers were again earning only a fifth more than the average. The reasons for this are somewhat complex but may be fairly summarized as follows. On the one hand, after an initial spurt during the War, government wage controls—accepted by the unions and the left for patriotic and antifascist reasons—resulted in an effective stagnation of steel wages (Weiss, 1967, pp. 189–191; Rees, June 1951, p. 391; Means, 1962, pp. 73–79). On the other hand, it was not simply that government controls boxed the steelworkers in. In part, the very success of the steelworkers in organizing a powerful union had the effect of encouraging other workers who where not yet organized to embark on the same course. Many did so during the favorable political conditions of the War, with the result that it was the turn of these newly organized workers to obtain "catch-up" raises. Thus, it was only natural, and a reflection of the generally strong position of the trade union movement during this period, that the special advantages won by the steelworkers in the first flush of the CIO be matched in industry generally. The result was that the wartime period and its aftermath saw a relative decline in the steelworkers' differential (Preis, 1972, pp. 157–256; Gordon and Persky *et al.*, n.d., p. 12; *The New York Times,* January 8, 1973).

But an additional distinction must be made with respect to what was happening to steel wages from 1939 to 1953, and this was the change in *real wages* of the steelworkers. From 1939 to 1945 real wages in steel rose by a third as a result of wartime prosperity. Then in the immediate post-War period of 1945–1948 real wages were either stable, or even declined slightly. Thereafter, real steel wages began to rise again with increasing rapidity, especially after 1953.

In the period from 1953 to 1958 the average manufacturing wage rose by 20 percent, but in steel dollar wages rose by 35 percent. Over the period from 1949 to 1960 the real wages of all production workers in manufacturing rose by 3.0 percent a year; but in steel wages rose at 3.8 percent a year. The result was that in 1960 the steelworkers had achieved a record differential over manufacturing workers generally—their average wage was 40 percent higher (Weiss, 1967, pp. 189–191, 304–305; Rees, June 1951, p. 391; Means, 1962, pp. 73–79; Gordon and Persky, *et al,* n.d., pp. 9–11).[24]

These unprecendented raises of the 1950's were rooted in the extraordinary success of American capitalism at the height of the Cold War. The worldwide hegemony of the United States made it possible for the leading oligopolistic firms which were earning record profits to share out a portion of these profits with their employees. As Len DeCaux put it:

> A formula emerged that—in a period of profitable United States expansion aboard, technological advance, and a growing domestic market—seemed to satisfy government, employers, and labor leaders alike. Big business benefited in rising profits from government planning, contracts, and labor discipline. Union leaders maintained standing with their members through regular wage increases and other improvements—relatively little resisted by employers who more than compensated by raising prices and cutting labor costs. If the formula depended on constant inflation, those who thought they were ''getting theirs'' didn't care; and the rest weren't organized enough to count (DeCaux, 1970, p. 453).

Needless to say, the implementation of this strategy both required and contributed to the destruction of the trade union left: a phenomenon initiated by the Taft-Hartley Act and culminating in McCarthyism (Green, 1976). Communist Party theorist Green summarizes the quality of such a period as follows:

> When times are relatively good for the ruling class, and when the labor market is tight, worker-boss relations are more ''peaceful.'' This is so even when more strikes occur. In periods of inflation, for example, when the employers believe they can write off a wage increase by an even larger price rise, they still try to whittle the increase down, but the battle itself is kept within certain agreed upon, prescribed bounds (Green, 1971, p. 167).

Based on the experience of firms such as United States Steel during the 1950's, Baran and Sweezy, (1966, pp. 67–78) actually went so far as to argue that a new economic law had come to characterize advanced capitalism: one in which ''the surplus tends to rise both absolutely and relatively as the system develops.'' Thus, increasing profits for the oligopolies, and ever-rising real wages for their workers, were asserted to have become a permanent feature of modern capitalism. With this model of development, the class struggle between labor and capital could be readily viewed as superceded.

Baran and Sweezy asserted that ''there is no reason to assume that the experience of steel in the mid-1950's is unique'' (Baran and Sweezy, 1966 pp. 81–88). This was an egregious error. Although perhaps not unique, the situation of the American steel industry during the 1950's was most unusual. After 1959 the ongoing economic cooptation of the industrial working class postulated by Baran and Sweezy was no longer possible for the steel industry. Rather, the traditional Marxist perspective appears more accurate:

> When the profit picture is not so bright, when there is greater competition from other industries or abroad, when growing unemployment begins to replace a tight labor market, or when inflation must be curbed in an attempt to hold wages down, then the struggle tends to sharpen and strikes become more protracted and bitter. Every demand of the workers for more pay is met by the demands of the employers for

> increased production. There is greater pressure for introduction of new laborsaving machines and for increased speed-up to lower the cost of production per unit at the expense of the working class. We have now entered a period of that kind. Wage increases are no longer keeping pace with rising prices and taxes. On-the-job tension increases and with it the rate of industrial accidents (Green, 1971, p. 167).

The steel strike of 1959 marked that precise turning point for the American steel industry. Due to the newly-competitive foreign steel competition, the American industry was no longer able to pursue the strategy of continual price rises. And as a result, it was unwilling to continue its tactic of granting substantial wage benefits. Despite the longest and one of the bitterest steel strikes in American history, the settlement achieved by the steelworkers provided less than half the benefits won in previous contracts (Adelman, February 1961, p. 34).

Moreover, since that time, there has been a marked intensification in the rate of labor exploitation. This is evidenced not only by the rapid increases in labor productivity (which is explicable in terms of more advanced technique)[25] but also by outright "speed-up."[26] As was already indicated, the secular trend in the steel industry has been toward a lower accident rate. By the late 1950's it had declined to almost half the average for American manufacturing. But in the 1960's there was a sharp reversal of this trend. While all manufacturing saw a rise in accident rates, that of steel rose even more rapidly—so that by 1970, the accident rates in steel were, whether measured in terms of frequency or severity, substantially *greater* than those in manufacturing generally (Ayler, June 1963, pp. 105–106; U.S. Bureau of Labor Statistics, 1929, p. 121, 1964, pp. 1, 6, 1969, pp. 7, 11; U.S. Department of Commerce, 1973, p. 239).[27]

Significantly, these steel industry accidents are concentrated among the lower ranks of the work force. Thus, black steelworkers experience an accident rate 30 percent higher than that of whites. This disproportionate accident rate is the result of industry racism and made possible by the special overall oppression of black workers in the labor market (Lloyd *et al.,* 1959–1961; Greer, September–October, 1976).[28]

Not only have working conditions deteriorated since 1959, but steel wages have lagged behind manufacturing averages too. In the period from 1960 to 1970, while manufacturing production wages rose by an average of 3.0 percent annually, those in the steel industry only rose by 1.3 percent a year (Gordon and Persky, *et al.,* n.d., pp. 10–11). Part of the reason for this relative deterioration in the situation of the steelworkers was the "class collaborationist" posture of the Steelworkers Union. But underlying the decline in union militancy has been a recognition that the flush days of the 1950's are over and that concessions from the industry are no longer obtainable without a different kind of working class movement.[29]

It seems a fair reading of the evidence to conclude that since World War II (except in the 1950's when wages may have run somewhat ahead of productivity), wages have generally risen in tandem with productivity increases (Weiss, 1967, pp. 303–310; Means, 1962, p. 123; Kefauver, 1965, p. 125; U. S. Bureau of Labor Statistics, 1956, 1966).[30] If this is true, then with wages accounting for less than half of the total costs of steel production, price rises proportionate to wage increases—which has been the post-War pattern in steel—result in increasing profits both absolutely and as a proportion of sales (Weiss, 1967, p. 310; Means, 1962, pp. 37–43; Blair, 1972, pp. 632–635).

PROFITS

After the costs of raw materials and labor, only taxes remain as a major burden to the steel industry. And effective tax rates are very low. For example, in 1973, all taxes combined, were only 3 percent of U.S. Steel's sales.[31] The remainder of the income of the steel corporation goes to the expanded reproduction of its capital or is paid out in dividends to its stockholders.[32]

The veil of corporate secrecy, along with secrecy and changes in the government tax laws and administration, prevent any conclusions as to the real profits of steel corporations in different historical periods. But available estimates suggest that the U.S. Steel Corporation made quite comfortable returns on its investments throughout the 1940's and 1950's. For instance, the Kefauver Antitrust Subcommittee concluded that U.S. Steel's after-tax profits for the 1940's—including the Wartime when strict price-controls were in effect—averaged 9.4 percent annually. For the period 1950–1956 the annual average was 11.5 percent (Baran and Sweezy, 1966, p. 111; Burcke, January 1956, p. 88; Kefauver, 1965, p. 111). *Fortune* Magazine indicated that the return on capital to the Corporation during the 1950's was adequate to finance its investment needs without resort to outside financing: in contrast to American manufacturing generally the steel industry obtains very little investment capital from outside sources (Silberman, December 1960, p. 254; Thorn, September 1968, p. 382; Sweezy, March 1941, pp. 63–68).

It was during this flush time of the 1950's that the Corporation tried to increase its profit margin above its historic rate by taking advantage of the oligopolistic industry structure. Price rises for steel were put into effect which far exceeded increases in labor and other costs. Their immediate impact was to substantially decrease the "break-even point" for steel production (from 47 percent in 1953 to 30 percent in 1959), and correspondingly to sharply increase the rate of profit at higher levels of production (Means, 1962, pp. 130–150; Blair, 1972, pp. 640–643; Baran and Sweezy, 1966, pp. 86–87; McConnell, 1963, p. 31).

The consequence was that while between 1953 and 1959 the wholesale price index exclusive of metals remained stable, that of steel went up by 36 percent. Steel price rises became the main cause of inflation in the economy (Means, 1962, pp. 113–16; Sorenson, 1965, pp. 443–444; Blair, 1972, p. 640; Adelman, February 1961, p. 20; McConnell, 1963, p. 27). But rather than this price policy becoming a general feature of the steel industry or American capitalism generally, it rapidly reached its limit and turned into its opposite.

To fully explicate this point, it is necessary to recapitulate the sequence of events in the aftermath of World War II. In 1945–1946 the first post-War Steel strike took place as the steelworkers attempted to make up for the foregone wage increases of the war period. The Truman administration wanted to permit the workers a modest wage increase to strengthen its political hegemony over the labor movement; it also wanted to maintain price and wage controls so as to prevent inflation. Truman asserted that "there is room in the existing price structure for business as a whole to grant increases in wage rates." Thus, he attempted to obtain a steel settlement in which there would be no price increase. In that event net profits for 1946 would still have been about 6 percent—a higher return than in 1945. The steel companies refused such an arrangement. To prevent an indefinite strike, President Truman capitulated and authorized a substantial price increase. "Rather than force the corporations to pay the wage increases from their profits, he permitted them to pass on the wage increases in the form of higher prices. Indeed, as a consequence, the corporations raised their profit ratios considerably above previous levels" (quote from Green 1976, pp. 30–31). The industry profits for 1946 were 9 percent. And wage-price controls were scuttled (Preis, 1972, pp. 157–320; Bernstein, March 1966).

This arrangement set the pattern for steel industry collective bargaining thereafter. Its net effect was to permit substantial increases in steel industry real wages and company profits—but to do so at the expense of the economy as a whole. During the Republican administration of the 1950's this pattern continued without government interference (McConnell, 1963, pp. 54–63; Harbison and Spencer, September 1954; Sorenson, 1965, p. 457; Domhoff, 1972, pp. 159–162).

Such a pattern of untrammeled steel price increases, however, could not continue indefinitely. The inflation it stimulated was dangerous to the overall political economy. The sharp rises in prices contributed to sagging domestic market demand for steel (with a resulting setback for national economic growth) and led to massive foreign competition (Schlesinger, Jr., 1965, pp. 620–634; Sorenson, 1965, pp. 434–450). Of these factors, the price competition of foreign steel producers was doubtless the most important. As *Fortune* Magazine recently put it:

> During most of the past fifteen years . . . foreign steel has supplied the main pressure . . . to keep steel prices down. Had imports not played that role, the big U.S. companies—which tend to act in concert on prices—might well have raised prices in the 1960's and early 1970's more than they actually did (Loomis, January 1976, p. 110).

The turning point for the industry's price policy was 1959. From that time on through the 1960's price increases essentially stopped. Indeed, from 1959 to

1961—*prior* to the Kennedy steel confrontation—average steel prices fell by 0.5 percent (Rippe, February 1970, pp. 40–41; Adelman, February 1961, pp. 24–30; Blair, 1972, p. 635).

It was falling sales consequent to international steel competition which compelled the companies to give up their tactic of substantial wage increases. That is why the 1959 steel strike was so long and bitter—and why it yielded the workers only minimal wage increases. The prosperity concensus of the 1950's had finite limits. Over the next decade steel prices rose at only half the rate of manufacturing prices in general (Blair, 1972, p. 640).

Thus, the role of the political intervention of the Kennedy administration during the steel crisis of April, 1962 was a limited one. Kennedy's purpose was to see that the steel industry—"a bellweather, as well as a major element in industrial costs"—not advantage itself at the cost of a disaster to the overall national economy. As soon as he achieved his immediate objective of preventing a steel price rise—whose feasibility under the extant market conditions was questionable in any event—his involvement ceased (McConnell, 1963; Schlesinger, Jr., 1965; Sorenson, 1965; Blair, 1972, pp. 635–643; Weiss, 1967, pp. 182–183).[33]

Throughout the 1960's the steel industry had to be satisfied with a relatively lower rate of profit as it made massive investments to remain competitive with its international competitors.[34] Starting in 1969, under a sympathetic Republican administration, the fortunes of the industry improved, particularly with the adoption of "voluntary quotas" which limited foreign competition (Sheperd, 1970, p. 129; Adams, May 1968, pp. 663–664). With the adoption of this quasi-tariff steel prices rose again at the rapid rate of the mid-1950's (Rippe, February 1970, pp. 44–45). Then came price controls during 1971–1973, followed by further rapid price rises which added to the inflation of the 1973–1974 period (*The New York Times,* December 16, 1973, December 17, 1974, December 18, 1974, December 24, 1974, January 5, 1975; Blair, 1972, p. 638). Most recently, the economic downturn in the economy has resulted in depressed conditions for the industry.

The fluctuations of the business cycle do not disguise the overall slippage of the American steel industry on the world scene. Mediated by the price system, American steel can be seen to have temporarily been able in the wake of World War II to satisfy the desires of its owners for higher profits and simultaneously make significant concessions to its employees. But that time seems to have passed, to have been only an historical interlude. The notion that the steel industry, as a central part of an affluent society, could resolve the problems of advanced capitalism in the general interest has been disconfirmed. Rather, it appears that to now wrest major concession from the industry—whether in conditions of work or in real wages—will require major structural changes in the political economy.

FOOTNOTES

1. In 1947, U.S. Steel was the third largest manufacturing firm; in 1973, it was eleventh. Between 1947 and 1967, Bethlehem Steel dropped from tenth to nineteenth. (*Fortune,* May 1973, pp. 222–223; Sheperd, 1970, pp. 78, 255) And among industry groups, steel earnings have shown a marked secular decline. However, the apparently low profit rates in steel may in part be an accounting illusion because it is particularly difficult to avoid ''distortions in the corporate profit series'' in the integrated primary metal industries ''that contain substantial extractive activities.'' (Rosenberg, 1969, p. 131; Sherman, 1968, pp. 85–89; McConnell, 1963, p. 117; *The New York Times,* August 31, 1973, December 14, 1973, November 1, 1974)

2. This loss of export markets was particularly serious since world trade in steel has been expanding even more rapidly than world production. Between 1960 and 1972, world output grew at 5 percent annually while exports increased 7.9 percent annually. The collapse of the American steel export market was concentrated in the 1950's as Japanese and other steel-producing nations achieved a competitive price position. Between 1953 and 1958 while world prices dropped, American prices rose by a third. The failure to retain any part of the rapidly growing world market in steel is part of the reason the American share of all world manufacturing exports declined from 25 percent in 1960 to 18 percent in 1973. (*The New York Times,* November 16, 1975; Kawahito, 1972, pp. 35, 165–167; Friden, 1972, p. 105; Green, 1976, p. 81)

3. A related view attributes steel industry backwardness in technique to its oligopolistic structure and desire to protect its existing capital investment. (Adams and Dirlam, September 1964, May 1966; Blair, 1972, p. 515)

4. The five industrial sectors of transportation including aircraft, electrical machinery, instruments, chemicals and nonelectrical machinery, absorb the vast bulk of federal R&D funds and dramatically raise the overall average. (Gruber, Mehta and Vernon, February 1967, pp. 22–25; Bell, 1973, pp. 250–259; Sheperd, 1970, pp. 87–88; Chandler, Jr., p. 277; *Hearings on Economic Concentration,* Part 3, pp. 1138–1143)

5. One particularly unfortunate consequence is the backwardness of the American steel industry in environmental matters. (Greer, 1974, June 1974)

6. As Senator Roman Hruska indicated by some sharp questioning of Blair (while as chief economist he was testifying before the Subcommittee on Antitrust and Monopoly of which Hruska was a member), Blair has been predicting imminent massive product substitution for steel since 1947, while the actual results heretofore have not borne out his analysis. U.S. Senate *Hearings on Economic Concetration,* Part 4, pp. 1565–1568)

7. From the outset of the CIO organizing drive, John L. Lewis grasped the point that coal industry wages were intimately tied to those of steel. Thus, unionization of the steel industry permitted great advances for the coal miners—advances which were lost after 1950 when the mineworkers union accomodated to the coal companies. (Alinsky, 1970, p. 64; Bethel, n.d.; United Mine Workers, 1974, pp. 13, 19)

8. The Senate Judiciary Committee—following up on the Kennedy Steel confrontation —reached a similar conclusion: that while there is a true cost of ''captive mine'' production, it is not available outside the industry. In explaining why he felt that Congress should not hold the steel companies in contempt for failing to honor the Kefauver Subcommitte's subpoena to produce this data, Senator Alexander Wiley of Wisconsin opined: ''I personally felt that in the state of the world at present, with Cuba, with Berlin and with the Near East, that this is no time for us to arrange things so that we will probably put a segment of our business out of business.'' (U.S. Senate *Hearings on the Refusal . . .,* 1963, pp. 121–129.)

9. As Stanley S. Surrey, former Assistant Secretary for Tax Policy in the Treasury

Department explains, ''In . . . industries such as steel . . . a zero tax may also occur although there are book profits. The reasons appear to be a combination of investment credits, excessive depreciation, and the benefits for natural resources, the latter obtained by subsidiaries engaged in that activity and included in a consolidated tax return so that their deductions are applied against the income of the consolidated group.'' (Surrey, 1973, p. 81) Thus, while the effective average federal corporation tax rate in 1963 was 39 percent, that of the coal industry consequent to depletion allowances was only 18 percent. (Siegfried, June 1974, pp. 245–255.)

10. The Truman Committee hearings detail how federal action during World War II (largely initiated by ''dollar-a-year'' men on loan from the steel industry) and Wall Street financial interests also played a role in preventing the entry of new firms into the industry. (U.S. Senate *Hearings before Special Committee Investigating* . . ., 1942, Part 14, especially pp. 5786–5932)

11. The commanding role of ore reserves is evidenced by the predominancy of iron ore mining companies among the joint subsidiaries set up by the major steel producers. Indeed, these subsidiaries largely determine the character of the industry's structure. (Fusfeld, May 1958, pp. 578–587.)

12. For instance, while U.S. Steel spent over $800 million on various capital expenditures between 1946 and 1949, a bare 1 percent of this sum was devoted to ore development. By contrast, half of the Corporation's capital expenditures in the current period are allocated to raw material developments. (U.S. Steel Corporation, 1954, p. 45; *Annual Reports, 1972, 1973)*

13. Recently U.S. Steel announced plans for a $200 million expansion of one of its taconite plants and signed a long-term contract with Litton Industries for the transport of Mesabi taconite to the Gary Works. (*The New York Times,* August 3, 1975; *The Wall Street Journal,* December 4, 1973)

14. However, when steel production reached new highs in the early 1970's and Japanese steelmakers bought large amounts of American scrap, its price set new records. (*The Wall Street Journal,* May 30, 1974)

15. Soviet iron ore production is currently two-and-a-half times that of the United States, and the U.S.S.R. is becoming a major exporter of iron ore. (*The Elements,* July 1975, p. 7; Manners, 1974, pp. 325–327)

16. The negative environmental effect is described in Mostert, 1974, especially p. 139.

17. Despite the opening of the larger St. Lawrence in 1969 the size of the Great Lakes ore fleet ships is still limited to such a degree that full advantage cannot be taken of the new economies of scale. Hence, over the period in question relative lake ore transport costs rose to such an extent that by the mid-sixties railroad transport of Mesabi ore to the Chicago steel district was actually competitive with shipping. (Manners, 1974, pp. 210–218; Hogan, 1972, Vol. 4, pp. 1493–1494)

18. The exact obverse of this relationship appears with respect to U.S. Steel's coal production. As a major producer of coal, the Corporation contracted in 1974 to sell the Hydroelectric Power Commission of Ontario, Canada, 90 million tons of coal over thirty years for a price in excess of $1 billion. To provide this coal, the Corporation will develop a $120 million new mine in Pennsylvania—to be jointly financed by Ontario Hydro and New York financial institutions.

Ironically, the American Iron and Steel Institute is attempting to obtain export quotas on metallurgical coal (which is selling well above domestic prices), presumably to make difficulties for Japanese and western European competitors who buy much of their coal in the United States. (*The New York Times,* March 2, 1974, October 21, 1974)

19. The two firms are Zeeruse Ltd. and Ferroalloys Ltd. (U.S. Steel *Annual Re-*

port, 1967; National Credit Office, *Specialized Credit Report USS,* January 23, 1968)

20. Significantly, U.S. Steel was also involved in a $17 million joint mining venture in Bolivia with Engelhard Minerals. The Engelhard interests are leaders in fostering American investment in South Africa. (*The Wall Street Journal,* May 3, 1971).

21. For a detailed study of U.S. Steel employment discrimination in the Gary Works, see Greer, September-October, 1976, pp. 45–66.

22. The U.S. Steel Corporation only opened the plant in 1915 after the progressive state legislature of Minnesota threatened substantial taxes on the Corporation's Mesabi ore; the plant was constructed in lieu of such taxes. (Warren, 1973, pp. 76–80; White and Primmer, February 1937, pp. 82–91) In the 1960's the steel companies asserted that they could not invest in the facilities necessary to utilize low-grade Mesabi ores unless they were guaranteed low taxes. So in 1964 the voters were intimidated into passing an amendment to the state constitution limiting taxes on taconite. Immediately thereafter U.S. Steel announced that it would begin construction of such plants. (Gerald Manners, an expert on iron ore production, dryly observes: "These investments might well have been made in any case.") And a few years later U.S. Steel—no longer threatened with substantial ore taxes—decided to shut down a major part of the mill. As a New York financial analyst observed: "U.S. Steel was forced to build it in the first place and I'm sure they'd love to close it down." (Manners, 1974, p. 155; Warren, 1973, pp. 262–263; *The Wall Street Journal,* September 10, 1971)

23. It should also be borne in mind that the first half of the twentieth century witnessed a marked secular tendency for wage differentials between skilled and unskilled blue-collar workers to decline. After 1950, however, this trend has not continued. (As with the failure of the work week to decline any further after World War II, despite its long-term tendency to do so until that point, it seems reasonable to attribute this stagnation in large part to the destruction of the American left, which had always been çentral to these class struggles.) In the steel industry, the skilled-unskilled differential declined most rapidly in the early days of the CIO. But thereafter no further change took place. Currently, skilled steelworkers earn perhaps a half more than their unskilled colleagues, a substantial gap—but far less than was the case before unionization. (Hamilton, 1972, pp. 396, 510; Stieber, 1959, pp. 236–244; Greer, September-October 1976; Green, 1976, p. 61)

24. These figures probably even underestimate the relative gains of steelworkers over other manufacturing workers in the 1950's because they are based upon hourly wages, exclusive of fringe benefits. But from 1950 to 1967 steelworkers' fringe benefits went from 12 to 24 percent of money wages, which probably exceeded the manfacturing average. Moreover, these fringe benefits—largely concentrated in the oligopolistic industries—have the additional feature of providing "tax expenditure" benefits under the tax code, so their addition to net real income is even greater. (Rippe, February 1970, pp. 34–35; Green, 1976, pp. 59–60; Surrey, 1973, p. 67.)

25. Between 1954 and 1970 the amount of labor necessary to produce a ton of steel fell by 50 percent. (Between 1904 and 1954, the decline was 83 percent.) (Boylan, Jr., 1975, pp. 190–191; Hiestand, 1974, p. 19)

26. *The Daily World* (April 4, 1974, November 7, 1974) reported a fatal accident in U.S. Steel's Gary Works on March 28, 1974. The accident occurred "in the wake of a record-breaking production run." Workers on the scene asserted it was consequent to the omission of safety procedures which were regularly disregarded during periods of high productivity. Corporation spokesmen insist that the overwhelming majority of accidents in their plants are caused by workers failing to take necessary precautions.

27. A parallel "speed-up" and concommitant rise in the accident rate has occurred in the western European steel industry. A particularly horrifying group of accidents has marked

the Usinor plant in Dunkerque. (The Scunthorpe Group, n.d., pp. 8–9; Segre, December 1972, p. 122; *Le Monde,* June 19, 1974)

28. Similarly, the dangerous conditions of work in the French steel industry are tied to the increasing proportion of foreign-born steelworkers whose ability to protect their working conditions is dimished by their subordinate political status. (Castles and Kosack, 1973; Gani, 1972; Castells, 1975)

This process repeats the pre-World War I American experience in which foreign-born steelworkers experienced far greater accident rates than native-born ones. (U.S. Bureau of Labor Statistics, 1918, pp. 131, 144–146.)

29. That there is a factor of trade union accommodation to management (and not simply a capitulation to inexorable market forces) is evidenced by the Abel leadership's agreement to the Experimental Negotiating Agreement—which essentially gives up the union's right to strike—during the early 1970's when steel profits were rebounding. This posture by the steelworkers' leadership has led to an unprecedented rank-and-file upsurge.

30. A variety of complex factors complicate any effort to arrive at a firm conclusion as to the actual rates of productivity increase in the post-war period. For instance, the number of blue-collar workers in the steel industry has been declining, while the number and proportion of white-collar workers has been increasing. Depending upon how one analyzes and classifies these workers, quite different conclusions about changes in productivity follow. (Bell, 1973, p. 133; *Political Affairs*, November 1973; Braverman, 1974)

31. In 1973 the federal corporation income tax constituted about one-third of the Corporation's total tax burden. Local property taxes—based on shamefully flagrant underassessments—made up the bulk of its tax liabilities. For the period 1969–1971, the U.S. Steel Corporation probably had no net federal tax liability. (U.S. Steel *Annual Report,* 1973; Vanik, July 1972, pp. 13–14; Greer, Fall 1975)

Incidentally, effective tax burdens on western European steelworkers are even lower, which causes much complaint among American steel manufacturers at how the government puts them at a competitive disadvantage. (Segre, December 1972, pp. 124–131; MacPhee, 1974, pp. 152–154)

32. Historically, from its formation in 1901 to 1931, U.S. Steel paid out $0.30 in dividends for every $1.00 it paid in wages. The sum would have sufficed to have assured a generation of its workers a decent livelihood instead of subsistence. (Davis, 1933, pp. 206–207.)

33. Kennedy then proceeded to implement the program of tax credits and liberalized depreciation allowances to American indusry worked out by Treasury Secretary Douglas Dillon—which effectively raised the overall profitability of American manufacturing capital. (Hall and Jorgenson, June 1967) And he refused to support the Kefauver Committee's efforts to discover the real costs of steel products (nor its attempt to cite for contempt of Congress the willful defiance of company executives of subpoenas to produce such data.) (U.S. Senate *Hearings before the Committee on the Judiciary,* especially pp. 74–75; McManus, 1967, pp. 70–71)

34. For the decade, the steel industry's average after-tax profits were reported to be the lowest of all major industry groups. (*The New York Times,* January 13, 1973; Blair, 1972, pp. 640–643)

REFERENCES

Adams, Walter (1961), "The Steel Industry," *The Structure Of American Industry: Some Case Studies*, edited by Adams, Walter, New York: Macmillian and Company.

———. (May, 1968), "The Military-Industrial Complex and the New Industrial State," *The American Economic Review,* Vol. 58.

Adams, Walter and Dirlam, Joel B. (September, 1964), "Steel Imports and Vertical Oligopoly Power," *The American Economic Review,* Vol. 54, No. 5.

———. (May, 1966), "Big Steel, Invention, and Innovation," *The Quarterly Journal of Economics,* Vol. 80, No. 2.

Adelman, M. A. (February, 1961), "Steel, Administered Prices, and Inflation," *The Quarterly Journal of Economics,* Vol. 75, No. 1.

Alexandersson, Gunnar (1956), *The Industrial Structure of American Cities: A Geographic Study of Urban Economy in the United States,* London: George Allen & Unwin Ltd.; Stockholm: Almquist & Wiksell.

———. (April, 1961), "Changes in the Location Pattern of the Anglo-American Steel Industry: 1948–1959." *Economic Geography,* Vol. 37, No. 2.

Alinsky, Saul D. (1970), *John L. Lewis: An Unauthorized Biography,* New York: Vintage Books.

Appleton, John B. (1927), *The Iron and Steel Industry of the Calumet Region: A Study in Economic Geography,* Urbana: University of Illinois.

Ault, David (March, 1973), "The Continued Deterioration of the Competitive Ability of the U.S. Steel Industry: The Development of Continuous Casting," *Western Economic Journal,* Vol. 11, No. 1.

Ayer, Hugh M. (June, 1963), "Hoosier Labor in the Second World War," *Indiana Magazine of History,* Vol. 59, No. 2.

Baran, Paul A., and Sweezy, Paul M. (1966), *Monopoly Capital: An Essay on the American Economic and Social Order,* New York: Monthly Review Press.

Barnes, Thomas and Lowie H. M. (1969), *A Cost Analysis of Air Pollution Controls in the Integrated Iron and Steel Industry,* Columbus: Battelle Memorial Institute.

Bell, Daniel (1973), *The Coming of Post-Industrial Society: A Venture in Social Forecasting,* New York: Basic Books, Inc.

Bernstein, Barton J. (March, 1966), "The Truman Administration and the Steel Strike of 1946," *The Journal of American History,* Vol. 52, No. 4.

Bernstein, Irving (1966), *The Lean Years: A History of the American Worker, 1920–1933,* Boston: Houghton Mifflin Company.

Berry, Brian J. L. and Horton, Frank E. (1970), *Geographic Perspectives on Urban Systems with Integrated Readings,* Englewood Cliffs: Prentice-Hall, Inc.

Bethel, T. N. (n.d.), *Conspiracy in Coal,* pamphlet, Appalachian Movement Press.

Blair, John M. (1972), *Economic Concentration: Structure, Behavior, and Public Policy,* New York: Harcourt Brace Jovanovich, Inc.

Boorman, Dean K. (1951), *The Impact of U.S. Steel in Buck's County Pennsylvania: A Regional Development Plan,* M.S., MIT.

Boylan, Jr., Myles G. (1975), *Economic Effects of Scale Increases in the Steel Industry: The Case of U.S. Blast Furnances,* New York: Praeger Publishers.

Braverman, Harry (1974), *Labor and Monopoly Capital,* New York: Monthly Review Press.

Brody, David (1960), *Steelworkers in America: The Nonunion Era,* Cambridge: Harvard University Press.

———. (1965), *Labor in Crisis: The Steel Strike of 1919,* Philadelphia: J. B. Lippincott Company.

Broude, Henry W. (1963), *Steel Decisions and the National Economy,* New Haven: Yale University Press.

Burcke, Gilbert (January, 1956), "The Transformation of U.S. Steel," *Fortune,* Vol. 53, No. 1.

Business Week (June 4, 1966), "Special Report: The World Battle for Steel."

Castells, Manuel (1975), "Immigrant Workers and Class Struggle in Advanced Capitalism," *Politics and Society,* Vol. 5, No. 1.

Castles, Stephen and Kosack, Godula (1973), *Immigrant Workers and The Class Structure in Western Europe,* London: Oxford University Press.

Chandler, Jr., Alfred D. (Spring, 1973), "The Structure of American Industry in the Twentieth Century: A Historical Overview," *Business History Review,* Vol. 43.

Citibank, (April, 1976), *Monthly Economic Letter.*

The Daily World.

Davis, Horace B. (1933), *Labor and Steel,* New York: International Publishers.

DeCaux, Len (1970), *Labor Radical: From the Wobblies to CIO, A Personal History,* Boston: Beacon Press.

Domhoff, G. William (1972), *Fats Cats and Democrats: The Role of the Big Rich in the Party of the Common Man,* Englewood Cliffs: Prentice-Hall, Inc.

Economic Priorities Report (June–July, 1973), "Steel—The Recyclable Material," Vol. 4, No. 3.

The Elements.

Estall, Robert (1972), *A Modern Geography of the United States,* Chicago: Quadrangle Books.

Fairless, Benjamin B. (1956), *It Would Only Happen in the U.S.,* reprinted from *Life Magazine* (n.p.: U.S. Steel, 1957).

Forbes.

Fortune (May, 1973), "The Fortune Directory," Vol. 87, No. 5.

Friden, Lennart (1972), *Instability in the International Steel Market: A Study of Import and Export Fluctations,* translated by Tanner, Roger, Stockholm: K.L. Beckmans.

Fusfeld, Daniel R. (May, 1958), "Joint Subsidiaries in the Iron and Steel Industry," Papers and Proceedings of the American Economic Association, *The American Economic Review,* Vol. 48, No. 2.

Gani, Leon (1972), *Syndicats et Travailleus Immigrés,* Paris: Editions Sociales.

Garraty, John A. (Winter, 1960), "The United States Steel Corporation Versus Labor," *Labor History,* Vol. 1, No. 1.

Gomez, Henry (1971), "Venezuela's Iron Ore Industry," in Mikesell, Raymond *et al.,* *Foreign Investment in the Petroleum and Mineral Industries,* Baltimore: The Johns Hopkins Press.

Gordon, David M. and Persky, Joseph J. *et al.,* "Economic Consequences on Steelworkers of Strikes and the Right to Strike in the Basic Steel Industry, 1949–1970." (Typescript, Appendix A to Plaintiff's Trial Memorandum on Hearing for a Preliminary Injunction.)

Green, Gil (1971), *The New Radicalism: Anarchist or Marxist?* New York: International Publishers.

———. (1976), *What's Happening to Labor,* New York: International Publishers.

Greer, Edward (1974), "Air Pollution and Corporate Power: Municipal Reform Limits in a Black City," *Politics and Society,* Vol. 4, No. 4.

———. (June, 1974), "Obstacles to Taming Corporate Polluters: Water Pollution Politics in Gary, Indiana," *Environmental Affairs,* Vol. 3, No. 2.

———. (Fall, 1975), "Racial Biases in the Property Tax," *Review of Radical Political Economics,* Vol. 7, No. 3.

———. (September–October, 1976), "Racism and U.S. Steel," *Radical America,* Vol. 10, No. 5.

———. (1978), *Big Steel, Little Steal: Limits of Black Reform in Gary, Indiana,* New York: Monthly Review Press.

Gruber, William, Mehta, Dileep and Vernon, Raymond (February, 1967), "The R & D Factor in International Trade and International Development of United States Industries," *The Journal of Political Economy,* Vol. 75, No. 1.

Gulick, Charles A. (n.p. 1924), *The Labor Policy of the United States Steel Corporation,* New York.

Hall, Robert E. and Jorgenson, Dale W. (June, 1967), "Tax Policy and Investment Behavior," *The American Economic Review,* Vol. 57, No. 3.

Hamilton, Richard F. (1972), *Class and Politics in the United States,* New York: John Wiley and Sons, Inc.

Harbison, Frederick H. and Spencer, Robert C. (September, 1954), "The Politics of Collective Bargaining: The Postwar Record in Steel," *The American Political Science Review,* Vol. 48, No. 3.

Heal, David W. (1974), *Industrial Britain: The Steel Industry in Postwar Britain,* London: David & Charles Ltd.

Heilbroner, Robert L. (Spring, 1973), "Economic Problems of a 'Postindustrial' Society," *Dissent.*

Hessen, Robert. (Autumn, 1972), "The Transformation of Bethlehem Steel, 1904–1909," *Business History Review,* Vol. 46, No. 3

Hiestand, Dale L. (1974), *High Level Manpower and Technological Change in the Steel Industry: Implications for Corporate Manpower Planning,* New York: Praeger Publishers.

Hines, L. Gregory (September, 1951), "Price Determination in the Lake Erie Iron Ore Market," *The American Economic Review,* Vol. 41, No. 4.

Hogan, William F. (1971), *Economic History of the Iron and Steel Industry in the United States,* Vols. I-V, Lexington: D.C. Heath and Company.

———. (1972), *The 1970s: Critical Years for Steel,* Lexington: D.C. Heath and Company.

Howe, Christopher (1973), *Wage Patterns and Wage Policy in Modern China,* Cambridge: Cambridge University Press.

Jones, Clarence Fielden and Darkenwald, Gordon Gerald (1965), *Economic Geogrpahy,* Third Edition, New York: The Macmillan Company.

Kawahito, Kioshi (1972), *The Japanese Steel Industry: With An Analysis of the U.S. Steel Import Problem,* New York: Praeger Publishers.

Keesing, Donald B. (February, 1967), "The Impact of Research and Development on United States Trade," *The Journal of Political Economy,* Vol. 75, No. 1.

Kefauver, Estes, (1965), *In a Few Hands: Monopoly Power in America,* Baltimore: Penguin Books.

Kimble, George H. T. (January, 1952), "The Geography of Steel," *Scientific American,* Vol. 186, No. 1.

King, L. *et. al.,* (July, 1971), "Optimal Transportation Patterns of Coal in the Great Lakes Region," *Economic Geography,* Vol. 47, No. 3.

Klein, Philip A. and Gordon, Richard L. (1971), *The Steel Industry and U.S. Business*

Cycles, University Park: The Pennsylvania State University.
Labor Research Association, Metalworker Facts.
Lippert, T. W. (1950), *Cerro Boliver: Saga of an Iron Ore Crisis Averted,* Reprinted from *Journal of Metals and Mining Engineering,* February, 1950, New York: United States Steel Corporation.
Lloyd, J. William *et al.,* (1959–1961), "Long-Term Mortality Study of Steelworkers," *Journal of Occupational Medicine,* Vols. 11–13.
Loomis, Carol J. (January, 1976), "Steel's Not-So-Solid Expansion Plans," *Fortune,* Vol. 93, No. 1.
McAteer, J. Davitt (1973), *Coal Mine Health and Safety: The Case of West Virginia,* New York: Praeger Publishers.
McCloskey, Donald N. (1973), *Economic Maturity and Entrepreneurial Decline: British Iron and Steel, 1870–1913,* Cambridge: Harvard University Press.
McConnell, Grant (1963), *Steel and the Presidency: 1962,* New York: W. W. Norton and Company, Inc.
McDonald, John (December, 1960), "Steel Is Rebuilding for a New Era," *Fortune,* Vol. 62, No. 6.
McManus, George J. (1967), *The Inside Story of Steel Wages and Prices, 1959–1967,* Philadelphia: Chilton Book Company.
MacPhee, Craig R. (1974), *Restrictions on International Trade in Steel,* Lexington: D. C. Heath and Company.
Manke, Richard B. (July, 1972), "Iron Ore and Steel: A Case Study of the Causes and Consequences of Vertical Integration," *The Journal of Industrial Economics* (Britain), Vol. 20. No. 3.
Manners, Gerald (1974), *The Changing World Market for Iron Ore 1950–1980: An Economic Geography,* Baltimore: The Johns Hopkins Press.
Manufacturers Hanover Trust (June, 1973), *Economic Report.*
Martin, David D. (1967), "Resource Control and Market Power," *Extractive Resources and Taxation,* edited by Gaffney, Mason, Madison: University of Wisconsin Press.
Means, Gardiner C. (1962), *Pricing Policy and the Public Interest: A Study Based on Steel,* New York: Harper and Brothers.
Mikesell, Raymond F. (1971), "Iron Ore in Brazil: The Experience of the Hanna Mining Company," in Mikesell, Raymond F. *et al., Foreign Investment in the Petroleum and Mining Industries,* Baltimore: The Johns Hopkins Press.
Miller, Roger Emile (1971), *Innovation, Organization, and Environment: A Study of Sixteen American and West European Steel Firms,* Sherbrooke: University of Sherbrooke.
Le Monde, (June 19, 1974), No. 9152.
Mostert, Noel (1974), *Supership,* New York: Alfred A. Knopf.
Murray, Robert K. (December, 1951), "Communism and the Great Steel Strke of 1919," *The Mississippi Valley Historical Review,* Vol. 38, No. 3.
National Credit Office, (January 23, 1968), *Specialized Credit Report,* USS.
The New York Times.
Organization for Economic Cooperation and Development, (1973), *The Iron and Steel Industry in 1971 and Trends in 1972,* Paris: O.E.C.D.
Parker, Geoffrey (1969), *An Economic Geography of the Common Market,* New York: Praeger Publishers.
Political Affairs (November, 1973), "The Working Class and the Class Struggle in the United States," Special Issue, Vol. 52, Nos. 10–11.

Preis, Art (1972), *Labor's Giant Step: Twenty Years of the CIO,* New York: Pathfinder Press.

Quillen, Isaac James (1942), *Industrial City: A History of Gary, Indiana to 1929,* Ph.D., Yale University.

Rees, Albert (June, 1951), "Postwar Wage Determination in the Basic Steel Industry," *The American Economic Review,* Vol. 41, No. 3

———. (1961). *Real Wages in Manufacturing 1890–1914,* Princeton: Princeton University Press.

Ridgeway, James (1973), *The Last Play: The Struggle to Monopolize the World's Energy Resources,* New York: E. P. Dutton & Co., Inc.

Rippe, Richard D. (February, 1970), "Wages, Prices and Imports in the American Steel Industry," *The Review of Economics and Statistics,* Vol. 52, No. 1.

Rodgers, Allan (January, 1952), "Industrial Inertia: A Major Factor in the Location of the Steel Industry in the United States," *The Geographical Review.*

Rogers, Barbara (1976), *White Wealth and Black Poverty: American Investments in Southern Africa,* Westport: Greenwood Press.

Rosegger, Gerhard (January, 1974), "Technological Change and Materials Consumption in U.S. Iron and Steel Manufacturing: An Assessment of Some Environmental Impacts," *Human Ecology,* Vol. 2, No. 1.

Rosenberg, Leonard Gerson (1969), "Taxation of Income from Capital by Industry Group," *The Taxation of Income from Capital,* edited by Harberger, Arnold C. and Bailey, Martin J., Washington, D.C.: The Brookings Institution.

Rowan, Richard L. (1970), "The Negro in the Steel Industry," *Negro Employment in Basic Industry: A Study of Racial Policies in Six Industries,* edited by Northrop, Herbert R., Philadelphia: University of Pennsylvania.

Arthur M. Schlesinger, Jr., (1965), *A Thousand Days,* Boston: Houghton Mifflin.

School and Society (October 20, 1923), "Educational Events: Undernourished Children," Vol. 18, No. 460.

Schroeder, Gertrude G. (1953), *The Growth of Major Steel Companies, 1900–1950,* Baltimore: The Johns Hopkins Press.

The Scunthrope Group (n.d.), *The Threat To Steelworkers,* Nottingham: Institute for Workers Control.

Segre, Henri (December, 1972), "La Sidérurgie Francaise: Crise et Perspectives," *Economie et Politique,* No. 221.

Sheperd, William G. (1970), *Market Power and Economic Welfare: An Introduction,* New York: Random House.

Sherman, Howard J. (1968), *Profits in the United States: An Introduction to a Study of Economic Concentration and Business Cycles,* Ithaca: Cornell University Press.

Siegfried, John J. (June, 1974), "Effective Average U.S. Corporation Income Tax Rates," *National Tax Journal,* Vol. 27, No. 2.

Silberman, Charles E. (December, 1960), "Steel: It's a Brand-New Industry," *Fortune,* Vol. 62, No. 6.

Sorenson, Theodore (1965), *Kennedy,* New York: Harper and Row.

Stieber, Jack (1959), *The Steel Industry Wage Structure: A Study of the Joint Union-Management Job Evaluation Program in the Basic Steel Industry,* Cambridge; Harvard University Press.

Stigler, George J. (December, 1949), "A Theory of Delivered Price Structures," *The American Economic Review,* Vol. 39, No. 6.

Stocking, George W. (1954), *Basing Point Pricing and Regional Development: A Case*

Study of the Iron and Steel Industry, Chapel Hill: The University of North Carolina Press.

Surrey, Stanley S. (1973), *Pathways to Tax Reform: The Concept of Tax Expenditures,* Cambridge: Harvard University Press.

Sweezy, Paul M. (March, 1941), "The Decline of the Investment Banker," *The Antioch Review,* Vol. 1, No. 1.

Temin, Peter (1964), *Iron and Steel in Nineteenth Century America: An Economic Inquiry,* Cambridge: The MIT Press.

Thorn, Richard S. (December, 1968), "Steel Imports, Labor Productivity, and Cost Competiveness," *Western Economic Journal,* Vol. 6, No. 5.

Ullman, Lloyd (June, 1958), "The Union and Wages in Basic Steel: A Comment," *The American Economic Review,* Vol. 48, No. 3.

United Mine Workers of America,Research Department, (1974), *Coal Miners and the Economy: A UMWA Research Report,* Washington, D.C.: UMWA.

U.S. Bureau of Economic Analysis (1973), *Long Term Economic Growth 1860–1970,* Washington: GPO.

U.S. Bureau of Labor Statistics (1918), BLS Bulletin No. 234, *The Safety Movement in the Iron and Steel Industry 1907 to 1917,* Washington: GPO.

U.S. Bureau of Labor Statistics (1929), BLS Bulletin No. 490, *Statistics of Industrial Accidents in the United States to the End of 1927,* Washington: GPO.

U.S. Bureau of Labor Statistics (1956), BLS Bulletin No. 1200, *Man-Hours Per Unit of Output in the Basic Steel Industry, 1939–55,* Washington: GPO.

U.S. Bureau of Labor Statistics (1964), BLS Report No. 278, *Injury Rates by Industry, 1958, 1959, and 1960,* Washington: GPO.

U.S. Bureau of Labor Statistics (1966), BLS Report No. 310, *Labor Productivity of the Steel Industry in the United States,* Washington: GPO.

U.S. Bureau of Labor Statistics, (1969), BLS Report No. 389, *Injury Rates by Industry,* Washington: GPO.

U.S. Department of Commerce, Bureau of the Census (1973), *Statistical Abstract of the United States, 1972,* Washington: GPO.

U.S. Senate, 62nd Cong., 1st Sess. (1913), Document No. 110, *Report on the Conditions of Employment in the Iron and Steel Industry in the United States,* in *Working Conditions and the Relations of Employers and Employees,* Vol. III, Washington: GPO.

U.S. Senate, 77th Cong. 2nd Sess. (1942), *Hearings Before Special Committee Investigating the National Defense Program,* in *Iron and Steel,* Part 14, Washington: GPO.

U.S. Senate, Senate Judiciary Committee, 87th Cong., 2nd Sess. (1963), *Hearings on the Refusal of Certain Steel Companies to Respond to Subpoenas,* Washington: GPO.

U.S. Senate, Senate Judiciary Committee, Subcommittee on Antitrust and Monopoly, 89th Cong., 1st Sess. (1965), *Hearings on Economic Concentration,* in *Concentration, Invention, and Innovation,* Part 5, Washington: GPO.

U.S. Steel Corporation, *Annual Reports.*

U.S. Steel Corporation, (1954), *U.S. Steel's Policies on Costs, Prices, Plants, Productivity,* New York: USS.

Vanik, Charles A. (July, 1972), "Corporate Federal Tax Payments and Federal Subisies to Corporations," Testimony before the Joint Economic Committee, 92nd Cong., 2nd Sess.

Walker, Charles Rumford (1922), *Steel: The Diary of a Furnance Worker,* Boston: The Atlantic Monthly Press.

The Wall Street Journal.
Warren, Kenneth (1973), *The American Steel Industry, 1850–1970: A Geographical Interpretation,* New York: Oxford University Press.
Weiss, Leonard W. (1967), *Case Studies inAmerican Industry,* New York: John Wiley and Sons, Inc.
White, Langdon and Primmer, George (February, 1937), "The Iron and Steel Industry of Duluth: A Study in Location Maladjustment," *The Geographical Review,* Vol. 27, No. 1.
Wittman, Michael et Thouvenot, Claude (1972), *La Mutation de la Siderurgie: Vers une Nouvelle Geographie de l'Acier,* Paris: Masson and Cie.
Yeates, Maurice H. and Garner, Barry J. (1971), *The North American City,* New York: Harper and Row.

UNPRODUCTIVE LABOR AND THE RATE OF SURPLUS VALUE IN THE UNITED STATES, 1947–1967*

Edward N. Wolff, NEW YORK UNIVERSITY

I
THE TENDENCY OF THE SURPLUS TO RISE

The movement of the surplus over time has been one of the principal concerns of Marxian political economy. Marx's own law of the tendency of the rate of profit to fall (Marx, 1967, Vol. 3, Ch. 13) states that the mass of surplus value will decline relatively to the value of constant capital over time. This law was argued on theoretical grounds and assumed a competitive economy and (implicitly) a negligible amount of unproductive activity in the economy.

Recognizing the dominant role played by monopoly power and the growing importance of unproductive activity in the American economy, Baran and Sweezy (1966, p. 72) proposed a new law of the tendency of the surplus to rise. The theorem is that "the surplus tends to rise both absolutely and relatively, as the system develops." The Baran and Sweezy concept of surplus includes not only enterprise profit but also government expenditure and "unproductive consumption." They did not attempt a systematic exposition of the concept of unproductive activity, but included such items as advertising and other sales costs, planned obsolescence, expense accounts and litigation costs. Moreover, they did not try to statistically verify their law of the tendency of the surplus to rise. However, a statistical appendix, compiled by Joseph Phillips, was provided, consisting mainly of national accounts data. Ironically, the data supplied did not provide any support for the law. Instead, they showed that the ratio of surplus to GNP dipped from .47 to .40 between 1929 and 1933, rose to .72 by 1943, dropped to .44 in 1947, increased to .55 in 1958, and then remained stable through 1963 (Baran and Sweezy, 1966, p. 389).

Moreover, there are conceptual problems involved in their measurement of the surplus. According to Marx, unproductive labor creates neither value nor surplus value. Therefore, the surplus recorded in an unproductive sector is a direct or indirect transfer of surplus from productive sectors and should not be included in the computation of the total surplus. On the other hand, the portion of workers' earnings spent on unproductive earings should be included in the surplus, since it constitutes a remittance to the capitalist class. Neither of these adjustments were made in the *Monopoly Capital* data.

In this paper, using a different body of data and a different measure of the surplus, it will be determined whether any empirical support exists for the law of the tendency of the surplus to rise. Since the data required are available only for years 1947, 1958, 1963 and 1967, the analysis will be confined to this period. In the next section, an accounting scheme will be proposed to measure the mass of surplus. In Section 3 a classification scheme for productive and unproductive activities will be developed. Section 4 will present the empirical results. The concluding section will present an evaluation and interpretation of the results.

II
THE MEASUREMENT OF THE SURPLUS

A. The Standard Framework

When an economy has no unproductive activity, the mass of surplus value can be computed directly from a standard input-output table as follows:[1]

a) A —interindustry flow matrix at market prices in current dollars;
b) W—row vector of wages and salaries, net of personal income taxes, paid out in each sector;
c) Π—row vector of "gross profits" generated in each sector, including profits gross of business taxes, net interest, rent, indirect business taxes and personal income taxes;
d) X—column vector of gross domestic output by sector;
e) M—column vector of "worker consumption"—that is, consumption financed out of wages and salaries[2];
f) Y—column vector of "surplus consumption" defined as the sum of capitalist personal consumption, net investment, government expenditure, and adjusted exports less competitive imports;
g) L—row vector of the labor employed in each sector;

h) N—total employment, where $N = \Sigma L_i$

Coefficient matrices and vectors are computed from the flow framework as follows:

i) a—inter-industry coefficient matrix, where $a_{ij} = A_{ij}/X_j$;

j) m—column vector, showing consumption per worker, where $m = M/N$;

k) l—row vector of labor coefficients, where $l_i = L_i/X_i$.

Therefore, the following identities hold:

$$\sum_i A_{ij} + W + \Pi = X' \tag{1}$$

$$aX + M + Y = X. \tag{2}$$

The total (direct plus indirect) labor requirements per dollar of output (λ) is then given as

$$\lambda = l\,(I - A)^{-1}. \tag{3}$$

The total surplus in market price terms is given by $\Sigma\Pi$, which equals ΣY. The mass of surplus value (S) in labor value terms is given by

$$S = \lambda Y \tag{4}$$

Total surplus value is thus a weighted sum of the elements of surplus consumption, where the weights are the labor content to the consumption items. The total wage bill is equal to ΣW, which equals ΣM. Total variable capital (V), the mass of labor valued advanced to hire labor, is given by

$$V = \lambda M \tag{5}$$

Variable capital is likewise a weighted sum of the elements of worker consumption, where the weights are the labor embodied in the consumption goods. The rate of surplus value (ϵ) with no unproductive activity in the economy, can then be computed as

$$\epsilon = \frac{S}{V} = \frac{\lambda Y}{\lambda M} \tag{6}$$

It is the ratio of the labor value of surplus consumption to that of worker consumption.[3] The analogous concept in market value terms in the ratio of gross profit to the wage bill. The rate of surplus value will differ from this ratio if the average labor content of a dollar's worth of surplus consumption differs from that of labor consumption.

B. The Introduction of Unproductive Sectors

When a distinction is drawn between productive and unproductive activity , the input-output framework must be considerably modified. Let subscript p refer to productive sectors and subscript u to unproductive sectors. Then, the inter-industry flow matrix, A, can be partitioned as follows:

l) A_{pp}—sales of productive output to productive sectors;
m) A_{pu}—sales of productive output to unproductive sectors;
n) A_{up}—sales of unproductive output to productive sectors;
o) A_{uu}—sales of unproductive output to unrproductive sectors.

The final demand vectors M and Y can likewise be split into two components:

p) M_p—productive output consumed by workers;
q) M_u—unproductive output consumed by workers;
r) Y_p—productive output consumed by the surplus classes;
s) Y_u—unproductive output consumed by the surplus classes.

On the income side, wage and gross profits can also be split into two components:

t) W_p—wages advanced in productive sectors;
u) W_u—wages advanced in unproductive sectors;
v) Π_p—gross profits generated in productive sectors;
w) Π_u—gross profits generated in unproductive sectors.

Moreover, the output vector X can be partitioned as follows:

x) X_p—gross domestic output of productive sectors;
y) X_u—gross domestic output of unproductive sectors.

As a result, the following accounting identities hold:

$$\sum_j (A_{pp} + A_{pu}) + M_p + Y_p = X_p \tag{7}$$

$$\sum_j (A_{up} + A_{uu}) + M_u + Y_u = X_u \tag{8}$$

$$\sum_j (A_{pp} + A_{up}) + W_p + \Pi_p = X'_p \tag{9}$$

$$\sum_j (A_{pu} + A_{uu}) + W_u + \Pi_u = X'_u \tag{10}$$

Let us define productive labor as that labor employed in productive sectors and unproductive labor as that employed in unproductive sectors. Then, the vector L and total employment, N, can be divided as follows:

z) L_p—labor employed in productive sectors (productive labor);
a′) L_u—labor employed in unproductive sectors (unproductive labor);
b′) N_p—total employment of productive labor ($N_p = \Sigma L_p$);
c′) N_u—total employment of unproductive labor ($N_u = \Sigma L_u$).

Moreover, for reason that will become apparent below, let us subdivide the two vectors M_p and M_u into that portion consumed by productive labor and that consumed by unproductive labor:

d′) M_{pp}—consumption of productive output by productive labor;
e′) M_{pu}—consumption of productive output by unproductive labor;
f′) M_{up}—consumption of unproductive output by productive labor;
g′) M_{uu}—consumption of unproductive output by unproductive labor;
Finally, let us subdivide the wage vectors into that portion spent on productive output and that spent on unproductive output:
h′) W_{pp}—earnings of productive workers spent on productive output ($\Sigma W_{pp} = \Sigma M_{pp}$);
i′) W_{up}—earnings of productive workers spent on unproductive output ($\Sigma W_{up} = \Sigma M_{up}$);
j′) W_{pu}—earnings of unproductive workers spent on productive output ($\Sigma W_{pu} = \Sigma M_{pu}$);
k′) W_{uu}—earnings of unproductive workers spent on unproductive output ($\Sigma W_{uu} = \Sigma M_{uu}$).

Then,

$$M_p = M_{pp} + M_{pu}; \tag{11}$$

$$M_u = M_{up} + M_{uu}; \tag{12}$$

$$W_p = W_{pp} + W_{up}; \tag{13}$$

$$W_u = W_{pu} + W_{uu}. \tag{14}$$

C. Measurement of Variable Capital and Surplus Value with Unproductive Sectors

The accounting identities presented above [Equations (7) through (14)] are only formal. With unproductive activity in the economy, the measure of output, national income, wages and surplus must be considerably modified. The reason is that unproductive labor creates neither value nor surplus value but merely transfers it (Marx, 1967, Vol. 2, Ch. 6). To understand the implications of this, let us first return to the standard framework.

In an economy without unproductive activity, the output in each sector in market flow price terms is the sum of the intermediate inputs, wages and gross profits of the sector. This output is sold to producing sectors, workers for their consumption, and surplus classes for their use. Total output in the economy is the sum of the output of each sector. The value added generated in each sector is the sum of wages and gross profits. The national income is the sum of the value added in each sector, which is the sum of total wages and total profits. The national product is the sum of total worker and surplus consumption, which equals national income.

With unproductive activity in the economy, these simple relations no longer hold. The reason is that unproductive sectors do not create value and therefore do not produce any output. Suppose, for example, a parent ''paid'' his child to do the family cooking. This activity would be unproductive since there is no market exchange of the output. But suppose ''family cooking'' was entered in the input-output table as a new sector. This sector would require certain inputs like food, utensils, pots and pans, gas or electricity for the stove, and building space, and labor. The cooking done by the child would be treated as a purchase of output by the parent from the cooking sector, and the food and utensils bought for cooking would be treated as a purchase of inputs by the cooking sector. In the unadjusted market flow framework, the output of the cooking sector would be included in the economy's total output. In a framework adjusted for unproductive activity, the output for the cooking ''sector'' would not be included in the the total output. Rather, the ''wage'' paid to the child would be treated as a transfer of income from parent to child, and the food, utensils and other items purchased would be treated as consumption of final output.

Consider as another example a case where a manufacturing firm buys ''protection services'' from a protection agency. The inputs in the ''protection'' activity consist of guns and ammunition, paper and other office supplies, uniforms and office space, as well as labor. Suppose this agency performs no real function but collects the money as a tribute. The protection services would therefore be unproductive. In the unadjusted market flow framework, this transaction would be recorded as a purchase from the protection sector by the manufacturing sector, and the output of the protection sector would be included in total output. In the adjusted market flow framework, the purchase of this unproductive output would be considered a transfer of part of the surplus generated in the manufacturing firm to another segment of the surplus class. The inputs purchased by the protection agency, like guns and ammunition, would be treated as part of surplus final demand, since they do not materially contribute to the production of any other output and thus leave the circular flow like exports.

With unproductive activity, then, the market value of a sector's output cannot be readily decomposed into intermediate, wage and profit components. Nor can the sale of the output be directly divided into intermediate, worker and surplus consumption. Instead, the accounting relations must be adjusted to account for unproductive activity. The "adjusted" framework is as follows:

1) A_{pp} show the purchases of productive inputs by productive sectors. These inputs directly contribute to the production of productive output and remain as intermediate flows in the adjusted framework.

2) A_{up} consist of flows of unproductive inputs into productive sectors. In standard input-output accounting they are recorded as enterprise costs. But they do not form intermediate flows in the adjusted framework since they do not materially contribute to production. Instead, they constitute purchases out of the surplus generated in the productive sectors. For example, "domestic cooking services" purchased by a firm for its owner may be recored as a cost to the firm but constitutes surplus consumption for its owner. The purchase of protection services by a textile firm constitutes a transfer of part of the firm's surplus to another set of individuals. Business entertainment expenses, also a cost to the firm, are, in effect, a supplementary form of income to the surplus class. The purchase of unproductive output like wholesaling and retailing services by the shoe industry, recorded as the sum of the mark-ups on the inputs, is a transfer of part of the shoe industry's surplus to the merchant capital class (see Marx, 1967, Vol. 3, Ch. 17). The flows recorded in the matrix A_{up} thus form part of the the gross surplus generated in the productive sectors.

3) A_{pu} are the flows of productive inputs into unproductive sectors. Since the inputs do not contribute to the output of anything else, they effectively form a portion of the final demand flows. For example, the food and utensils purchased by the "domestic cooking services" sector are part of the consumption of the firm's owner. The guns and ammunition purchased by the protection services sector do not materially contribute to the production of textiles and are thus part of final consumption. (Analogously, defense expenditures are considered part of final consumption.) The inputs into the business entertainment sectors—restaurant and hotel expenses, theater tickets, alcohol and the like—are part of the personal consumption of the surplus classes. Inputs into trade services, like building space, electricity and gas, and display equipment, do not materially aid production and are therefore part of final consumption. Since the inputs into these unproductive activities are not part of workers' consumption, they constitute part of surplus consumption.

4) A_{uu} are the sales of unproductive output to unproductive sectors. The flows

constitute a transfer of surplus from one group to another. For example, the revenue received by the trade sector is a transfer of surplus created in other sectors. If part of this revenue is spent on protection services, part of the surplus received by the trade sector is transferred to the owners of the protection agency. No new output or surplus is thereby created; only a transfer of money. These flows thus fall out in the adjusted framework, since their inclusion would constitute double-counting.

5) W_u are the wages received by unproductive labor. Though received by labor, the income is effectively a transfer of surplus. For example, the wages received by protection personnel are part of the surplus transferred to the protection sector from other sectors. The labor employed in the sector does not produce any output that is directly or indirectly consumed by other workers or the surplus class. Rather, the workers are supported out of the surplus generated in other sectors. Likewise, sales personnel are paid wages out of the surplus transferred to the trade sector. They do not contribute to the production of any output directly or indirectly consumed by others. They, too, are supported out of the gross surplus. The wages received by unproductive labor are thus a transfer payment from the surplus class and must be netted out in computing the total gross surplus.

As a result, the consumption of unproductive labor (M_{pu} and M_{uu}) forms part of surplus consumption, since it is paid for out of the surplus. Suppose a factory owner hires a domestic cook and buys him his food, clothing and other consumption items. The cook produces nothing that is sold. Therefore, his consumption is paid for directly out of the surplus income of the factory owner and, in effect, constitutes a part of the owner's consumption that is *shared* with someone else. Likewise, the consumption of the workers in the protection agency, though paid for directly by them, is part of surplus consumption since their income comes from the gross surplus. It is the source of the expenditure, not the people or class that spends it or the items that are purchased, that determines whether the expenditure constitutes worker or surplus consumption.[4]

6) W_p are the wages received by productive workers. Part of the wages are spent on productive output (W_{pp}) and the remainder on unproductive output (W_{up}). Let us first consider the portion spent on unproductive output. Suppose workers were required to pay a fee to a protection agency, though they received nothing in return. The fee would be paid out of the workers' wages but would not provide the workers with any use-value. The fee, in fact, would be a remittance of wages to the surplus class. It can alternatively be thought of as an additional sales tax on the workers' purchases, a tax that is appropriated by a segment of the surplus class. Likewise, the trade mark-up on goods bought by workers is effectively a surcharge on the purchase price of the goods which provides no use-value to the workers. The expenditures by productive labor on unproductive output is thus an indirect transfer of part of the surplus generated in the productive sectors to other members of the surplus class. W_{up}, as a result, forms part of the surplus of the productive sectors.

The value of labor power is then the labor value of the productive output consumed by productive labor (M_{pp}). The variable capital advanced by the capitalist thus corresponds to the wages paid to productive labor for the consumption of productive output (W_{pp}). The wages paid to productive labor for the purchase of unproductive output (W_{up}) is part of the surplus. As a result, the purchase of unproductive output (M_{up}) disappears in the adjusted framework, since it is a bookkeeping device that indicates the transfer of surplus and does not represent the consumption of use-values. Likewise, M_{uu} also disappears in the adjusted framework, since it does not indicate the exchange of use-values. W_{pu} and W_{uu}, as we argued above, are netted out, since they are an indirect transfer of surplus.

7) Π and Y are respectively the gross profit and the surplus final demand vector. The gross profit generated in productive sectors (Π_p) is part of the sectors' gross surplus. The gross profit generated in unproductive sectors (Π_u) is, as we have argued above, a transfer of gross surplus from productive sectors and is netted out when computing the gross surplus in the economy. The purchase of productive output by the surplus classes (Y_p) is part of the economy's surplus consumption. The purchase of unproductive output by the surplus classes (Y_u) is a bookkeeping entry, respresenting an intraclass transfer of surplus, and disappears in the adjusted framework.

With unproductive activity in the economy, then, the market flow matrix must be adjusted as follows:

$$A^* = A_{pp} \tag{15}$$

$$W^* = W_{pp} \tag{16}$$

$$\Pi^* = \Pi_p + W_{up} + \sum_i A_{up} \tag{17}$$

$$M^* = M_{pp} \tag{18}$$

$$Y^* = Y_p + M_{pu} + \sum_j A_{pu} \tag{19}$$

$$X^* = X_p \tag{20}$$

$$L^* = L_p \tag{21}$$

A* is the adjusted intermediate flow matrix, W* the adjusted wage bill vector, and Π* the adjusted gross profits vector. The market value of output (X*) is the sum of adjusted input costs, adjusted wages and adjusted profits:

$$(X^*)' = \sum_i A^* + W^* + \Pi^*. \tag{22}$$

This output is bought by intermediate users (A*), productive workers for their consumption (M*), and surplus classes for their use (Y*).
Therefore:

$$X^* = \sum_j A^* + M^* + Y^*. \tag{23}$$

Total output is the sum of the output of each (productive) sector. The value added in each sector is the sum of the adjusted wages and adjusted profits; and the adjusted national income is the sum of value added in each sector. The adjusted national product is the sum of adjusted worker and surplus consumption. Since ΣM^* equals ΣW^* and ΣY^* equals $\Sigma \Pi^*$, the adjusted national product equals the adjusted national income.

D. The Conversion to Labor Values in the Adjusted Framework

The conversion follows the same pattern as in the standard framework. Let us form the following coefficient matrices.

1′) a*: adjusted interindustry coefficient matrix, where $a^*_{ij} = A^*_{ij}/X^*_j$,

m′) 1*: row vector of adjusted labor coefficients, where $1^*_j = L^*_j/X^*_j$.

The total (direct plus indirect) labor required per dollar of output is then given as:

$$\lambda^* = 1^* (I - a^*)^{-1}. \tag{24}$$

The mass of surplus value (S*) and total variable capital (V*) are given by

$$S^* = \lambda^* Y^* \tag{25}$$

$$V^* = \lambda^* M^* \tag{26}$$

The rate of surplus value, with unproductive activity in the economy, is therefore

$$\epsilon^* = \frac{S^*}{V^*} = \frac{\lambda^* Y^*}{\lambda^* M^*} \tag{27}$$

The adjusted rate of surplus value will differ from the ratio of adjusted gross profits to adjusted wage if the average labor content of the adjusted surplus consumption vector differs from that of the adjusted worker consumption vector.

III
The Classification of Sectors

Our data consist of standard 87-sector U.S. input-output tables for years 1947, 1958, 1963 and 1967. Since the sectors are highly aggregated, most are a conglomeration of activities. In the case where a sector consists of both productive and unproductive activity, it will be classified as productive. This will serve to understate the actual level of unproductive activity in the economy and provide a lower bound on the estimate of the rate of surplus value.[5] Moreover, some activities serve different purposes as intermediate and household consumption. An activity like entertainment that is productive consumption for households may constitute an unproductive expenditure for firms. Some sectors are therefore split into a household and a nonhousehold portion.

The principle on which to classify sectors into productive and unproductive ones has been a matter of some controversy in both the Marxian and non-Marxian literature. Rather than entering the theoretical fray in this article, I have decided to use four generally accepted criteria for unproductive activity.[6] First, the expenses of circulation are unproductive. This principle Marx discussed at great length (Marx, 1967, Vol. 2, Ch. 6), and derives from his more general law that "all costs of circulation which arise from changes in the forms of commodities do not add to their value" (Marx, 1967, Vol. 2, p. 149). Here, circulation is understood to refer to the selling of goods and the transferring of titles, not to the physical movement of goods, which is generally productive. Here, moreover, it is crucial to distinguish between activities that are *necessary* in capitalism and activities that are *productive*. Circulation activities are by and large necessary for the functioning of capitalism but not productive. The reason is that capitalism itself is characterized by competition and a lack of social planning, which makes the sale of commodities a problem. Thus, a part of the society's capital and labor force must be diverted to realizing the value (and surplus value) contained in commodities though this activity does not add any value to the commodities.

Second, certain fringe benefits and perquisites recorded as costs by firms are in fact supplementary forms of income to the surplus classes. These costs should therefore be treated as unproductive expenses, since they are not materially involved in the production process. Third, government activity not directly or indirectly related to providing a use-value are unproductive. Thus, legislators, other government bureaucrats and their staff, judges, and the like do not provide any consumable services and are therefore unproductive (Marx, 1963, Ch. 4). Fourth, household servants and other domestic help are unproductive, since they do not produce any exchangeable commodity.

The resulting classification scheme is shown in Table 1. Agriculture, mining, construction and manufacturing (1–64) all produce use-values and are productive.[7] Transportation is generally productive, since it creates a new use-value by altering a good's spatial relation to its purchaser (Marx, 1967, Vol. 2, Ch. 6). However, insofar as the transportation of goods is generated by the peculiar trade patterns arising in capitalism, including cross-shipping, it is unproductive. Likewise, warehousing is productive insofar as it is part of the normal operation of moving goods (Marx, 1967, Vol. 2, Ch. 8). Insofar as it is necessitated by the uncertainties associated with realization within a capitalist economy, it is unproductive. Since sector (65) has some productive activity, it was classified productive. Communications except broadcasting (66) is productive, since the flow of information is a necessary ingredient in production. Radio and televison broadcasting (67), though paid for almost exclusively by advertisers, is also productive, since it provides a use-value to households. Utilities (68), like water, sanitation and power companies, are productive.

Wholesale and retail trade (69) is a cost of circulation and is unproductive (Marx, 1967, Vol. 3, Ch. 17). Some movement and storage of goods is necessary in any mode of production, but this is captured in sector (65). Moreover, some display of goods and transmittal of information to customers is required in any mode of production, but this seems a relatively minor function of the trade sector in modern American capitalism. Most of the activity of this sector seems necessitated by the competition and uncertainties peculiar to capitalism. This includes the complex trade networks for the distribution of goods, including cross-shipping, the presence of numerous middlemen between producers and final consumer, transaction costs, advertising and other marketing expenses, and the long periods of time inventories of goods are tied up. It is probably true that with the development of larger and larger retailing and wholesaling outlets, the trade sector has become increasingly more efficient over time. On the other hand, with the growing affluence of consumers, the marketing effort has probably grown in relative importance and size to the production effort.[8]

Financial, insurance, and real estate services (70, 71) are unproductive, since they are involved in the transfer of titles and claims to use-values. Hotel, personal and repair services (72, 75) provide use-values to households and therefore constitute productive consumption for households. Moreover, repair services are a necessary ingredient in the production process and are a productive intermediate flow. Personal services and, to some extent, hotel services "purchased" by firms are unproductive, since they very likely constitute a fringe benefit to the surplus classes. Since Sector (72) is partly productive, it was classified as productive. Business services (73) consist of advertising, legal and other professional services (except health) and are unproductive, since they perform a circulation function. Research and development (74), though not directly involved in the production process, may contribute to increased productivity in the future and is therefore productive. Amusements (76) provide a use-value to households and that portion is therefore productive. Amusements purchased by firms constitute surplus consumption and are therefore unproductive.

Table 1.
The Classification of Productive and Unproductive Sectors

Productive	Unproductive
Agriculture (1–4)	Wholesale and Retail Trade (69)
Mining (5–10)	Finance and Insurance (70)
Construction (11–12)	Real Estate Rentals (71)
Manufacturing (13–64)	Business Services (73)
Transporation and Warehousing (65)	Amusements (76b), excluding Households
Communications, except Broadcasting (66)	Government Industry (84)
Radio and Television Broadcasting (67)	Rest of World (85)
Utilities (68)	Household Industry (86)
Hotels, Personal and Repair Services, except Automotive (72)	Inventory Valuation Adjustment (87)
Research and Development (74)	
Automotive repairs (75)	
Amusements (76a) : Households only	
Medical and Education Services and Nonprofit Institutions (77)	
Federal Government Enterprises (78)	
State and Local Government Enterprises (79)	
Allocated Imports (80)	
Business Travel (81)	
Office Supplies (82)	
Scrap (83)	

Note: Sector numbers from the standard Bureau of Economic Analysis 87-order input-output tables are shown in parentheses.

Medical and educational services purchased by households are a use-value to them and therefore productive. Such services purchased by firms are productive if they improve worker efficiency and performance but are unproductive if they constitute only extra consumption. Since Sector (77) has both a productive and unproductive component, it was classified as productive. Federal, state and local government enterprises (78, 79) include utilities, transit systems and other public services and are productive since they provide use-values to the public. Allocated imports (80) was also classified as productive, since it consists of goods produced abroad. Business travel (81), insofar as it is required for the coordination of production, is productive (Marx, 1967, Vol. 3, Ch. 23), but insofar as it functions as surplus consumption it is unproductive. Since it is very difficult to disentangle these two components, Sector (81) was classified as productive.

Office supplies (82) and scrap (83) are material inputs in the production process and are therefore productive. Government industry (84) is a value added sector consisting almost exclusively of wages paid to nonenterprise government employees and is therefore unproductive. Household industry (86) is also a value added sector consisting almost entirely of wages paid to domestic help and is therefore unproductive. The rest of the world (85) and inventory valuation adjustment (87) sectors are likewise value added sectors but consist exclusively of property income. Since this surplus is not generated by or connected to labor activity, it is treated as a transfer of surplus in the adjusted framework and thus, from an accounting standpoint, the same as an unproductive sector.

IV RESULTS

To estimate the rate of surplus value and compute related statistics, 87-sector input-output tables of the U.S. economy were used for years 1947, 1958, 1963 and 1967 (see the Appendix for details on data sources and adjustments). Of particular interest is the relation between the level of surplus and the amount of unproductive activity in the economy. To isolate this relation, I first calculated an "unadjusted" rate of surplus value, assuming no unproductive activity in the economy.[9] I then calculated the rate of surplus value adjusting for the presence of unproductive activity. The movement of this "adjusted" rate of surplus value can then be broken down into two effects: the first from the change in the ratio between surplus and necessary labor time and the second from a change in the level of unproductive activity.

A. The Rate of Surplus Value Unadjusted for Unproductive Activity

The unadjusted rate of surplus value rose slowly but at a relatively constant rate between 1947 and 1967 (Table 2). The ratio between uncompensated and compensated labor time was approximately 100 percent throughout the period. The rate of

Table 2.
The Unadjusted Rate of Surplus Value and Related Statistics

	1947	1958	1963	1967
1. Rate of Surplus Value (ϵ)	1.01	1.05	1.10	1.12
2. Gross Profits/Wages ($\Sigma\Pi/\Sigma W$)	0.93	0.93	0.99	0.98
3. Average Labor Content of Surplus Consumption ($\lambda Y/\Sigma Y$)*	0.27	0.17	0.13	0.11
4. Average Labor Content of Worker Consumption ($\lambda M/\Sigma M$)*	0.25	0.15	0.12	0.10

*Statistics are in man-years per thousand dollars (in current prices).

surplus value in the U.S. was of approximately the same magnitude as those estimated for other countries. Calculations for the 1951 Japanese economy yielded an estimate of 0.93, though only manufacturing sectors were included (Okishio, October 1959). Kyn, Sekerka and Hejl (1967) estimated a rate of surplus value of 1.35 for the 1962 Czechoslovakian economy, though it is unclear how "profits" were handled. I computed a rate of surplus value of 0.97 for the 1948 Puerto Rican economy and one of .93 for the 1963 economy, though before-tax, as opposed to after-tax, labor earnings were used.

The second line shows the ratio of gross profits to wages, which is the market price analogue of the unadjusted rate of surplus value.[10] This ratio remained steady between 1947 and 1958, rose between 1958 and 1963, and then fell off slightly by 1967. This ratio, too, was close to 100 percent throughout the period but was uniformly smaller than the unadjusted rate of surplus value. This was a phenomenon I had also found in my study of the Puerto Rican economy (Wolff, October 1975). The reason for it is that the average labor content of the surplus consumption vector is higher than that of the worker consumption vector (lines 3 and 4 of Table 2). In fact, the labor embodied in the surplus consumption basket per thousand dollars was approximately 10 percent greater than that embodied in the worker consumption basket. This accounts for the approximately 10 percent discrepancy between the unadjusted rate of surplus value and the ratio of the gross profits to the wage bill.[11]

B. The Rate of Surplus Value Adjusted for Unproductive Activity

The U.S. input-output matrices were partitioned into productive and unproductive components, according to the classification scheme in Table 1. The Amusements Sector (76) was proportionately split into a household and nonhousehold vector. The worker consumption vector (M) and the wage vector (W) were divided into productive and unproductive componements under the assumption that the proportion of wages spent on unproductive services is the same for both productive and unproductive workers (and, more generally, that the consumption mix is the same for the two classes of labor).

The resulting "adjusted" rates of surplus value are shown in Table 3. The adjusted rate of surplus value rose steadily and at a roughly uniform rate during the period (line1). It averaged roughly 2.6 over the period, considerably higher than the unadjusted rate (line 2). The ratio between the adjusted and unadjusted rates increased between 1947 and 1958, declined slightly by 1963, and then rose between 1963 and 1967. The rate of increase of the adjusted rate of surplus value was thus considerably greater than the unadjusted rate over the 1947–1967 period. The ratio of adjusted gross profits to adjusted wages, the market price analogue of the adjusted rate of surplus value, also rose steadily during the period (line 3). It averaged roughly 2.8 over the period, considerably higher than the ratio of gross profits to wages (line 4). The spread between the adjusted and unadjusted "class

Table 3.
The Adjusted Rate of Surplus Value and Related Statistics

	1947	1958	1963	1967
1. Adjusted Rate of Surplus Value (ϵ^*)	2.25	2.67	2.80	3.02
2. Adjusted/Unadjusted Rate of Surplus Value (ϵ^*/ϵ)	2.23	2.55	2.54	2.70
3. Adjusted Gross Profits/Adjusted Wages ($\Sigma\Pi^*/\Sigma W^*$)	2.43	2.85	3.03	3.14
4. Adjusted/Unadjusted "Class Shares" $[(\Sigma\Pi^*/\Sigma W^*)/(\Sigma\Pi/\Sigma W)]$	2.61	3.07	3.06	3.10
5. $\epsilon^*/(\Sigma\Pi^*/\Sigma W^*)$	0.93	0.94	0.92	0.96
6. Average Productive Labor Content of Adjusted Surplus Consumption ($\lambda^* Y^*/\Sigma Y^*$)[a]	0.23	0.12	0.10	0.08
7. Average Productive Labor Content of Adjusted Worker Consumption ($\lambda^* M^*/\Sigma M^*$)[a]	0.25	0.13	0.11	0.08

[a]Statistics are in man-years per thousand dollars (in current prices).

Table 4.
The Decomposition of Adjusted Wages

	1947	1958	1963	1967
1. Adjusted Wages/Total Wages ($\Sigma W^*/\Sigma W$)	0.42	0.36	0.35	0.33
2. Productive Labor/Total Labor (N_p/N)	0.68	0.58	0.57	0.55
3. Productive/Overall Mean Earnings ($\bar{W}_p/\bar{W}$)	0.98	1.05	1.06	1.07
4. Productive Consumption/Total Consumption ($\Sigma M_p/\Sigma M$)	0.63	0.59	0.58	0.57

Note: $$\frac{\Sigma W^*}{\Sigma W} = \frac{N_p}{N} \cdot \frac{\bar{W}_p}{\bar{W}} \cdot \frac{\Sigma M_p}{\Sigma M}$$

shares'' increased sharply between 1947 and 1958, fell slightly by 1963, and then rose less sharply between 1963 and 1967. Over the entire period, the growth rate of the adjusted shares was higher than that of the unadjusted shares.

The ratio of adjusted profits to adjusted wages was uniformly higher than the adjusted rate of surplus value, though the spread between the two narrowed somewhat over the period (line 5). The reason for the difference in the two statistics is that the average productive labor content of the adjusted surplus consumption vector differed from that of the adjusted worker consumption vector (lines 6 and 7). The average productive labor content of the former was, in fact, uniformly less than that of the latter, but the percentage difference between the two narrowed somewhat over the period.

C. Decomposition of Adjusted Wages and Adjusted Gross Profits

The difference in results between Tables 2 and 3 suggests that the rate of surplus value is highly related to the presence of unproductive activity. Moreover, the results in Table 3 strongly suggests that the magnitude and movement of the adjusted rate of surplus value is largely governed by the magnitude and movement of the ratio of adjusted gross profits to adjusted wages. To understand how the rate of surplus value is related to the level and composition of unproductive activity, I have therefore decomposed the wage bill and the gross profits into their component parts. This will allow an assessment of the relation of each to the rate of surplus value.

Adjusted Wages. The ratio of total adjusted wages (W^*) to total wages (W) can be expressed as follows:

$$\frac{\Sigma W^*}{\Sigma W} = \frac{N_p}{N} \cdot \frac{\bar{W}_p}{\bar{W}} \cdot \frac{\Sigma M_p}{\Sigma M} \tag{28}$$

where the first term on the righthand side is productive workers as a percentage of total workers, the second term the ratio of the mean earnings of productive workers to the overall mean earnings, and the third term the percentage of total wages spent on productive output. The percentage of productive workers in the employed labor force declined from about two-thirds in 1947 to a little over a half by 1967, with 76 percent of the decrease occurring between 1947 and 1958 (Table 4, line 2). Productive workers earned slightly less than average in 1947 but by 1958 they were earning slightly more than average, with relatively little change after 1958 (line 3).[12] The percentage of money wages spent on productive output declined moderately during the period with 57 percent of the decline occurring between 1947 and 1958 (line 4). The proportion of wages spent on unproductive services during the 1947–1967 period was quite high, averaging roughly 40 percent. Since wages spent on unproductive output are, in effect, part of the surplus, this means that roughly 40 percent of workers' take-home pay was remitted to the surplus class during the period. As a result of the high proportion of unproductive workers in the labor force and the high proportion of wages remitted to the surplus class, the proportion of the total (after-tax) wage bill that actually went to support prouctive workers was quite small, averaging less than 40 percent in the 1947–1967 period (line 1). Moreover, the proportion declined over the period, due to the relative increase in unproductive activity and in unproductive consumption.

Adjusted Gross Profits. Adjusted gross profits can be broken down on the income side into three components:

$$\Sigma\Pi^* = \Sigma\Pi_p + \Sigma A_{up} + \Sigma W_{up} \tag{29}$$

The percentage breakdown of the gross surplus in each of the four years is shown in Table 5. Gross profits accounted for about half of adjusted gross profits, with the other part roughly split in half between intermediate purchases of unproductive output and unproductive consumption by productive workers. The proportions were fairly constant over the period, except for a drop in profits as a percentage of adjusted profits between 1947 and 1958 and an offsetting percentage rise in unproductive expenditures by productive sectors.

In order to understand how adjusted gross profits were related to changes in the relative level of unproductive activity in the economy, Equation (29) was further decomposed as follows:

$$\frac{\Sigma\Pi^*}{\Sigma\Pi} = \frac{\Sigma\Pi_p}{\Sigma\Pi} + \left(\frac{\Sigma A_{up}}{\Sigma\,(A_{pp} + A_{up})}\right)\left(\frac{\Sigma(A_{pp} + A_{up})}{\Sigma A}\right)\left(\frac{\Sigma A}{\Sigma\Pi}\right) + \left(\frac{\Sigma W_{up}}{\Sigma W_p}\right)\left(\frac{\Sigma W_p}{\Sigma W}\right)\left(\frac{\Sigma W}{\Sigma\Pi}\right) \tag{30}$$

Table 5.
Percentage Breakdown of Adjusted Gross Profits

	1947	1958	1963	1967
1. Gross Profits of Productive Sectors ($\Sigma\Pi_p/\Sigma\Pi^*$)	0.54	0.49	0.50	0.48
2. Unproductive Purchases by Productive Sectors ($\Sigma A_{up}/\Sigma\Pi^*$)	0.22	0.28	0.26	0.27
3. Unproductive Consumption by Productive Labor ($\Sigma W_{up}/\Sigma\Pi^*$)	0.24	0.24	0.24	0.24

Note: $\Sigma\Pi^* = \Sigma\Pi_p + \Sigma A_{up} + \Sigma W_{up}$.
Rows 1 through 3 sum to one.

Adjusted gross profits were slightly greater than gross profits but the ratio between the two remained fairly constant over the 1947–1967 period (Table 6, line 1). The reason for this stability can be seen in the decomposition. The percentage of the total profits generated in productive sectors averaged a little more than half but fell over the period with the increase in unproductive activity (line 2).[13] For the second component, unproductive expenditures by productive sectors, the increase in unproductive activity resulted in counteracting changes. The percent of intermediate purchases by productive sectors that was spent on unproductive output was relatively small but increased by over a third between 1947 and 1963 (line 3). The percent of total inputs purchased by productive sectors was quite high and declined by less than 5 percent over the period (line 4). The result was that the fraction of intermediate flows forming part of the gross surplus (on the income side) increased over the period. Moreover, the ratio of intermediate flows to gross profits remained relatively constant (line 5). For the third component, unproductive consumption by productive labor, there were also counteracting changes from increased unproductive activity. On the one hand, the proportion of total wages spent on unproductive output increased by 18 percent (line 6). On the other hand, the percentage of total wages received by productive labor declined by 11 percent (line 7). On balance, the percentage of total wages forming part of the gross surplus increased slightly over the period. Moreover, the ratio of total wages to gross profits was approximately unity and declined slightly over the period.[14]

The Ratio of Adjusted Gross Profits to Adjusted Wages. The relative level of unproductive activity in the economy thus exerts counteracting effects on adjusted gross profits. In the 1947–1967 period in the U.S., the fraction of gross profits generated by productive sectors declined, causing profits as a percentage of

Table 6.
The Decomposition of Total Adjusted Gross Profits

	1947	1958	1963	1967
1. Adjusted Gross Profits/Gross Profits ($\Sigma\Pi^*/\Sigma\Pi$)	1.09	1.11	1.07	1.07
A. Gross Profits				
2. Gross Profits of Productive Sectors/Gross Profits ($\Sigma\Pi_p/\Sigma\Pi$)	0.59	0.59	0.54	0.52
B. Unproductive Disbursements by Productive Sectors				
3. Unproductive/Total Purchases by Productive Sectors ($\Sigma A_{up}/\Sigma(A_{pp}+A_{up})$)	0.11	0.14	0.14	0.15
4. Intermediate Purchases by Productive Sectors/Total Intermediate Flow ($\Sigma(A_{pp}+A_{up})/\Sigma A$)	0.87	0.84	0.84	0.83
5. Intermediate Flow/Gross Profits ($\Sigma A/\Sigma\Pi$)	2.43	2.62	2.46	2.38
C. Unproductive Consumption by Productive Labor				
6. Unproductively Consumed/Total Wages of Productive Labor ($\Sigma W_{up}/\Sigma W_p$)	0.37	0.41	0.42	0.43
7. Wages of Productive Labor/Total Wages ($\Sigma W_p/\Sigma W$)	0.66	0.61	0.60	0.59
8. Total Wages/Gross Profits ($\Sigma W/\Sigma\Pi$)	1.07	1.08	1.01	0.02

Note:

$$\frac{\Sigma\Pi^*}{\Sigma\Pi} = \frac{\Sigma\Pi_p}{\Sigma\Pi} + \left(\frac{\Sigma A_{up}}{\Sigma(A_{pp}+A_{up})}\right)\left(\frac{\Sigma(A_{pp}+A_{up})}{\Sigma A}\right)\left(\frac{\Sigma A}{\Sigma\Pi}\right) + \left(\frac{\Sigma W_{up}}{\Sigma W_p}\right)\left(\frac{\Sigma W_p}{\Sigma W}\right)\left(\frac{\Sigma W}{\Sigma\Pi}\right)$$

adjusted gross profits to increase (Table 5). The unproductive portion of productive labor's consumption increased but productive labor as a percent of the labor force declined. On balance, the "loss" in profits from increased unproductive activity was counterbalanced by an approximately corresponding "gain" in unproductive intermediate inputs and unproductively spent wages. The result was a ratio of adjusted gross profits to gross profits approximately equal to unity over the 1947–1967 period.

The increased unproductive activity in the post-War period led to a steady decline in the ratio of adjusted wages to total wages. This was due to a growing percentage of unproductive labor in the labor force and an increasing proportion of unproductive consumption. There was one counteracting tendency, a rising ratio between the mean earnings of productive workers and the mean earnings of unproductive workers, but this effect was not sufficient to offset the effects of the first two factors. Given a fairly constant ratio of gross profits to total wages, the result was an increasing ratio of adjusted gross profits to adjusted wages and an increasing (adjusted) rate of surplus value.

V
CONCLUSION AND INTERPRETATION

A. The Tendency of the Surplus to Rise

Between 1947 and 1967 the relative level of unproductive activity in the U.S. economy increased sharply. As measured by the percentage of unproductive employment, it rose by 39 percent, and as measured by the percentage of unproductive output, it rose by 23 percent (Table 7, lines 1 and 2). By most indicators, the major part of the shift toward unproductive activity occurred in the 1947–1958 period. By the percentage of unproductive employment, 76 percent of the shift occurred between 1947 and 1958, and by the percentage of unproductive output, 58 percent. After 1958, the rate of change slowed down appreciably, suggesting a major structural shift in the economy immediately after the War, and relative stability thereafter.

Gross surplus as a fraction of total (adjusted) national income stood at over 70 percent in the post-War period (line 3). Moreover, the ratio of gross surplus to national income rose steadily during the 1947–1967 period, with 63 percent of the increase occurring between 1947 and 1958. Gross surplus as a fraction of total output averaged about a third and rose throughout the period (line 4). In labor value terms the results were almost identical. Surplus value as a fraction of national income in labor value terms averaged over .7 and rose steadily throughout the

Table 7.
The Relative Level of Surplus in the Economy

	1947	1958	1963	1967
1. Unproductive/Total Employment (N_u/N)	0.32	0.42	0.44	0.45
2. Unproductive/Total Output ($\Sigma X_u/\Sigma X$)	0.24	0.28	0.28	0.30
3. Gross Profits/National Income ($\Sigma\Pi^*/\Sigma(W^*+\Pi^*)$)	0.71	0.74	0.75	0.76
4. Gross Profits/Total Output ($\Sigma\Pi^*/\Sigma X^*$)	0.32	0.33	0.34	0.35
5. Surplus Value/Labor Value Added ($\Sigma S^*/\Sigma(V^*+S^*)$)	0.69	0.73	0.74	0.75
6. Surplus Value/Total Value Output ($\Sigma S^*/\Sigma(C^*+V^*+S^*)$)	0.31	0.33	0.34	0.36

period. Moreover, total surplus value as a fraction of total output in labor value terms averaged about a third and rose continuously throughout the period. Thus, by all measures, the Baran and Sweezy law of the tendency of the surplus to rise was confirmed for the post-War period in the U.S.

B. The Relation of Unproductive Activity to the Surplus

The empirical results in the paper indicate a strong association between the relative share of surplus in the economy and the relative level of unproductive activity. As unproductive activity increased in the U.S., particularly between 1947 and 1958, so did the share of surplus. This increase occurred despite the fact that the unadjusted rate of surplus value remained almost constant. Thus, the increased share of surplus was attributable to increased unproductive activity, rather than to an increased ratio of uncompensated to compensated labor time.

The existence of a direct relation between unproductive activity and the surplus does not indicate which is cause and which effect. However, some reflection will suggest that causation runs both ways. On the one hand, a certain level of surplus is necessary to support unproductive activity. The ratio of surplus to necessary labor time must be high enough for classes other than labor to subsist. If total labor time was just sufficient to support the direct producers, then a surplus class could not be sustained. In fact, both the level of productivity and the rate of exploitation must be sufficiently high to support a surplus class and, in particular, unproductive activity. This is true in any form of society—primitive, feudal, capitalist or socialist.

On the other hand, unproductive activity may increase according to its own dynamic and thereby cause an increase in the surplus. This is particularly true in capitalism, given its unplanned and competitive nature, and is even more characteristic of monopoly capitalism, given its reliance on marketing techniques and legal and financial maneuvers as forms of competition. In fact, unproductive activities like business and trade services are necessary in modern capitalism, and their relative increase derives from the competitive nature of capitalism itself. Their relative increase will have the effect of increasing the relative share of surplus in the economy and holding down the increase in the real (that is, productively consumed) wage. Moreover, unproductive government activity, though initially requiring a certain level of surplus, may also develop according to its own dynamics. The increasing size of the government bureaucracies and the increasing share of government expenditure, particularly defense expenditures, in GNP that have characterized the post-War economy in the U.S., may, in part, have been conditioned by the form of American capitalism, particularly its intrusion and expansion into foreign markets. The effect of this has also been an increase in the relative size of the surplus and a depression of real wages.

C. Unproductive Activity as a Contradiction of Capitalism

Baran and Sweezy suggest that increased unproductive activity is in the interests of the capitalist class, since it alleviates the realization problem. A large portion of the social product is absorbed in unproductive activities like defense and this keeps effective demand high. Unproductive activity thus helps ensure the continued reproduction of capital.

But as Zarembka (1977) and others have argued, unproductive activity is in fact detrimental to capitalism, since it reduces the amount of surplus available for accumulation. Though unproductive activity increases the relative share of surplus in the economy, it diminishes the proportion disposable by *productive capitalists* and thus the proportion available for capital expansion. The product absorbed by other segments of the surplus classes—merchant and financial capitalists, landlords, unproductive workers and the government—does not aid the accumulation process. On net, it appears that the increased unproductive activity in the U.S. economy between 1947 and 1967 reduced the rate of accumulation (though further analysis is required).

Unproductive activity thus appears a contradiction of the advanced capitalist system. It threatens the reproduction of the system by reducing the rate of accumulation. Its one apparent virtue is that it absorbs part of the social product and thus alleviates the realization problem. But this product could also be absorbed by increased accumulation (and, of course, increased personal consumption by workers and capitalists). Moreover, unproductive activity is a feature of advanced capitalism that benefits neither workers nor capitalists. Workers (both productive and unproductive) are not benefited, since their wages are depressed by the increasing share of surplus and the increasing portion of their wages remitted to the surplus class in the form of taxes and unproductive expenditures. (Indirectly, their wages are kept low by the reduced rate of accumulation and the consequently lowered rate of productivity increase). The individual capitalist, moreover, is not benefited. The portion of this profits paid out in taxes is a loss to him. His disbursements on unproductive items like business services, though part of gross profits, are a cost from his standpoint and reduce the amount available for investment. The unproductively consumed portion of wages, also part of gross profits, is still a cost to the individual employer. Unproductive activity thus does not increase the amount of surplus at the disposal of the capitalist class.

Why, then, the dramatic increase in unproductive activity in the post-War U.S. economy if neither capitalist nor worker benefits? It is that for the individual capitalist such unproductive expenditures are required for competition. For the individual capitalist such purchases are necessary expenses. From the social point of view, however, such activity constitutes unnecessary and wasteful uses of the economy's labor-power and resources. It is the capitalist system itself that manufactures such needs that provide no useful social function. It is then in the contradictory nature of advanced American capitalism that so much of society's manpower and output is devoted to unproductive activities while so many real social needs go unsatisfied.

APPENDIX

The 1947 input-output table was obtained from the Bureau of Economic Analyis (BEA), which updated the original 1947 Bureau of Labor Statistics (BLS) version and reconciled it with national accounts data. The 1958, 1963, and 1967 tables are the BEA versions obtained from Professors Ann Carter and Peter Petri of Brandeis University. Additional data sources and adjustments are as follows:

1. Depreciation Row

Sectoral depreciation coefficients were estimated by Stephen Dresch and Robert Goldberg on an 86-sector level for their IDIOM model (see "IDIOM: A User's Manual, Annex II-B," National Bureau of Economic Research, February, 1975, Mineo, Table A-1). Their 86-sector classification was reconciled with the BEA standard 87-sector classification scheme. Though the coefficents were estimated with 1963 data, they were used for each of the four years and then adjusted by a scalar so that total depreciation equalled the national account estimate for the total capital consumption allowance (see *Economic Report of the President,* 1972, Table B-13, p. 210).

2. Value Added

The value added in each sector was divided into a wage and salary component, net of income taxes, and a residual, gross profits. For 1947 and 1958 partial estimates of gross labor earings by sector were obtained from BEA worksheets. Gaps were filled in with estimates obtained from employment and industrial wage bill data (see *Employment and Earnings, 1909–1966,* Bureau of Labor Statistics). Data for 1963 were published in "The Composition of Value Added in the 1963 Input-Output Study," by Albert Walderhaug (*Survey of Current Business,* April 1973, p. 36). The value added in the 1967 input-output table was already divided into employee compensation, indirect business taxes, and property-type income. Total wage and salary earning were reconciled with national accounts data (*Economic Report of the President,* 1972, Table B-12, p. 209). In order to net out personal income taxes from total wages and salaries, personal income taxes (Table B-15, p. 212) were computed as a percent of total personal income (Table B-12). This percentage was then applied to total wage and salary earnings for each year.

3. Labor Coefficients

Labor Coefficients for 1947, 1958 and 1963 were obtained from the Brandeis group. Gaps in the data existed for 1947 and 1958 and were filled in with estimates from the *BLS Employment and Earnings, 1909–1966*. Labor coefficients for 1967 on a 125-order scheme were obtained from the BLS' *The Structure of the U.S. Economy in 1980 and 1985* (Bulletin 1831, 1975). The 125-order scheme was aggregated to the BEA 87-order scheme.

FOOTNOTES

*This paper was originally presented at the Allied Social Science Association Meetings in Atlantic City, New Jersey, September 1976. I would like to thank those present at the session for their comments, particularly John Eatwell. I would also like to thank Wassily Leontief, William Baumol and Paul Zarembka for their helpful suggestions, and Ann Carter and Peter Petri for supplying the data used in the study.

1. Actually, the input-output matrix used here differs from the standard one in two respects. First, a depreciation row is added to the matrix, since in Marxian theory depreciation is not part of value added but part of constant capital (produced inputs). Depreciation is estimated using the capital consumption allowance totals in the National Accounts and thus may overstate the actual amount of economic depreciation, since the capital consumption allowance figures are estimated by businesses for income tax purposes. The depreciation row is counterbalanced by a new activity (colum), "depreciation replacement," estimated from the column vector of gross capital formation, such that the column sum of depreciation replacement equals the row sum of depreciation. Second, the noncompetitive import row is counterbalanced by a column of "endogenous exports" so that the sum of endogenous exports equals the sum of noncompetitive imports. See Wolff (1975)) for an explanation of this adjustment.

2. This vector is computed by multiplying the household consumption column in final demand by a scalar so that the sum of worker consumption equals the sum of wages and salaries.

3. It can also be interpreted as the ratio of surplus (or uncompensated) to necessary (or compensated) labor time. To see this, note that:

$$N = \lambda M + \lambda Y$$

since total value added is the newly added labor time. Therefore,

$$\epsilon = \frac{N - \lambda M}{\lambda M} \cdot .$$

Dividing by N, we obtain:

$$\epsilon = \frac{1 - \lambda m}{\lambda m}$$

which is the ratio of uncompensated to compensated labor time.

4. By the same reasoning, expenditures on food, clothing and other necessities for armed forces personnel are part of surplus consumption, even though the beneficiaries of the expenditures are members of the working class.

5. Empirically, the "ambiguous" sectors are very small and make a very minor difference in the computed rate of surplus value.

6. See Gillman (1957), Mage (1963), Becker (1971), and Wolff (1976) for other discussions of unproductive labor.

7. Sector numbers from the standard Bureau of Economic Analysis input-output tables are shown in parentheses.

8. In an input-output table in producers' prices, trade costs are recorded as the sum of the mark-up on inputs. This is the appropriate table for our analysis, since the transfer of surplus to merchant capitalists is the mark-up on the inputs.

9. This will also allow a comparison of estimates of the rate of surplus value in the U.S. with existing estimates for other countries. See below.

10. This ratio is also close in concept to the traditional factor share or class share ratio. In our case, gross profits include not only property income but also tax receipts and, implicitly, the balance of trade deficit.

11. The sizeable decrease in the average labor content of both surplus and worker consumption over the period indicates a dramatic increase in labor productivity between 1947 and 1967. (See Morishima, 1973, Ch. 1.) This has several important implications, particularly concerning the movement of the organic composition over time.

12. The ratio in mean earnings between productive and unproductive worker was as follows:

	1947	*1958*	*1963*	*1967*
$\bar{W}p/\bar{W}u$	0.93	1.13	1.16	1.17

This result is significant because some Marxists have recently argued that the relatively higher earnings of unproductive workers has been one factor in the slowdown of accumulation.

13. The precentage of total profits originating from unproductive sectors was substantially higher than the relative level of unproductive activity in the economy, as measured by the percentage of unproductive labor in the labor force. The reason is that unproductive sectors were over twice as profit-intensive as productive sectors:

	1947	*1958*	*1863*	*1967*
Gross Profits/Total Output: Productive Sectors ($\Sigma\Pi_p/\Sigma X_p$)	0.17	0.16	0.17	0.17
Gross Profits/Total Output: Unproductive Sectors ($\Sigma\Pi_u/\Sigma X_u$)	0.37	0.36	0.37	0.37

14. A similar decomposition can be done on the product side:

$$\Sigma Y^* \ (= \Sigma\Pi^*) = \Sigma Y_p + \Sigma A_{pu} + \Sigma A_{pu} + \Sigma M_{pu}, \text{ and}$$

$$\frac{\Sigma Y^*}{\Sigma Y} = \frac{\Sigma Y_p}{\Sigma Y} + \left(\frac{\Sigma A_{pu}}{\Sigma(A_{pu}+A_{uu})}\right)\left(\frac{\Sigma(A_{pu}+A_{uu})}{\Sigma A}\right)\left(\frac{\Sigma A}{\Sigma Y}\right) + \left(\frac{\Sigma M_{pu}}{\Sigma M_p}\right)\left(\frac{\Sigma M_p}{\Sigma M}\right)\left(\frac{\Sigma M}{\Sigma Y}\right)$$

With the increased unprodctive activity between 1947 and 1967, the fraction of surhlus consumption spent productively declined. The fraction of productive inputs into unproductive sectors declined but the fraction ot total inputs purchased by unproductive sectors increased. Moreover, the fraction of worker consumption accounted for by productive labor declined.

REFERENCES

Baran, Paul and Sweezy, Paul (1966), *Monopoly Capital,* New York.

Becker, James (Winter 1971), "On the Monopoly Theory of Monopoly Capital," *Science and Society*.

Gillman, Joseph (1957), *The Falling Rate of Profit,* London.

Kyn, O., Sekerka, B. and Hejl, L. (1967), "A Model for the Planning of Prices," *Socialism, Capitalism, and Economic Growth,* edited by Feinstein, C.H., Cambridge.

Mage, Shane (1963), *"The Law of the Falling Tendency of the Rate of Profit,"* (Columbia University: Ph.D. dissertation, unpublished.

Marx, Karl (1967), *Capital,* New York.

———. (1963), *Theories of Surplus Value,* Part I, Moscow.

Morishima, Michio (1973), *Marx's Economics,* Cambridge.

Okishio, Nubuo (October, 1959), "Measurement of the Rate of Surplus Value," *Economic Review,* 10, Hitotsubashi University Institute of Economic Research.

Wolff, Edward N. (October, 1975), "The Rate of Surplus Value in Puerto Rico," *Journal of Political Economy,* 83, 935–949.

———. (April, 1976), "Production and Reproduction: The Classical Juncture," presented at the 1976 Eastern Economics Association Meetings. *Mimeograph.*

———. (1977), "Capitalist Development, Surplus Value, and Reproduction: An Empirical Examination of Puerto Rico," *A Second Critique of Economic Theory* edited by Schwartz, J., Goodyear Publishing Co.

Zarembka, Paul (1977), "The Capitalist Mode of Production: Economic Structure," *Research in Political Economy,* edited by Zarembka, P., Vol. 1, Greenwich, Conn.: JAI Press.

MONOPOLY ACCUMULATION, HEGEMONIC CRISIS AND FRANCOIST DICTATORSHIP*

Juan-Pablo Pérez Sáinz

I. INTRODUCTION

If we were to characterize, in a condensed way, the nature of the class struggle that has taken place in the Spanish State from 1939 to the present, we could say that the existence of hegemonic crisis has been its main and permanent manifestation —a crisis that has expressed the antagonisms between the power bloc and the people in general, but especially between monopoly capital and the proletariat. Such a crisis has not been reduced to this general or global level, but it has developed to some extent within the dominant classes. Although it is not possible to talk about an internal hegemonic crisis in the power bloc because the same fraction appears as hegemonic during the whole period considered, it is true that from a certain moment new fractions have appeared inside monopoly capital implying the end of an absolute hegemonism in the power bloc. Therefore, any analysis on the hegemony question in the Spanish State should take into account such antagonisms at the level of the dominant classes in order to offer a complete picture.

The object of this article is not the analysis of the hegemonic crisis by itself but rather the analysis of essential characteristics of the structures which have generated and the maintenance of which has perpetuated such an hegemonic crisis. In other words, we will try to analyze the main contradictions which have defined the accumulation process and the superstructure which has reproduced it, i.e., the Francoist dictatorship.

Before starting off with the analysis of the essential features of the accumulation process, an historical remark is necessary. The hegemonic crisis is not a particular characteristic of this period. We should remember that the origin of the Francoist dictatorship was a civil war which was no more than the fill of the generated contradictions by the absence of a solution to the hegemonic crisis—a product of the development of the accumulation process which started at the beginning of the current century. If the monarchy of the Restoration (1874) meant the definitive consolidation of the capitalist mode of production, and it allowed the appearance of a monopoly capital, the contradictory nature of the accumulation process of such a capital eroded that superstucture. Its necessity of metamorphosing in the Primo de Rivera dictatorship (1923–1929), as an adjustment attempt, meant its death certificate (Tamames, 1973b, p. 7).[1] The Republic (1931–1936) gave way to an equilibrium situation. On the one hand, the power bloc, forced to established different power relationships, became weaker. On the other hand, the popular classes, and especially the proletariat, were not yet ready for seizing power through a revolutionary road (Bandera Roja, May 1972, p. 1768). In such an equilibrium situation, the petty bourgeoisie emerged as the ruling class. The bursting failure of the power block in its attempt to impose hegemony during the Republic, the so-called "Bienio Negro" (Black Biennium), and the appearance of the proletariat as a revolutionary social force (The Asturias Commune in October, 1934), left only one way open to the dominant classes: the coup d'etat. The electoral victory of the Popular Front (February, 1936) accelerated such a need. The armed opposition of the proletariat to the coup (July 17–18) forced the power bloc to three bloody years of civil war, the outcome of which was the Francoist dictatorship—the superstructure that the power bloc required.

II. THE PROCESS OF MONOPOLY ACCUMULATION

The essential characteristics of the monopoly accumulation process, which has taken place in the Spanish State since the end of the civil war, can be understood through the analysis of four basic elements: 1) the form of articulation of the "Spanish"[2] social formation in the imperialist chain; 2) the development of the accumulation base; 3) the relationship between the industrial and the agrarian branches; and 4) the nature of the fusion between the banking and the industrial capital. Let us analyze each of these.

Autarky and economic liberalization

There is unanimous agreement in pointing out two stages in the process of monopoly accumulation in the Spanish State. One is the period which runs from 1939 to 1959, characterized as autarchical; and the other is a period which started in 1959 and arrives at the present, and is qualified as liberalization. The famous Stabilization Plan in July 1959 is recognized as the dividing line. Obviously the break was not immediate, but that Plan meant the culmination of a process which had begun in 1951—a process which progressivly made the contradictions emerge that characterized the autarchical situation until imposing its overcoming, in order not to risk the accumulation process as such.

The origins of the autarchical frame have to be found in the civil war itself, on the side of the rebelled militaries against the Republic, in the support received from the fascist nations (Germany and Italy). Such a fact determined that the Francoist dictatorship concentrated its relationships with the imperialist chain mainly[3] with Germany and Italy.[4] The outcome of World War II implied the disapperance of those fascist states, and the Francoist dictatorship found itself suddenly cut off from its main articulation. The reaction was bewilderment, and the process of redefinition was not immediate. A product of such bewilderment was the autarky (Clavera, *et al.*, 1973, Vol. I, p. 90). Its maintenance produced a large intervention from the State. One thing implied another (Clavera, *et al.*, 1973, Vol. I, pp. 97–98). Interventionism did not need to be improvized. The existence of a monopoly accumulation supposed it. In the case of the Spanish State, during the period of Primo de Rivera's dictatorship, there was an attempt to consolidate a large interventionism. Moreover, there was a very close historical circumstance—the civil war. To some extent, interventionism was a prolongation of the war economy.

Such an interventionism was mainly materialized in the direct control on supplies and prices. That is to say, market mechanism was distorted. Obviously, the subsequent parallel black market arose, which gave the opportunity for surplus-profits. Facing such a situation, the tendencies determining the accumulation process were deformed, and extra-economic elements played a fundamental role in the accumulation process during the forties.

As we shall see later, dealing with the productive process, the accumulation stopped. One of the limits to be overcome was the import liberalization concerning raw materials and capital goods. From 1951, those imports increased notably. Their financing was possible thanks to the existing reserves in foreign exchange, and to the U.S. economic aid. This help accompained the mutual defense agreement.[5] Such a fact meant a first attempt in redefining the articulation in the imperialist chain. The appearance of some flexibility in the autarchical frame made explicit the contradictions of the forties and, athough allowed an initial relief, accelerated them in the mid-fifties. Precisely, the balance of payments was a previleged place of materialization of those contradictions (Rojo, October-December 1967, p. 948). The above-mentioned Plan of Stabilization culminated in a series of measures taken since 1957, intended to overcome the autarchical frame. The main measures contained in that Plan were, briefly: 1) no further expanison of credit and public expenditure; 2) no more emission of automatic amortizable public debt; 3) establishment of a realistic foreign exchange ($1 = 60 pesetas); 4) gradual liberalization of imports which led to the new tariff; and 5) new legislation on foreign investment (Tamames, 1973a, pp. 495–496).

The so-called liberalization stage did not mean the renunciation from protectionism, a fact which has characterized the monopoly accumulation in the Spanish State since 1883—the year of the tariff promulgation. The exacerbated protectionism has expressed the fragility of the monopoly accumulation in the "Spanish" social formation.[6] Foreign capital, which had played a primordial role in the middle of the nineteenth century, was progressively displaced by the raising of a local monopoly capital, which occupied the predominant place in the accumulation process. This situation was maintained until 1959. As we have seen, in the Stabilization Plan it was decided to suppress obstacles against the entry of foreign capital. This was performed during the following years through a generous and copious legislation which transformed the Spanish State into one of the most attractive places for foreign capital. The capital inflow was not delayed and increased progressively during the whole decade of the sixties and the beginning of the present decade. Therefore, the liberalization stage implied that foreign capital appeared as one of the fundamental elements of the monopoly accumulation process.

The overcoming of the autarchical frame meant a greater liberalization of imports, not only of capital goods and raw materials, but also of consumer goods as a response to the inability of the local production to meet demand. Equally, an export promotion policy was set up with a certain success. During 1966–1973 exports grew 1.4 times faster than imports, reversing the previous trend. But the low productivity relative to other imperialist centers made incompetitive the commodities in external markets. A large set of measures of a fiscal, trade and credit nature tried to compensate such a deficiency, but the balance of trade reflected a permanent deficit during all these years. This could only be filled by two elements external to the accumulation process itself. On the one side, the development of tourism was spectacular and constituted an inexhaustible source of foreign currency. On the other hand, an increasing migratory outflow took place to certain European imperialist centers where the high technical progess had created, in some branches, an overqualification of the local labor power. This migratory outflow not only consitituted a second main source of foreign currency, but was also an ideal solution with regard to a too large (in terms of possible social unrest) relative surplus population in the depressive phases of the accumulative cycle. These two phenomena, tourism and emigration, are very significant elements in the articulation of the Spanish State in the imperialist chain. Together with the importance of foreign capital and the permanent deficit of the balance of trade, these two facts express the structural weakness of the accumulation base that we are going to analyze next.

The fragility of the accumulation base

As it has been mentioned, autarky meant interventionism. Production and realization spheres were affected by this fact. In the first place, the State's control on raw materials and import licenses was the main factor in deciding who produced and who did not. Therefore, the dynamics of the accumulation process were distorted because it was not competition through the introduction of technical progress and other indirect means that characterized competition in the monopolistic stage, but the mere possibility of producing. Once obtained, the reduced number of capitals did not find big difficulties on the realization side, although the consumption level in the intervened official market was very low. As we pointed out, it raised a parallel black market wherein the selling of commodities was more interesting because it was possible to realize substantive surplus-profits. That is to say, with the distortion provoked by the State's intervention, the number of capitals was reduced and the profits high. Thus, a centralization of capitals took place by extra-economic means, and not as a result of technical progress and the formation of a competitive rate of profit. Therefore, the subsequent process of capital concentration did not occur. Such a situation was made possible, not only by the distortion of competition, but also due to the kind of exploitation which existed in that period. The accumulation was based upon the extraction of absolute surplus value through the extension of labor hours, made feasible by the ferocious repressive frame which covered the relationships of exploitation. The decade of the forties was the epilogue of the civil war, wherein, during the first years, a tremendous repression was still exercised on the working class who needed time to recover itself, even in biological terms (Gallo, 1969, Vol. I, p. 224). Privation in the official market and astronomic prices in the black one submitted the working class and the majority of the population to the situation of absolute pauperism.

The forties, therefore, meant a very particular accumulation. Given the autarchical frame—that is to say, of a minimal articulation in the imperialist chain, which allowed an abnormal State's intervention (until the point of controlling the entry in the productive process) and the conditions of an extreme repression, making possible exploitation mainly based on the extraction of absolute surplus value—the accumulation process appeared totally distorted. The outcome was an increased monopolization in the majority of branches, because only big firms had access to licenses and financing (Esteban, 1976, p. 91). This last fact implied the reinforcement of the hegemonic monopoly capital which totally controlled the banking sphere.

The reinforcement of monopoly capital, implied at the same time the continuity of its main weakness. The fragile productivity from the prewar period, a product of extreme protectionism and of the nature of monopoly capital, as we shall see, was maintained by the distortions caused by the interventionist mechanisms. The low productivity reflected the slow development of productive forces and permits us to characterize the decade of the forties as a stagnant period, i.e., a period of simple reproduction. With the autarky a certain process of substitution of imports took place, but focused on light goods without concerning basic industries. This fact, together with the bad quality of the raw materials, inadequate equipment and rudimentary industrialization, was the cause of such a low productivity. Moreover, the produced surplus was spent on luxury consumption, circulating capital and real estate development (Esteban, 1976, p. 92). The nature of such an accumulation originated a burden for its ulterior enlarging.

It is not difficult to imagine that such a situation could not last too long. Once the centralization process in the productive sphere was completed, the accumulation needed to continue. Its enlargement met two immediate obstacles. On the one side was the level underconsumption of the majority of the population. The existence of food intake certificates (on a family basis until 1948, and individual ones until 1951) was the best expression of such a phenomenon.[7] At the end of the forties the symptoms of an overproduction crisis were evident. On the other side, if the State's interventionism had helped initially through its discriminatory nature, to consolidate positions, it appeared in the fifties as a bureaucratic obstacle opposing a minimum of flexibility in order to carry out the accumulation process. As we pointed out, in 1951 a certain liberalization on raw materials and capital goods imports began. Vis-à-vis the first obstacle, the accumulation by its monopoly nature needed to transform the absolute pauperism into a relative one. Wages and salaries increased on several occasions. It was clear for monopoly capital that the exploitation should be based on the extraction of relative surplus value. Efforts were devoted to increasing productivity (creation of the National Commission on Productivity in May 1952) accompanied by essays in qualifying the labor power (Law on Professional Training in July 1955). This minimal decompression of the autarchical and interventionist frame was translated into a fluctuant growth with price stability between 1951 and 1954. But once this initial enlargement was realized, the accumulation process met the same boundaries. The realization of capital faced not only the autarchical frame, but also the rise in wages. The only way out for its valorization was the increase of prices. The period 1955–1957 was a biennium of fast growth and strong inflation. The real level of wages and salaries decreased in spite of its important increase in October 1956. The spectrum of overproduction appeared again, but now the contradictions were amplified because the accumulation base had grown. It was obvious that the maintenance of the accumulation process required a different frame. The Plan of Stabilization responded to that.

The already mentioned liberalization frame allowed an accelerated accumulation of monopoly capital. Not only the productive sphere expanded but also the unproductive ones. Thus, unproductive labor reached a considerable magnitude. The so-called new petty bourgeoisie with its different fractions developed considerably in the sixties, but such a frame did not imply by itself a radical change in the nature of the productive process. The original vices persisted to a considerable extent in spite of attempts to eradicate them. During all this period the process of productive capital concentration was not enough. Technical progress was mainly imported and penetrated in a very uneven way because many branches were still protected.[8] Therefore, productivity could not reach levels of other imperialist centers and competitive capacity was seriously affected. Such facts reflected not only the origins and formation of the productive base but also its partial maintenance, due to the nature of monopoly capital.

During the period 1959–1967 the increase of wageearners, a product of the expansion of the accumulation base, implied an important raising of the demand. This could not be satisfied by the corresponding increase in the productive base. Imports of consumer goods, as we have already indicated, and inflation were the adjustment mechanisms. In 1967 the limit of such a process was reached, making a second Plan of Stabilization necessary, which banned the "developmentalist" optimism of the beginning of the decade. In addition to the peseta's devaluation—the measure with most publicity—wages and salaries were frozen. The magnitude of such an impact (affecting more than five million workers) implied that a revision was required the following year, imposing a certain degree of flexibility. There followed a period of recession from 1967 to the end of 1971, with the exception of 1969. The biennium 1972–73 was an expansion with no comparison. As it has been said, it was the peak in the whole history of monopoly capital accumulation in the Spanish State (Muñoz *et al.*, 1974, p. 17). The expansion was followed by a generalized recession, as in other imperialist centers. The economic policy measures of November 1973 responded to the beginning of this recession, and again freezing wages and salaries appeared as the axis of the economic policy, showing once more that the "stabilization" of the accumulation cycle is done on the shoulders of the wageearner classes.

Summarizing, it can be said that the liberalization stage implied an acceleration of the accumulation process, leading to its definitive consolidation. We think that the 1967 crisis, although it was the outcome of the contradictions defining the accumulation process exacerbated by its acceleration, meant also the beginning of its consolidation as an irreversible process. The 1972–1973 boom showed it. Acceleration and definitive consolidation led to a clear reallocation of contradictions around monopoly capital. No doubt the main one was its antagonism with the working class, but this was not the unique one. Contradictions started to develop in the different reproductive spheres, making other dominated classes, besides the proletariat, antagonistic to monopoly capital. The difficulties in the extraction of relative surplus value, given the weakness of the productive base, were expressed not only in the necessity of inflation, but also in the slow and painful process of wage increases. The evolution of the so-called *salario mínimo interprofesional garantizado* (minimum guaranteed wage), that in this period constituted the keystone of the laboral system, is the best proof in this respect.[9] The results of this process of reallocation of contradictions were the extension and intensification of the struggle of the popular classes that would lead, as we will see, to the crisis of the dictatorship itself.

The slow capitalization of the land rent

The penetration of capitalism into agriculture started in the nineteenth century.[10] The road was the Prussian one, but its development was slow because no pressure was exercised by a sufficiently strong industrial branch (Viñas, 1972, p. 23). The two disentailments, affecting ecclesiastical and communal property, created a powerful landowning class which emerged as hegemonic. Its protectionist necessity, as an outcome of the decrease of wheat prices in the world market due to the transport revolution, led to joint interests in the last quarter of the past century with the nascent burgeoisies, namely the Basque bourgeoisie and the Catalan bourgeoisie. Although it has not been established that the rent contributed to the monopoly capital formation, the hypothesis of a relative but important capitalization of the land rent seems reasonable (Viñas, 1972, p. 29). During the first four decades of the current century, the power bloc presented a shared hegemony: big landowners-monopoly bourgeoisie. Such a repartition could be explained by the close relationships between the two classes, but it seems correct not to dissolve the landowning class in the monopoly capital. In fact, such a situation would reflect the particularity of the monopoly accumulation in the Spanish State from the standpoint of the articulation of the agrarian and industrial branches, showing from a different angle the fragility of the accumulation process—i.e., it can be said that the process of land capitalization was quite slow. From this point of view the characterization of agriculture as feudal is dangerous because it does not perceive the incorporation of agriculture into the capitalist mode of production as a productive branch, a fact which does not require a complete development of capitalist relations of production in this branch. The kind of precapitalist relations production that emerged as the tenant or the sharecropper (*arrendatario* and *aparcería*) were rather transitional, expressing the low level of development of productive forces in agriculture, a fact that has to be analyzed within the whole frame of the accumulation process before one will be able to grasp its meaning (Martinez Alier, October-November 1967, pp. 12–13).[11]

The period of the Francoist dictatorship, accelerating and consolidating the monopoly accumulation, inclined the balance on the industrial branch side. The fraction of the landowning class closer to monopoly capital was integrated and dissolved into it.[12] After the forties, the landowning class began the decline toward a secondary position inside the power bloc. But the process of the land rent capitalization, although with a faster rhythm than in the prewar period, was not fast enough for the requirements of monopoly capital accumulation. This fact reflected the persistent fragility of the productive base. It was in 1972 that the first signs of completion of capitalization of land rent appeared. At this conjuncture, for the first time in the history of development of capitalism in the Spanish State, an agrarian crisis did not affect the development of the industrial branch (Muñoz, *et al.*, 1973, p. 68).

The stages of land rent capitalization during the Francoist dictatorship correspond to those of the accumulation process. The land property was restored in the rebel zone during the civil war through an authentic agrarian counterreform carried out by the *Servicio de Reforma Económica y Social* (Service of Social and Economic Reform). The height of the autarchical period (1939–1951) meant the stabilization of the agrarian interests due to the practically nonexistent pressure from the industrial branch in this period of simple reproduction. As has been said, this was a period of reruralization (Esteban, 1976, p. 86). The agrarian branch was equally submitted to State's interventionism. Occultation of surfaces and production also allowed important profits in the black market, although it was argued that the stagnation of production was due to other kinds of factors (weather, lack of fertilizers, etc.). Less rigidity in the autarchiacal frame, with the subsequent development of the industrial branch, affected the relationship between the two branches. The exchange relationship between agriculture and industry began to deteriorate to the disadvantage of the former. The expansion of the industrial branch began to absorb important quantities of labor power from agriculture, which was there as a latent form of relative surplus population, giving way to an important rural exodus to urban centers.[13] Industrial commodities started to compete with agrarian ones as main components of consumer goods.

Such modifications had impacts on the agrarian branch through several attempts to accelerate the capitalization of land rent. Among them it is worthwhile to mention, first, the so-called colonization policy implemented by the institute of the same name. Started already in the forties, it was only at the end of the decade, through the promulgation of the law on *Colonización y distribución de la propiedad de las zonas regables* (colonization and distribution of land in irrigated areas) that the link between the colonization policy and the irrigation program was set up. These programs were a necessary element for the success of the colonization policy. But very little land irrigated was "colonized," only the so-called *tierras en exceso* (superfluous land), and not all with favorable conditions for the acquisition of the land property. The people who benefited most were the affected big landowners because the majority of irrigated lands belonged to them (Sevilla-Guzmán, 1976, pp. 107–108; Tamames, 1964, pp. 50–51).

A second attempt worth pointing out was the policy of small plot consolidation, which geographically was mainly reduced to Old Castilla because of its support the Francoist side in the civil war (Sevilla-Guzmán, 1976, p. 111), and which favored mainly the biggest parcellary producers (Anlló, 1967, p. 66). This policy addressed against *minifundia* was not complemented with any measure on *latifundia*. The law of *fincas mejorables* (improvable real estates) made no attempt at implementation whatsoever, a fact which showed the power of the big landowners.

During the decade of the sixties the already known accelaration of the accumulation process imposed the need of the development for productive forces in the agrarian branch. The increasing number of capitalist productive units introducing mechanization reflected such a fact, a process which was supported in the first two "Plans of Development," and specifically through the credit policy which tended to favor this type of productive unit. The outcome was the appearance of the tendency to minimization of the absolute rent. But the landowning class had been able, during all this period, to maintain, through a policy of agrarian prices, a monopoly rent expressed as differential between them and the parcellary producers (Anlló, 1967, p. 190). Such a level of agrarian prices has been one of the main causes of inflation during the considered period, although it has been attempted to divert the attention to the circulation sphere (the question of commercial margins).

The increase in rural wages has generated an effect of dissolution of the parcellary form of production (especially those units not too much capitalized) because the levels of reproduction are higher in the capitalist mode of production than in that form of production. In that way a process of proletarianization of the peasantry appears (Naranco, June-September 1967, August-September 1968).[14] Moreover, this tendency of proletarianization is reinforced by the increasing control of the exchange sphere by capital (Sevilla-Guzmán, 1976, p. 120 ff), transforming these parcellary producers into a sort of domicilliary worker.

Summarizing, we can say that capitalist development in agriculture in the Spanish State appears today as an irreversible process but the too long duration of this process has been linked dialectically to the existence and maintenance of a weak base in the accumulation process.

The nature of monopoly capital and its process of inner differentiation

As we have pointed out several times, the formation of a monopoly capital in the Spanish State can be dated at the beginning of this century. Several processes met in its formation. First, the existing accumulation in the mining branch, extended later to siderurgy (and even to shipbuilding), already presented a fusion of banking with industrial capital. That was the case with the Asturian and, above all, the Basque capital. Second, there was the transference to local hands of the credit institutions, which were the first ways of financing of foreign investment half a century ago. Third, there was channeling of overseas remittance flows, and especially the repatriation of capitals with the definitive loss of the last colonies in America and Asia. Finally, there was the above mentioned process of land rent capitalization. Those processes gave way to the formation of an important banking capital, partially merged with industrial capital, as was the case of the Basque capital; but its constitution,as mixed banks, gave the possibility for progressively dominating industrial capital. This fusion was materialized with the industrial expansion that took place with the favorable conjuncture of World War II. The domination of banking capital was consolidated, appearing as financial capital in the strict sense of the term. In this process there was an important absence: the most pioneering capital, the Catalan one. Too much linked to the colonial markets, its attempt to overcome its basically competitive nature, through the creation of the Banco

Hispano Colonial, failed with the loss of the last colonies. Thus, the Catalan capital was condemned to a nonmonopolistic form. The banking crisis in the twenties of the present century consolidated the positions of the Basque and Madrid capitals, displacing the Catalan one to a nonhegemonic position inside the power bloc.[15]

Monopoly capital, the so-called "financial oligarchy," found its adequate superstructure with the Francoist dictatorship. With the promulgation of the status quo in 1942, ratified by the Banking Law of 1946, it consolidated its totally dominant position in the banking sphere. The prohibition of creation of new banks permitted the famous big six (Banco Español de Crédito, Hispano Americano, Urquijo, Central, Bilbao and Vizcaya) an unprecedented process of centralization.[16] With the 1946 Law, the *Consejo Superior Bancario* (High Banking Council) was constituted, an institution of which the main function was to minimize possible intrabanking competition (Tamames, 1974, pp. 29–30). This centralization allowed this capital to become the main beneficiary of the automatic amortization of the public debt, which constituted the usual way of financing the permanent budget deficit. In this way, an important share of surplus value was channelled to banking capital emerging as the only one to finance the accumulation. Thus, the already existing domination on the industrial capital was reinforced and expanded when the accumulation process started to enlarge in the fifties. This monopoly capital dominated the main productive branches (electricity, siderurgy, cement, chemicals, etc.).

The fundamental idea to have in mind regarding this capital is its peculiar nature, because given its hegemonic position it is possible to understand the specific characteristics of the accumulation process in the Spanish State. Such a nature can be expressed mainly be three features. First, there is its historical conformation. On one side, parts of its constitutive elements had a clear speculative nature; and, on the other side, the domination on industrial capital took place in a pronounced protectionist frame. There was no threat from competition of foreign capital and therefore its fusion with industrial capital could present an "external" nature—i.e., not deep integration. The autarky of the immediate postwar period accentuated such a protectionist frame. Second, the possible internal competition among its different components was reduced to its minimal expression, as we have seen. And, third, its possibility of reproduction, through the mechanism of the automatic amortization of the public debt, implied a large autonomy as banking capital vis-à-vis the industrial one—i.e., in relation to the determination in the last instance of the productive capital. It is in this threefold sense that the peculiar nature of monopoly capital has to be understood. Its reproduction is centered mainly on the banking sphere which presents a pronounced relative autonomy from the productive sphere, a fact which is materialized in the superficial articulation of both capitals characterized by an external domination of banking capital over the industrial one. Thus, the contradictions affecting the latter did not immediately and directly reach the former, a fact which did not neglect the determination in the last instance of productive capital but, on the contrary, specified it for the case of the Spanish State. Only in this way can it be understood why this capital opposed, in a certain way, the Plan of Stabilization, without knowing to differentiate its immediate interest from long-term ones.

We think it is possible to talk about a process of differentiation inside monopoly capital, which started in the autarchical period, and the outcome of which was the emergence of a distinct fraction of this capital.[17] Such a fact was possible because of the external domination of the hegemonic fraction, that from now on we shall label "traditional," in opposition to the "new" one. On its origins two hypotheses, that do not exclude each other, are possible. On the one hand the extra-economic elements in the forties, affecting the accumulation process, namely State interventions, favored such a formation playing the function of a certain "primitive accumulation." On the other hand, with a certain degree of flexibility introduced in the next decade, some capitals, mainly allocated in the productive sphere, could develop with no opposition from the hegemonic fraction allocated in the banking sphere, as we have pointed out. We think that this "new" fraction, through its representation in the State apparatus—the famous Opus Dei to which we shall refer later—imposed the overcoming of the autarchical frame with the Plan of Stabilization. Although its weight was minimal at that time compared to the hegemonic fraction,[18] its pertinent effect took place because of the conditions of its existence. Such an existence was threatened by the contraditions affecting the accumulation process. In this way, this capital represented, at that conjuncture, the interests of monopoly capital and capital as a whole, materializing the determination in the last instance of the productive sphere.

But the liberalization frame, its necessity of expansion, trying to develop also in the banking sphere, opposed it to the hegemonic fraction. The *Bases de ordenación del crédito y de la banca* (Credit and Banking Law) in 1962, and the *Ley de Incompatibilidades* (Law of Incompatibilities) in 1968, were two clear pertinent effects of this "new" fraction facing the hegemony of the "traditional" one. Although the latter was not seriously affected, it could not avoid the consolidation of the former through its representation in the State's apparatus.[19] Given its nonhegemonic position, this capital was forced to show a deeper articulation between the banking and industrial spheres. In this sense it represented, to a certain extent, the necessity of restructuring the nature of monopoly capital as a whole, a fact which was the necessary result of its existing conditions and not the outcome of a deliberate wish of its representative members in the State's apparatus—i.e. the Opus Dei. We will come back later to this point, which deals with the question of the famous Opus. Actually, the limits of the "project" of this fraction express its objective nonhegemonic position.

We have pointed out that since the sixties the massive entrance of foreign capital implied that a third element must be taken into account in the process of monopoly accumulation. This flow of capital was mainly materialized by transnationals which occupied first order positions in some key branches such as chemicals, motorcars, electrical and electronic material and oil (Suarez, May-June 1973). Among foreign capital, doubtless the U.S. capital got the dominant place[20], although its rhythm of investment declined in 1970. In order to overcome the autarchical frame, foreign investment inflow was desirable in terms of monopoly accumulation. For the ''new'' capital implied more degrees of freedom vis-à-vis the ''traditional'' one (Fernández de Castro and Goytre, 1974, p. 175). As far as the new capital was reduced to the productive sphere, as was the case[21], not attacking its banking ''fief,'' it implied a certain complementarity. But the definitive consolidation of local monopoly capital has created antagonism with foreign capital. On the one side this latter capital has hegemonic pretentions, especially the U.S. one; and on the other side, in the case of the ''new'' monopoly capital, once it is consolidated, and due to its closer integration between banking and industrial capitals, its further ampliation is seriously affected by foreign capital. In the case of the ''traditional'' fraction, it is because the definitive consolidation of the process of monopolistic accumulation has implied the relative disappearance of its peculiar nature. The sharpening of contradictions in the productive sphere, and the presence of other monopoly capitals, had forced it to redefine in a closer way than articulation of banking and industrial capitals. Such a fact implied that the initial complementarity with foreign capital had ceased and, therefore, antagonisms started to develop. In our opinion, the reticencies on the presence of foreign capital which led to the revision and abolishment, in October 1973, of the generous decree-law of April 1963, suppressing all limits to foreign participation in local firms, should be understood in this sense (Muñoz *et al.,* 1974, p. 433 ff). In spite of their mutual antagonisms, both local monpolistic fractions jointly opposed a possible hegemony of foreign capital, a fact which would demonstrate again the imperialist nature of the Spanish State, although as the center of an inferior order, and therefore not peripheral or semiperipheral, thus making it one of the weakest links in the imperialist chain today.

III. THE FRANCOIST DICTATORSHIP

The form of the Spanish State in the postwar period has been twofold. On one side it has been an intervention form corresponding to the monopolistic stage of the dominant capitalist mode of production in the ''Spanish'' social formation; and, on the other side, the contradictions generated by such an accumulation, giving way to the appearance and conservation of a deep hegemonic crisis, implied the corresponding exception form. The analysis of the former will show the nature of the State's economic function, while the analysis of the latter relates to the essential features of the ideological and political functions.

The economic function in the monopoly accumulation

We can date the appearance of a form of intervention from the beginning of Primo de Rivera's dictatorhsip. In the postwar period the State interventionism was extended, following the development of a process of monopoly accumulation. In this sense, the nature of this function had an equal evolution with the accumulation process. During the autarchical period we have already seen which were the main interventions, and the causes which originated them. It is worthwhile also to mention two other interventions that had relevance in terms of the accumulation process. The first one, above mentioned, was the mechanism of automatic amortization of public debt, an intervention which gave a large relative autonomy to banking capital in its reproductive dynamics. The second one was the direct intervention in the productive process with the creation of the *Instituto Nacional de Industria* (National Institute of Industry). This institution, responding partially to autarchical goals, was reduced to playing a fundamental role in those branches where the private accumulation was deficient or partial.[22] In this respect it tried to reinforce the process of monopolistic accumulation at its weakest point: its productive base.

This accentuated and distorted intervention corresponded with the fascist ideology dominant in the Francoist bureaucracy at the end of the civil war. But one of the biggest problems was the lack of suitable staff to carry out those interventions. Actually, at the beginning, it was necessary to incorporate persons linked with Primo de Rivera's dictatorship because, given their experience, they could respond to such necessities.[23]

The liberalization stage implied an adjustment of State's intervention to more normal patterns. In this period also, new interventions appeared that were more typical and an attempt was made to coordinate the various existing interventions. Such an attempt was materialized, as in other capitalist countries, through programing experiences. Several ''Plans of Development'' responded to this; but with the meager result of the first one, their limits were pointed out, although they contributed to the appearance and formalization of important interventions. Among them it is worthwhile mentioning the system of concerted action, authentic substitute for nationalizations (Lopez Muñoz, 1971, p. 77), the public credit, the poles of promotion and development, and the program of public investments. Through them it was intended to contribute to the acceleration and consolidation of the process of monopoly accumulation, but, as we have seen, the monopoly capital in that period was not homogeneous. State's interventions tended, to some extent, to favor the ''new'' fraction. The clearest case was the public credit policy, an outcome of the already mentioned new banking law of 1962,[24] which contributed to the development of this new fraction, avoiding being absorbed by the traditional and hegemonic one.

The remodelling of the State's economic function was mainly due to the famous Opus Dei. This organization, incorporated in the State's apparatuses in the forties, specifically in the University and in research, was moving progressively toward the State's apparatus: in concrete, the civil administration branch. Vis-à-vis the impasse created by the autarky, it appeared as the only fraction of the bureaucracy able to offer an alternative of change. The administrative reform at the end of the fifties, which restructured the civil administration branch—creating the appropriate institutional frame to face the new stage—was inspired by the Opus displacing the project presented by the Falange. In this sense the interests of the new monopoly capital were reflected in its way of formation. The Opus presented a big advantage from an ideological point of view: it combined "modernist" elements ("technocratism") with "traditional" ones ("integrist catholicism" and "authoritarianism") (Ynfante, 1970, p. 135 ff; Le Vaillant, 1971, p. 204 ff and 232 ff). In this way there was perfect combination of the necessity of change in the base maintaining intact the essence of the superstructure. Its secret nature,[25] added to the fact that it was the dominant social force in the State's apparatus, distorted its true importance. We do not try to minimize it because of the fact that it represented the new monopoly capital which achieved to consolidate it, but we want to emphasize that the Opus Dei phenomenon has to be understood as a result of an objective process. That is to say, the emergence, formation and necessity of consolidating this new fraction of monopoly capital, in relation to the process of accumulation as a whole, is the explanation of the large relative autonomy reached by the Opus Dei as a social force. So, when this fraction was consolidated vis-à-vis the traditional and hegemonic fractions, and the State apparatus was able to generate its own bureaucratic stratum for the management of the State's economic function,[26] the Opus was displaced, although at the end of 1969 it occupied the majority of all ministerial posts.

Repression and crisis of the ideological function

If we talk about dictatorship it is because there is no doubt that the authentic support of the State has been the repressive branches, and especially the Armed Forces. It is the branch which has been the dominant one during the whole Francoist period, although sharing with other branches and apparatuses the dominant function. The irrefutable expression of such domination has been the dictator himself: Franco. Franco's role should mainly be understood as the personalization of the Armed Forces, the victorious Armed Forces from a (civil) war whose "chief" emerged as *caudillo*. Actually, one of the basic elements of cohesion of Spanish Armed Forces has been the loyalty to Franco. In this way it was prevented that any other military "personality" could stand out, unless they were unconditonals of the dictator, as were the cases of Muñoz Grande and Carrero Blanco. Only in this way can Franco's role of "arbiter" on the different social forces that developed from the State's apparatuses be explained. This fact has caused the majority of analyses on Franco's role to fall down to subjectivism, appearing as homologous, although the starting point and the conclusions (condemnatory or apologetic) were adverse.

It can be argued that the Armed Forces have been reduced to their traditional function (defense of the integrity of the national territory vis-à-vis an external aggression). From a superficial perspective it would seem so. The Armed Forces, with the exception of the initial period (the civil war), have usually been maintained marginalized in the repressive tasks. Other repressive branches, namely *Guardia Civil, Policía Armada* and *Cuerpo General de Policía*[27] (due to its number of effectives, an authentic internal "second Army"), have coped with such repressive tasks. But that does not mean that the Armed Forces have not participated in the performance of that function. The interchangeability of posts in the high strata of the various repressive branches mentioned (to which it is necessary to add the juridical one, as it is shown by the war tribunals), has allowed the dominant fraction of the Armed Forces, that could be called the "rightist",[28] to participate directly in the represssion (Soler, November-December 1969, p. 8). Any attempt, as the tendency of "liberal" or "professional" shade[29] which started to configurate at the end of the fifties[30], and which was grouped around the Staff Army chief, Díaz Alegría, was condemned to impotence, as long as it stayed in the frame of the Armed Forces of the dictatorship, being unable to constitute itself as a social force. Only the break with the dictatorship, as seems the case of the recently created *Unión Democrática Militar (Military Democratic Union)* can allow its constitution as a social force and menace the domination of the rightist faction, if they know how to articulate the inner dissatisfaction in the Armed Forces[31] with the current crisis of the dictatorship.

To the supremacy of the repressive branches[32] corresponded a progressive and clear crisis of the ideological function. The two assigned social forces of the ideological tasks, the Falange and the Church, failed in their attempts. The Falange, at the beginning, besides occupying a large part of the civil administration branch, and partially the repressive ones[33] controlled the majority of the State's ideological apparatuses. It lost some of them to the benefit of other social forces, as was the case of the mass media. Others did not perform any ideological function at all vis-à-vis the dominated classes. That was the case with the Movimiento,[34] which never became a fascist mass party and was only reduced to the control of the Francoist bureaucracy. Finally, there were those appartuses in which it was tried to carry out the assigned function. Among them the Trade Unions should be mentioned above all; on second level, the University. Trade Unions of vertical structure, resisted the time that the working class got organized as a result of struggles leading to the reconstruction of its movement. Thus, with the appearance of the *Comisiones Obreras* (Workers Commissions), the official Trade Unions were overrun. The same happened with the University where the first important symptom of crisis of the dictatorship manifested itself in 1956. The attempt of the Falange to impose its fascist student organization, S.E.U., was another failure due to the opposition offered by the student movement which had developed since the beginning of the sixties.

The Church, which "sanctified" the military rebellion against the Republic, "baptized" it as a "crusade" raised as the main social force carrying out the ideological function since the middle of the forties. The displacement of the Falange by the Church responded to the outcome of World War II, forcing the dictatorship to replace its fascist component by the clerical one.[35] Therefore, the Church, which always had strong control of one of the key apparatuses of the State—the school—felt a large portion of the weight of the ideological function. That implied that it was the Church which was going to suffer the pressure of the hegemonic crisis, a fact which explains the deep crisis that struck it during the sixties. The second Vatican Council created the inner conditions accelerating the split between a part of the low clergy and the high strata of the hierarchy. But the deepening of contradictions reached also the latter, a process which was manifested at the end of the sixties. The liberals gained position in 1971 with the National Commission of Peace and Justice. In the same year, the Joint Assembly of bishops and priests showed a clear division in relation to the question of the bishops' presence in Las Cortes (Francoist parliament) and the historical position of the Church during the civil war (Cooper, 1976, pp. 73–74). Since that moment the fraction close to the dictatorship started to lose terrain, becoming minoritarian.

Summarizing, we can say that the maintenance of the dictatorship has meant a constant deterioration of the State's ideological function, showing the inability of imposing hegemony. This process has been materialized in the cracking of the concerned apparatuses. An example of this fact has been the Trade Unions, the University, the press (since the moment that it got a minimum of freedom in 1966), etc. Only those that did not perform the assigned function, such as the Movimiento or the political system (Las Cortes) were not affected, but it only served as a control, or the political scene of the dominant social forces. This crisis mainly affected the two social forces in charge of the ideological function. The Falange impotently took refuge in the State's apparatus dreaming with the autarchical period. The Church, affected in a deeper way, started its decomposition as an ideological apparatus of the dictatorship to rebuild as a distant social force and, therefore, not representing any longer one of the main pillars of the dictatorship that it used to be.

IV. CONCLUSIONS: HEGEMONIC CRISIS, CRISIS OF THE DICTATORSHIP.

It is doubtless that the Francoist dictatorship has been the "adequate" superstructure for the definitive consolidation of the accumulation process (Solé-Turá, 1974, p. 4). But such a consolidation does not mean that contradictions defining this process have disappeared. It is true that some of them, as could be the case of the slow capitalization of the land rent have been minimised. Others, although tempered, have generated new contradictions. Thus, the overcoming of the autarchical frame meant that inter-imperialist contradictions were reflected in a more direct and clear way inside the ''Spanish'' social formation. Equally the redefinition of the articulation between industrial and banking capitals, being the result of the appearance of new elements in monopoly capital, has generated new contradictions inside the power bloc. But the essential point, in our opinion, is the reallocation of contradictions around monopoly capital and above all its antagonisms with the proletariat.

It is precisely the antagonisms between the two classes which materializes the essence of the hegemonic crisis. The difficulties at the level of the relations of exploitation have made necessary extreme relations of political domination with the subsequent crisis of the ideological relationships. In the autarchical period, as we have pointed out, the extraction of absolute surplus value and the maintenance of absolute pauperism were only possible in the ferocious repressive frame which followed the civil war. It was the too-long maintenance of such a situtation which generated, at the beginning of the fifties, the first important manifestion of the popular classes, especially the proletariat, in the class struggle field.[36] Since that conjuncture, and in the frame of transformations affecting the accumulation process, the struggle of the working class started to develop progressively. Monopoly capital tried to delimit the frame of those struggles (Law on Collective Agreements in 1958), but it failed. The low productivity implied a reduction of the margins of action on the terrain of economic struggles. The increasing repression at the end of the fifties (Law on Public Order, Law on collective responsibility in case of strike, installment of the so-called *consejo sumarísimo* (drum-head courtmartial), etc.) counterbalanced such a deficiency. This second stage is closed in approximately 1962, when the first mass strike took place, located mainly in Asturias and the Basque country.[37] The response was the proclamation of the exception state. So a third stage was opened, corresponding to the period of acceleration of the accumulation process. In this third stage new contradictions appeared around monopoly capital. On one side the (traditonal) petty bourgeoisie was submitted to a deep process of dissolution, as a result of the acceleration and extension of the base of monopoly accumulation. Its oppositon to such a process was reflected in the reapperance of nationalism: mainly Basque and Catalan. Depending on the position of the corresponding bourgeoisie in the power bloc, such nationalism took a radical (Basque) or a moderate (Catalan) form (Bandera, Roja, May 1973, p. 1803).[38] On the other side, as we have already pointed out, a large new petty bourgeoisie emerged in this period. This class was also submitted to the contradictions of the monopoly accumulation, through the erosion of salaries, although in an unequal way according to its different fractions, being incorporated in the struggle. Therefore, the extension and acceleration process, inside a similar framework of inability of monopoly capital in the terrain of economic struggles, corresponded with an extension and intensification of popular classes, especially the proletariat. This third period ended with the crisis of 1967, a conjuncture to which monopoly capital responded with the exacerbating repression and reinstallation of the state of exception at the beginning of 1969.

As we have said, several times, the 1967 crisis was the outcome of the contradictions due to the acceleration of the accumulation process. But such an acceleration had, in our opion, a qualitative effect: the definitive consolidation of the monopolistic form of the Spanish State, as an irrevertible process. Although such a fact was not immediately evident—because, as we said, the following years were years of recession—1972–1973 showed that such a consolidation was a fact. In this sense the Francoist dictatorship has fulfilled its "historical mission" regarding monopoly capital. Such a fact implies that the material basis for an hegemonic attempt existis. But the means used in order to achieve such a consolidation had led to a reduction of terrain of economic struggles and, therefore, to the ineluctable politization of these struggles. Thus, the allocation more often of struggles on the political terrain, impacting directly on State's apparatuses, led to a definition of a new objective of those struggles: the disappearance of the dictatorship. This process is reflected in the evolution of the dictatorship itself. Losing progessively ideological apparatuses and suffering crackings in some of the branches, as is the case of the juridical one and to some extent the Armed Forces, it reduced itself to its purest expression: its most reactionary elements and the unavoidable repression that accompanied them (the metaphor of the bunker). The rhythm of amplitude of the struggles continued to be determined by the accumulation cycle. Thus began the recession years at the end of the sixties, 1970 being the peak of a first wave. After the favorable conjuncture of 1972–1973, and entering the process of generalized recession that has affected imperialism as a whole, 1975 was the second peak.[39] The reaction of the dictatorship was the proclamation of the antiterrorism law in August of that year, having its first victims in October with five executions. During that tense conjuncture Franco's illness began, which led to his physical disappearance, accelerating the process of crisis due to the fundamental role that he played, as we have seen before.

This event can be taken as the dividing line in the crisis of the dictatorship. We could consider the first stage to start at the end of 1973—the period that constituted the second big wave of popular unrest mentioned above; although, in our opinion, the origins of this crisis lie in 1966–1967. In this first stage, the popular movement, having as its main axis the working movement, developed important struggles, in spite of the ferocious repression, as has been shown by several mass strikes in the Basque country and in the Baix Llobregat in Catalonia. Monopoly capital, and through it, capital as a whole, and the power bloc, took some distance from the dictatorship, perceiving the danger of a possible identification between the hegemonic crisis and the crisis of the dictatorship itself that could open the road to a revolutionary process. At the level of State's apparatuses, the crisis of the dictatorship implied a regroupment of the different social forces. On one side were the so-called "ultras," representing the most rightist elements, and on the other side, the *asociacionistas* (associationists), representing a certain consciousness of such a crisis and the necessity of overcoming it. But the false nature of these solutions (a mere evolution of the dictatorship through the *asociaciones*—caricatures of political parties loyal to the principles of the Movimiento), and above all the offensive of the popular movement, made for the raising of the "ultras" as the dominant social force inside the State's apparatuses. The increased repression, to which we have referred previously, was the normal consequence of such a domination.

Franco's death made possible the incorporation of a third social force into the constellation of the dictatorship: The so-called *reformistas* (reformists) who, occupying key ministerial posts (Interior, Foreign Affairs, Justice, among others), countervailed the domination of the ultras. The first government of the monarchy appeared to be composed of these three elements; those inherited (ultras and *asociacionistas*) and the new coming one (*reformistas*), with an inner equilibrium between its first and third force, but without an arbiter or inner "Bonaparte" because King Juan Carlos cannot exercise such a role.[40]

What is relevant is to understand that this reformist force is the expression of power bloc interests in the second stage.[41] Distant from the dictatorship, in order to avoid a possible identification of the two crises, and trying not to hypothecate its future, the dominant classes cannot prescind from the materialization of their power relationships existing for forty years. Although a part of the opposition, through its "democratic" road,[42] could represent its long-term interests better, the power bloc condenses them in the reformists.[43] The main goals of such a reformist strategy are two: first, to give time to the bourgeoisie for its future political organization vis-à-vis a new form of State; and second, to create conditions for bourgeois hegemony. To accomplish it entails a twofold operation. Internally, to isolate the ultra elements, and even to expell them, through the alliance of the *asociacionista* elements, in order to avoid the identification of the two crises. Externally, to break the democratic opposition, attracting the Christian Democrats and the Socialists (with whom it will be tried to create an important loyal workers' party acting as a dam against the Communist Party and other extreme left parties or organizations) to try to isolate the Communists (Fraser, 1976, p. 22). For the moment the ultras inside the State's apparatus have strong positions and the *asociacionistas* are not allies by principle: they will move toward the strongest. Up to now the opposition remains united and the attempts to isolate the Communists have not succeeded.[44] But the most important element in the reformist strategy, because it is its major weakness, is its assumption about the development of class struggle. It is its belief that a certain flexibility of the dictatorship would imply the recovery of margins in the economic struggle, making it possible to maintain the working class within them.[45] But in the situation of an economic crisis, and in view of the drastic measures taken in November 1975 regarding the freezing of wages and salaries, events led to the most important strike movement since the end of the civil war: the huge walk-out of January/February 1976. Confronted with such a movement, the government has responded in the classical way, as the tragic events of Vitoria (March 1976) and other examples have shown. But the pressure of the popular classes is mainly channelled by the democratic opposition, especially by the workers' parties and trade unions. Therefore the impact of these struggles depends on the path to be followed by these organizations. In this sense, it is quite likely that the final road to post-Francoism and the posible solution to the crisis of the dictatorship, will be the confrontation of the reformists with the democratic opposition, i.e. reform vs. democratic rupture. But this process can be as the agony of the dictator himself, long and painful.

FOOTNOTES

*Author's warning: The absence of sufficient studies on some crucial aspects of the Francoist period, due to obvious historical resasons, implies that some of the points of our analysis have a purely tentative character.

1. Primo de Rivera's dictatorship was a response to the Summer events of 1917, the year in which the working class appeared for the first time as an autonomous social force (Fernández de Castro, 1968, p. 155).

2. We shall use the adjuctive "Spanish" in relation to the concept "social formation" in order to avoid redundancies with the term "Spanish State." But we are conscious of its inaccuracy due to the existence of several national facts. That is the reason why we use quotation marks.

3. Mainly, but not exclusively. Food and oil imports from Great Britain and the U.S.A., respectively, were important enough for maintaining Franco during the Second World War in a position of no belligerency or neutrality.

4. The military aid had to be compensated by unfavorable economic relationships with the Francoist dictatorship. The most evident case was the mining with Germany. This country achieved a mining trust to be formed (MONTANA) wherein it controlled 75 percent in the three main firms. We have to remember that the existing legislation allowed only 25 percent of foreign participation, a percentage which was already raised to 40 percent in March 1937. It is obvious that Germany had pretensions of economic domination in the Spanish State for the postwar period (Jackson, 1972, p. 416; Gallo, 1969, Vol. I, p. 116).

5. The agreement on economic aid was 500 million dollars. In 1951 the U.S. Congress had already granted 100 million. In 1952 it added 25 million, to which was added 62.5 million Import-Export credit. And, finally, in 1953, aid was complemented with 20 million in wheat, which helped the country to face the bad harvest year.

6. The existence of protectionism at that time is an argument in favor of the monopolistic nature and therefore imperialistic nature of capital in the Spanish State. We have to remember that during that period all the imperialist centers implemented protectionist policies expressing the sharpening of their mutual contradictions which led to World War I. The fragility of the Spanish capital was reflected in the fact that tariffs were the highest in Europe (Carr, 1970, p. 379).

7. Besides, the threefold distinction of these certificates (upper, medium and low) had immediate and clear antiredistributive effects.

8. In the sixties, the protectionism was still maintained, although through new forms not so visible as the previous ones (Tamames, 1973a, p. 307 ff).

9. Regulated by law in 1963, it was only revised seven times for a period of ten years when it was stipulated yearly. Its maximum increase was 9.3 percent, and even in 1969 it suffered a decrease of 1 percent (Cruz and Serrano, 1972, p. 162 ff).

10. This process was quite heterogeneous given the different types of development in the various parts composing the Spanish State. Brenan (1962, p. 73 ff) has given a perspective of such a diversity. In relation to the genesis of this phenomenon, as a product of the different phases of the Reconquest, see Malefakis (1970, p. 50 ff).

11. The majority of the contracts were short-term (Martínez Cuadrado, 1973, pp. 155–156), which shows its instability. Moreover, the spreading of tenants and sharecroppers responded also to political reasons, because they could play a certain neutralizing role against the agrarian proletariat (Sanz, 1972, p. 52).

12. In this way the twofold process of aristocratization (a relevant number of landowners were aristocrats) of the bourgeoisie and bourgeoisization of the aristocracy was completed. Moya (1975, p. 181 ff) has qualified this fusion as "financial aristocracy."

13. Nevertheless, we can point out the existence of this migratory flow already in the forties in spite of the measures, like passes and safe-conducts for traveling, taken in order to avoid it (Sevilla-Guzmán, 1976, pp. 104–105).

14. If this process is sharpened, the outcome will be the disappearance of the differential rent, leaving only the monopolistic one the existence of which is a matter of favorable State's interventionism in the formation of agrarian prices.

15. Such a fact made the Catalan bourgeoisie turn to catalanism (Solé-Turá, 1974). In the autarchical period following the Civil War, this capital suffered an important discrimination through the system of import licenses. Moreover, Barcelona was broken as the major stock market in the Spanish State, and Catalan banks were absorbed by banks of Madrid (Jones, 1976, p. 238).

16. The number of absorptions by those banks for the period 1941–1960 was 69; while for the periods 1915–1940 and 1960–1966, it was respectively 12 and 0 (Muñoz, *et al.*, 1974, pp. 29–30).

17. This is one of the most important questions to investigate in the period of the Francoist dictatorship. The existence of this fraction has been pointed out by one of the few analytical attempts from a Marxist perspective on social classes in the Spanish State for that period (Fernández de Castro and Goytre 1974, p. 165).

18. In 1959 it represented only 1 percent of the stock companies and did not account for more than 1.6 percent of total disbursed capital. In 1970 this last figure had increased to 15 percent (Muñoz, 1975, p. 20).

19. The main constituent elements of this fraction could be the banking group Popular-Atlántico; to a certain extent the Santander group (Fernández de Castro and Goytre, 1974, p. 175); and the Rumasa group, famous through its spectacular growth in the sixties (Cuadernos de Ruedo Ibérico, 1972, p. 22 ff).

20. This capital represented 40.3 percent of the total between 1959 and the middle of 1973. In the second place came the Swiss capital with 20.7 percent, which, in many cases, is no more than disguised U.S. capital. Therefore, it can be said that more than half of the capital inflow during this period was U.S.

21. The existing foreign banks were very insignificant. With the creation of industrial banks the foreign penetration has increased, but the weight of this kind of bank in the total banking context is not relevant. Only the connections between the Bank of America and the Bank of Santander merit to be mentioned (Tamames, 1974, p. 27).

22. Moreover, there were two other goals: on the one side, to struggle against monopolistic situations; and on the other side, to create and maintain national war indus-

tries. In both goals, as well as in the one concerning autarky, the I.N.I. failed (Tamames, 1973a, p. 200 ff).

23. According to De Miguel (1975, p. 176), the *primoriveristas* were partially the ''technicians'' of the beginning of the Francoist dictatorship, along with the ''technicians'' in a strict sense (De Miguel, 1975, p. 268 ff). The latter are qualified by Moya (1975, p. 268) as the ''military managers.''

24. This law broke with the monopoly exercised by the ''traditional'' fraction on the credit, reinforcing the role of public credit which emerged as a possible competitor of the private one. Moreover, it made the famous ''status quo'' of 1942 disappear. Also, the law on incompatibilities (1968) was an attack on the hegemonic fraction in High Banking Council and its control over I.N.I.'s enterprises.

25. Cooper (1976 p. 39) has attributed such a secrecy of great deal to the Cooperatores, one of the four categories of Opus members, who are persons working for the good of the organization having Opus' priests as confessors.

26. This new bureaucratic stratum has been named the second generation of ''technicians'' (De Miguel, 1975, pp. 232–233).

27. It is in this last body that the political police is located.

28. This fraction can be roughly identified with the so-called ''blue generals,'' i.e., those who fought as volunteers on the Nazi side in the Soviet Union.

29. In a very interesting article published in *Le Monde Diplomatique* of June 1976, giving a detailed description of the structuring of the different repressive branches, it is pointed out how they are actually controlled by a tiny group of ''ultras'' or rightist'' officers of the Staff Army. Moreover, since the death of Carrero Blanco, the increasing repressions have been coordinated by the S.E.I.S. (Security and Infomation Special Service), reinforcing the unity among the different repressive banches.

30. This tendency reflected the postwar generation and therefore is not connected directly with the war experience which gave birth to the Francoist dictatorship (Busquets, 1971, p. 154 ff).

31. Such a dissatisfaction can be summarized in the following points: 1) lack of resources; 2) dependency on war material supplies from the U.S.A., supplies insufficient in qualitative and quantitative terms; 3) a vague defense policy; and 4) the new generations do not enjoy the privileges of those who fought in the Civil War (García, 1976, p. 46).

32. This function has been exercised permanently during the dictatorhsip, but it reached its peak in the immediate postwar period (1939–1943). In this bloody epilogue of the Civil War the calculations vary from 100,000 executions and 200,000 trials (Thomas, 1965, p. 760 ff) to 200,000 deaths by execution or illness in prison (Jackson, 1972, p. 539).

33. An investigation service of the Falange was created at the beginning of the forties, copying the Gestapo, which collaborated in its creation. It disappeared as a practicing service after World War II.

34. The unique party created in April, 1937, fusing the rest of the rightist parties, and the two unique organizations that resisted such a process of political disintegration of the right—i.e., the Falange and the Carlismo. In both cases the ''radical'' wings were suppressed, the Falange (an insignificant fascist organization during the Republic) becoming the main axis.

35. The Church participated directly in different governments through ministers belonging to the Asociación Católica Nacional de Propagandistas. These will be the politicians able to finish off with the political and economic blockade imposed on the dictatorship in the second half of the forties. The agreement with the U.S.A. and the Concordat with the Vatican in 1953 were their work.

36. We refer to the stike and boycott of public transports in Barcelona in 1951, which is usually considered the first important manifestation of protest since the end of the Civil War; although strikes developed prior to this, in Vizcaya in 1947. Moreover, in the forties, it is necessary to mention the guerrillas, who did not last long because they had no chance to link with a popular movement, nonexistent in that period.

37. The result of it was the appearance of "Comisiones Obreras," an autonomous organization of the working class, which henceforth constituted the main axis of the workers' movement.

38. Thus it can be explained why, in the Basque country, the national question finds its solution in a revolutionary frame. The petty bourgeoisie is more attracted by the strong proletariat, because the Basque monopoly capital is part of the hegemonic fraction and, therefore, not nationalistic, and the possible "national" bourgoisie (nonmonopolistic) is too weak. The Marxist splits of the E.T.A. (Basque nationalistic organization developing armed struggle) reflect such a phenomenon. In the case of Catalonia, the bourgeoisie rises as a strong pole of attraction and, therefore, the national question does not find solution in a revolutionary framework. At this moment, this predominant influence of the bourgoisie is clear in the formation of Consell de Forces Politiques, which tries to countervail the Assembly of Catalonia, wherein the P.S.U.C. (Unified Socialist Party of Catalonia, the Catalan Communist Party) is dominant (Fraser, March-April 1976, p. 7). We should add that another national question exists: to wit, the Galician one; and recently regional questions are developing in response to Madrid's repressive centralism.

39. It is difficult to evaluate the consequences of this recession, which seems to have deeper structural consequences for the accumulation process than previous ones (Muñoz *et. al.,* 1975, p. 81). Such a fact is crucial in order to know how much the material basis of capital for imposing hegemony has been deteriorated. A fundamental element that reinforces bourgeoisie's hesitations vis-à-vis the post-Francoist road to be followed.

40. The delimitation of the attributes of the Chief of State, defined in the Organic Law in 1966, shows the impossibility of Franco's successor to play the same role as the dictator himself. Also, and more important, Juan Carlos cannot be what Franco was: the personalization of the Army that provided him the basis for such a role.

41. The only dominant class that follows a different strategy is the Catalan bourgeoisie, due to its very particular situation, as we have pointed out before.

42. Today in the Spanish State it is possible to talk about five roads toward "post-Francoism":

1) The "ultra" road of the extreme right, characterized by immobility and regression. It pretends the maintenance of the dictatorship in its purest conception.

2) The "associationist" road, which implies continuation and evolution through the "associations," caricatures of political parties which took form under President Arias Navarro.

3) The "centrist" road, which represents the "reform" without "rupture."

These three roads correspond respectively to the three already mentioned social forces which define the dictatorship in the period immediately following Franco's death—i.e., "ultras," "associacionistas" and "reformistas."

4) The "democratic" road, implying the "rupture" with the previous form of State and the establishment of a nonexception form in its whole amplitude which groups the majority of the opposition.

5) The "revolutionary" road, which pretends to take advantage of the crisis of the dictatorship in order to enter into a revolutionary process that will culminate in the establishment of a dictatorship of the proletariat—i.e., a new State's power.

The formulation of each road in terms of strategy and tactics varies according to the several groups and parties.

43. The "democratic" road implies for the dominant classes the risks of a potentiation of the class struggle (Equipo de Estudio, 1976, p. 61) and, therefore, a reduction of their possibilities of imposing hegemony.

44. The main two pacts of the "democratic" road, the Junta Democratica (dominated by Communists) and the Plataforma de Convergencia Democratica (dominated by Christian Democrats and Socialists) have joined efforts with the creation of a unitary organism of coordination. This pact shows the reinforcement toward unity. But this unity is contradictory with the different interests present. Therefore, such a unity is not totally immune to the "reformist" attacks.

45. Since 1973 and 1974 there have been attempts in this sense through a remodelling of official trade unions, granting them more autonomy; the promulgation of a new law of collective agreements; and the proposal of a law on labor relations. But in all cases the State's action has been characterized by a paralysis, by an immobility, thus failing to overcome the inherent limits of the dictatorship (Muñoz, *et al.*, 1975, p. 222).

REFERENCES

Anlló J. (1967), *Estructura y problemas del campo español,* Madrid: Edicusa.

Bandera Roja (May, 1972), "La lutte de classes en Espagne entre 1939 et 1970," *Les Temps Modernes,* 310.

Brenan, G. (1962), *El laberinto español,* Paris: Ruedo Ibérico.

Busquets, J. (1971), *El militar de carrera en España,* Barcelona: Ariel.

Carr, R. (1970), *España, 1808–1939,* Barcelona: Ariel.

Clavera, J., Esteban, J. M., Mones, M. A., Montserrat, A. and Ros Hombravella, J. (1973), *Capitalismo español: de la autarquía a la estabilización (1939–1959),* 2 vols., Madrid: Edicusa.

Cooper, N. (1976), "The Church: from Crusade to Christianity," *Spain in Crisis,* edited by Preston, P., Hassocks: The Harvester Press.

Cruz, I. and Serrano, A. (1972), "Algunos problemas de economía laboral española durante 1971," in Muñoz, J., Roldán, S. and García Delgado, J. L. *La economía española 1971,* Madrid: Edicusa.

Cuadernos de Ruedo Ibérico (1972), "Rumasa o los mecanismos del crecimiento español," *Horizonte español 1972,* Vol. 3, Paris, Ruedo Ibérico.

De Miguel, A. (1975), *Sociología del franquismo,* Madrid: Euros.

Equipo de Estudio (1976), *Lucha política por el poder,* Madrid; Elías Quejereta.

Esteban, J. (1976), "The Economic Policy of Francoism: an Interpretation," *Spain in Crisis,* edited by Preston, P., Hassocks: The Harvester Press.

Fernandez de Castro, I. (1968), *De las Cortes de Cádiz al plan de desarrollo,* Paris: Ruedo Ibérico.

Fernandez de Castro, I. and Goytre, A. (1974), *Clases sociales en España en el umbral de los años 70*, Madrid: Siglo XXI.

Fraser, R. (March–April), "Spain on the Brink," *New Left Review,* 96.

Gallo M. (1969), *Histoire de l'Espagne franquiste,* 2 vols., Verviers: Marabout.

García, M. G. (1976), "The Armed Forces: Poor Relations of the Franco Régime," *Spain in Crisis,* edited by Preston, P., Hassocks, The Harvester Press.

Jackson, G. (1972), *The Spanish Republic and the Civil War, 1931–1939,* Princeton: Princeton University Press.

Jones, N. L. (1976), "The Catalan Question since the Civil War," *Spain in Crisis,* edited by Preston, P., Hassocks: The Harvester Press.
Le Monde Diplomatique (June, 1976), "L'appareil repressive de l'Etat franquiste reste intact."
Le Vaillant, Y. (1971), *Sainte Maffia. Le dossier de l'Opus Dei,* Paris: Mercure de France.
López Muñoz, A. (1971), *Capitalismo español: una etapa decisiva,* Vizcaya: Zero.
Malefakis, E. (1970), *Agrarian Reform and Peasant Revoluton in Spain,* Yale: Yale University Press.
Martínez Alier, J. (October–November, 1967), "El latifundio en Andaulcía y América Latina," *Cuadernos de Rudeo Ibérico,* 15.
Martínez Cuadrado, M. (1973), *La Burgesía conservadora (1931–1974),* Madrid: Alianza Universidad.
Moya, C. (1975), *El poder económico en España (1939–1970),* Madrid: Túcar Ediciones.
Muñoz, J. (1970), *El poder de la banca en España,* Vizcaya: Zero.
———. (July, 1975), "Políticos y banqueros," *Doblón extraordinario.*
Muñoz, J., Roldán, S. and García Delgado, J. L. (1973), *La economía española 1972,* Madrid: Edicusa.
Muñoz, J., Roldán, S., García Delgado, J. L. and Serrano, A. (1974), *La economía española 1973*, Madrid: Edicusa.
———. (1975), *La economía española 1974*, Madrid: Edicusa.
Naranco, J. (June-September, 1967), "La agricultura y el desarrollo económico español," *Cuadernos de Ruedo* Ibérico, 13–14.
———. (August-September, 1968), "Los aumentos de salarios y la crisis de la pequeña explotación," *Cuadernos de Ruedo Ibérico,* 20.
Rojo, L. A. (October-December, 1967), "Le commerce extérieur de l'Espagne," *Revue Tiers Monde,* 32.
Sanz, G. (1972), "La cuestión agraria en el Estado español," *Horizonte español 1972,* Vol. 2, Paris: Ruedo Ibérico.
Sevilla-Guzmán, E. (1976), "The Peasantry and the Franco Régime," *Spain in Crisis,* edited by Preston, P., Hassocks: The Harvester Press.
Solé-Turá, J. (1974), *Catalanismo y revolución burguesa,* Madrid: Edicusa.
Soler, R. (November–December, 1969), "The New Spain," *New Left Review,* 58.
Suárez, M. (May–June, 1973), "Une économie en voie de dépendence: le cas de l'Espagne," *Economies et Societés,* 5–6.
Tamames, R. (1964), *Estructura económica de España,* Madrid: Guadiana.
———. (1973a), *Introducción a la economía española,* Madrid: Alianza.
———. (1973b), *La república. La era de Franco,* Madrid: Alianza Universidad.
———. (1974), *Los monopolios en España,* Vizcaya: Zero.
Thomas, H. (1965), *The Spanish Civil War,* Middlesex: Penguin.
Viñas, M. (1972), "Franquismo y revolución burguesa," *Horizonte español 1972,* Vol. 3, Paris: Ruedo Ibérico.
Ynfante, J. (1970), *La prodigiosa aventura del Opus Dei. Génesis y desarrollo de la Santa Mafia,* Paris: Ruedo Ibérico.

THE CHANGING CLASS STRUCTURE OF SOUTH AFRICA: THE AFRICAN PETIT-BOURGEOISIE

Harold Wolpe, UNIVERSITY OF ESSEX

INTRODUCTION

The relationship between class and race and, therefore, between the class struggle and the national struggle has been, for obvious reasons, the central theoretical issue confronting the revolutionary movement in South Africa since its inception (with the formation of the South African Communist Party) in 1921. The issue, of course, is by no means merely theoretical: the history of the revolutionary movement is the history not only of its political policies and strategies, but also of the different analyses of the South African social formation proposed from time to time and from which these policies and strategies have been derived.

While it is not intended to attempt to provide here an account of this history, nonetheless it is necessary, in order to situate the discussion which follows, to summarize briefly the main elements of the analysis upon which the general political strategy of the South African Communist Party (SACP) and the African National Congress (ANC)—has been based since the end of World War II.

At the center of the analysis stands the concept of "internal colonialism" or "colonialism of a special-type" which serves to characterize the South African social formation (see SACP, 1962, and ANC, 1969). The essentials of this characterization may be expressed in the following way[1]:

(1) The South African social formation is dominated by the capitalist mode of production and, at one level, displays the usual features of advanced capitalism—industrial monopolies, the merging of industrial and finance capital, capitalist agriculture and links with foreign imperialist interests.

(2) Yet the development of capitalist productive relations and the ensuing dominance of productive capital within South Africa occurred under highly specific conditions which determined the special charcter of the social formation. The crucial condition was an already existing racial structure which had its origins in the early days of slavery at the Cape. That is to say capitalist production was inserted into a structure in which the white population dominated the black people. With the ending of British colonial rule, itself a consequence of the emerging dominance of the capitalist mode of production *within* South Africa, political power passed to the white settlers who

> . . . assumed more and more of the functions of the British ruling class toward the black majority whose subject and colonial status as a group dominated the whole subsequent process of class formation, class mobility, and class exploitation. (Slovo, 1976, p. 135).

The effect of this is that while "white South Africa," therefore, has all the features of advanced capitalism, "nonwhite South Africa," assumes a colonial status:

> The indigenous population is subjected to extreme national oppression, poverty and exploitation, lack of all democratic rights and political domination by a group which does everything it can to emphasize and perpetuate its alien "European" character. (SACP, 1962, p. 26.)

Clearly, this description of the social formation has important implications for the analysis of the class structure, class alliances and political conflict. Thus, in the first instance, while capitalist production in South Africa produces and reproduces a dominant capitalist class and a subordinate and exploited working class, this class division is "overdetermined" by racial, political and ideological structures and practices. The effect of this is that, without destroying the dominance of capital, the class structure takes on a special form which is determined by the political and ideological levels:

> Explicit provisions in the law and state-backed social practice have ensured that while not every white man is a full member of the ruling class proper, no black man, whatever his economic status, can participate on equal terms with his white equivalent at any level of the social structure . . . In each contemporary class category—whether it be capitalist, worker or peasant—the black man is fenced off from his white counterpart by a multitude of state-imposed boundaries. (Slovo, 1976, p. 119.)

More specifically the following features of the class structure may be noted:

(a) The capitalist class is virtually entirely white and there is "a total extra-economic bar to blacks acquiring productive property in the existing preserves of the white group." (Slovo, 1976, p. 121.)
(b) The black and white working class stand in distinct "and color defined positions in relation to the means of production" and, indeed, white workers "play an active role in maximizing the exploitation of the black worker." (Slovo, 1976, p. 121.)
(c) The African petit-bourgeoisie, new and old, with the possible exception of those in the Bantustans, are hampered and restricted by laws which favor their white counterparts.
(d) In agriculture there is an almost perfect racial division: capitalist agriculture is completely in the hands of white capitalists and at the same time there are no white rural laborers; the entire labor force (excluding manager and supervisors) is black. By contrast there are no white peasants or small producers—these classes are virtually restricted to improverished African rural producers in the Bantustans, although here there are signs of a slowly emerging richer peasant stratum.

Clearly it follows from this characterization of the class structure that while all white groups and/or classes have a vested interest in maintaining the existing racial structures, all black groups and/or classes share a more or less common objective basis for wishing to destroy these structures:

> The destruction of this structure is, at the moment, the factor which gives a common content to the aspirations of all the social groups among the black people except, perhaps, those who have a vested interest in Bantustan separatism. (Slovo, 1976, p. 141.)

The interests, politically, economically and ideologically defined, of all classes and fractions of classes among the whites (whatever the secondary conflicts between them) depends upon an alliance which opposes and is opposed by an alliance of all classes and class fractions among the blacks (whatever the secondary conflicts between them). Hence the centrality of the national liberation struggle and the importance of antiracist and nationalist policies as a means of mobilizing the entire black people in this struggle.

However, despite the fact that all the classes within the subordinate "colonial" group are in some (not necessarily identical) way and to some degree oppressed/exploited, it does not follow that the opposition of these classes to that oppression/exploitation will be of the same nature or extent. Indeed, both the ANC and the SACP, as Slovo (Slovo, 1976, pp. 139–140), points out insist upon the special and indispensable role of the African working class in ensuring the full achievement of the national and social goals of the liberation struggle and in preventing "any tendency for the national struggle to fall under bourgeois hegemony." (Slovo, 1976, p. 140.)

This special role relates both to the conduct of the immediate struggle against the apartheid regime which "at the moment" unites all "social groups among the black people" and more particularly to the moment, after the defeat of the regime, when the struggle for the construction of a socialist order comes to the forefront and generates divergent interests between the black working class and its class allies on the one side, and the black bourgeois or petit-bourgeois classes on the other. (See Slovo, 1976, pp. 144–149.)

It must be emphasized again, however, that according to the analyses based on the notion of internal colonization, *at the moment* there is a common interest among all classes within the black groups to destroy the racial structure of South Africa. This common interest is deduced from the structure of internal colonialism itself as I have suggested above. That this is so is shown by the fact that classes in the social formation are situated in the class structure and class struggle almost entirely by reference to "racial exclusiveness" with little reference to the specific economic, ideological and political relations within which they are embedded.

The theory of internal colonialism is questionable in a number of respects but I do not intend to discuss these here. (See Wolpe, 1975, already cited.) Rather, I want to question, on two grounds, the adequacy of an analysis which moves from the description of the internal colonial structure to the assumption that the very existence of that structure produces a common, more or less inevitable and total opposition to it of all classes in the colonial population at each moment of its existence. First, internal colonialism specifies, at best, only one aspect of the structure of the South African social formation; it says nothing about the specific structure of capitalism in the present phase of its development. But, and this brings me to the second point, even an account of the general structure which includes both aspects would be insufficient. The general characterization of a social formation, in terms of the dominant structural relations which define historically specific epochs in its development, is undoubtedly a necessary prerequisite for the analysis or specific conjunctures. That is to say, the delineation of the economic structure (for example, in terms of the dominance of either competitive or monopoly capital), the specification of the ideological/institutional structure (for example, in terms of racial differentiation) and the analysis of the political structure (in terms, say, of its internal colonial character) are clearly of fundamental importance to an analysis of a particular conjuncture and the struggles occurring within it, since the structures specify the *possible* limits and content of the conflicts and struggles. But the actual conflicts which occur, and the *actual* content of class interests defined in the course of struggle cannot be read off from the general character of a social formation. This point becomes clear if we think of the following analogies: Just as the political and ideological position of the working class, at a given moment, cannot be inferred from the mere fact of its exploited condition within a capitalist social formation (it may be in part reactionary, reformist or revolutionary), so the political and ideological position, at a given moment, of different classes within a colonial territory or neocolonial state cannot be inferred from the mere fact of their presence within the colony (reformist opposition, revolutionary struggle and collaboration are all possible positions vis-à-vis the colonial or neocolonial power).

Thus, it cannot be assumed that within a given conjuncture the interests of *any* of the groups or classes which are subject to a structure of oppression and exploitation will be represented in the course of struggle, in terms of the complete destruction of that structure. This means, more concretely, that the interests and, consequently the political involvement of each class and class fraction within the black population, can only be determined through an analysis of the concrete economic, political and ideological conditions in the social formation.

This, of course, is not to deny that there may be, during a particular phase, a convergence of interests between different classes or class fractions. But, the crucial question here relates to the conditions which produce such a convergence. In the light of this clarification it is now possible to turn to a discussion of the African petit-bourgeoisie in South Africa.

II THE AFRICAN PETIT-BOURGEOISIE, 1948 TO MID 1960's

The African political scene in the post World War II period was, in fact, marked by an alliance of all black classes. This alliance reflected a convergence of class interests in the struggle against racial discrimination and the structure of political domination. Insofar as the black petit-bourgeoisie became part of this alliance (within the organizational framework of the Congress Alliance) which united the African National Congress, South African Congress of Trade Unions, South African Congress of Democrats, Colored People's Congress and the illegal Communist Party, then its political position and the formulation of its class intersts cannot be explained simply by reference to the internal colonial structure of the South African social formation, but by the concrete conditions of the conjunctures in that period. No adequate analyses exist of the period and nothing like a full analysis can be attempted here. It is necessary, however, to at least indicate the main conjunctural conditions insofar as they bear directly on the African petit-bourgeoisie. The significant features can be roughly summarized as follows.

The economic expansion which was nourished by the circumstances of World War II served to consolidate the position of dominance of the English-speaking section of the white population at all levels in the economy. That is to say, by the end of the war, the fraction of each class which was composed of English-speaking whites had extened and entrenched their positions of control and economic power. This applied equally to their position in the dominant classes—banking, industrial, finance and merchant capital—and in the subordinate classes where members of the English speaking-group filled the highest paid and most skilled industrial jobs, the supervisory, h8g . .-level administrative and managerial positions in the new petit-bourgeoisie and had considerable control of small commerce including trade. Only, perhaps, in capitalist agriculture and in the middle range of civil service posts was there a powerful intrusion of Afrikaans-speaking whites. Despite the activities of various Afrikaans nationalist organizations, Afrikaners occupied a relatively weak position in the "traditional" petit-bourgeois sectors of trade and commerce and in the ranks of the "new" petit-bourgeoisie. (See Van Wyk, 1968.)

The electoral victory of the Nationalist Party in 1948, representing in the main an alliance of Afrikaner agricultural and banking capitalists, and the Afrikaner petit-bourgeoisie and workers, established the political condition for the penetration of Afrikaners into, inter alia, the spheres of finance, industrial and banking capital and also on an expanded scale into the new and traditional petit-bourgeois sectors. With respect to these latter sectors, the policies of the Nationalist Government operated positively to foster the advancement of Afrikaners and negatively to curtail or impede competition from black people. The positive measures were both direct and indirect. Thus, on the one hand, for example, a policy of Afrikanerization was practiced vis-à-vis the higher posts in the civil services, the army, in the appointment of judge and in state enterprises, and steps taken to encourage the development and extension of secondary and higher education for Afrikaans-speaking students. Similarly, favorable conditions were directly created for Afrikaner traders, particularly in the smaller towns, through preferential treatment in the allocation of trading licences, the advancement of capital and in other ways. On the other hand, by providing the means for the rapid expansion of Afrikaner capitalist interests, and, therefore, the development of large scale finance, banking and other enterprises, the state, at the same time, established the conditions for a considerable increase in the Afrikaner new middle class in the private sector, for here recruitment was virtually totally from the Afrikaner population.

Coupled with such positive steps, the Government also took measures to undermine competitive threats in the sphere of both the traditional and the new petit-bourgeoisie from the direction of the black population. First, the politically weak but economically tenacious Indian traders who had established themselves in many towns, villages and cities, were brought under attack by means of the Group Areas Act. The Act provided for the residential and business segregation of all races and the effect was, inter alia, to prohibit Indians from trading in white (or African) areas and to relegate them to trade only among Indian people in the Indian group areas. The Act also affected African traders who were restricted to trading in black townships; and, in addition, a whole series of disabilities (which will be referred to below) began to be imposed upon them. Furthermore, a series of measures were taken which operated to inhibit the entrance of Africans into the new petit-bourgeoisie, despite considerable shortages of manpower. These measures included: the prohibition upon blacks from continuing to attend the then established "mixed" universities; the exclusion of African professionals from occupying offices in the white urban areas; the job reservation clause of the Industrial Conciliation Act of 1956 which enabled the Minister to reserve any occupation for whites; the virtual ending of exemptions from the pass laws and so on.

In the period under discussion, then, the position of the black (and particularly the African) petit-bourgeoisie, which was in any event small in number and generally economically weak, must be seen against the background of these policies of aggressive state support for the Afrikaner petit-bourgeoisie and an equally aggressive hindrance of the blacks.

There is, however, a further factor to be considered—the rise of the national liberation movement. From late in the 1940's to early in the 1960's the political scene was dominated by the ever increasing mass struggles of the black people and the growing strength of their organizations and of their mass support. The struggles were organized under the leadership of the African National Congress with its allies in the Congress Alliance. The national liberation movement constituted an alliance of the black working class, improverished African petty agricultural producers, and the new and traditional petit-bourgeoisie among the Indian, Colored and African people. The economic interests of the petit-bourgeoisie and petty producers was reflected in the major policy document of the period, *The Freedom Charter,*[2] which stated:

> All people shall have equal rights to trade where they choose, to manufacture and to enter all trades, crafts and professions.
>
> Restriction of land ownership on a racial basis shall be ended, and all the land redivided among those who work it, to banish famine and land hunger.
>
> The State shall help the peasants with implements, seeds, tractors, and dams to save the soil and assist the tillers.

In summary, the relatively small and weak black petit-bourgeoisie, repudiated by the white fractions of this class and crippled by state policies, entered into an alliance with the black working class and poor agricultural producers. In the circumstances, these classes given their growing strength and antiracialist policies, their struggles against racial discrimination, were the natural allies of the black petit-bourgeoisie. There were, of course, small collaborationist groups particularly within the Indian petit-bourgeoisie; but this does not disturb the main point of the above analysis, which suggest the conditions that produced a convergence of class interests between the black petit-bourgeoisie and other classes.

There is no reason to suppose that these conditions should persist. One writer has recently made the point in this way:

> The emergence of a vocal bourgeois grouping going-it-alone outside the mainstream of the nationalist movement signals the need for the national movement to clarify its long term aims beyond the stage thus far reached in South Africa. Up to now, the national movement has spoken for, and represented the aspirations of all classes within the ranks of the oppressed; its aims have been clear and sufficient—to abolish every vestige of race discrimination in the national life, and to win full equality of opportunity for all citiizens. As the assemblage of the whole nation, the economic aims of the national movement have always been those to which every class grouping could subscribe—workers, peasants and bourgeois alike—equality and the abolition of color discrimination. For a time, that simple formuation was enough. (Touissant, 1976.)

Slovo's analysis (Slovo, 1976) identifies various classes in the social formation but his adherence to the overriding importance of the internal colonial structure in determining class interests, at the present moment, leads him into an ambiguous analysis. He insists that while

> South Africa's ruling class, is of course, able to find *individual* collaborators among black people through the lure of status, more lucrative jobs etc. (Slovo, 1976, p. 141.) (Italics mine.)

nonetheless, to repeat part of a passage quote above:

> The destruction of this structure [i.e., the present racial structure,] is, *at the moment,* the factor which gives a common content to the aspirations of all the social groups among the black people. . . . (Slovo, 1976, p. 141.) (Italics mine.)

The only possible exception to this resides in the emergence of a black petit-bourgeoisie or small capitalists and "farming entrepreneurs." Now, with regard to these, Slovo appears to argue two separate points. In the case of the white areas, the mobility of the black middle strata, unlike that of the "normal" petit-bourgeoisie is restricted by race and not by economic factors. Indeed the ruling class is compelled "by its very nature to resist any incursion into its existing sources of wealth and the state power which underwrites it" (Slovo, 1976, p. 142.) Hence:

> Objectively speaking, therefore, the immediate fate of the black middle sections is linked much more with that of the black workers and peasants than with their equivalent across the color line." (Slovo, 1976, p. 126.)

He merely adds that if the impossible were to occur, if some of the black middle strata were taken into the "white fold," they would simply become "collaborators in a continued system of race repression" (Slovo, 1976, p. 142).

In the Bantustan, however, there is "emerging a significant group of petty capitalist" (Slovo, 1976, p. 126) who aspire "to greater rights of participation at the top of the exploitative machine than is permitted in white South Africa" (p. 143). However, despite its significance, this class is "pathetically small and has arrived too late on the historical scene to play a classic class role either as a leading element in the national struggle or as the main beneficiary of mass revolutionary sacrifice" (p. 143). Therefore, it is relegated, in furthering its own interests, to a dependent role "outside the mainstream of the national struggle." (p. 144).

Thus, in Slovo's analysis, the urban black petit-bourgeoisie (he appears to be referring only to the traditional and not also to the new petit-bourgeoisie) remains small in size and tied by the structure of racial domination to the liberation movement. On the other hand, in the Bantustan, the emergent petit-bourgeoisie is placed outside of the liberation movement and seen as incapable of establishing a social base among the popular masses. The conclusion which follows is that either the petit-bourgeoisie (in the white areas) is objectively linked to the liberation movement (because of the internal colonial structure) or (despite that structure) the Bantustan petit-bourgeoisie falls outside of that movement but is doomed to political insignificance.

The validity of both these conclusions can be determined only by a conjunctural analysis which is really only hinted at in Slovo's account. In what follows, my purpose is threefold: first, to sketch out (with such data as is available) the growth in the size of both the new and traditonal African petit-bourgeoisie; second, to discuss in a tentative way some of the conditions which both produced this development and account, in the case of the traditional petit-bourgeoisie, for the shift in its political allegiance in the white areas and the Bantustans; and, third, to comment on the political singificance of this shift.

III THE GROWTH OF THE AFRICAN PETIT-BOURGEOISIE

In this section of the paper, insofar as both official and unofficial statistics and accounts allow, a description of the emergence of a relatively large African petit-bourgeoisie will be provided. As always with information relating to the class structure and, in the case of South Africa, particularly where the information concerns black people, both the inadequacy of the concepts in terms of which the statistics are provided and the paucity of the statistics requires to be noted. Consequently, the account which follows is both incomplete and uneven and must be read bearing these problems in mind.

In presenting the material, a distinction will be drawn between the traditional and new petit-bourgeoisie.

As is well-known, the problem of the new middle class has become the focus of a considerable debate. From the Marxist standpoint, the discussion has revolved largely around the question of productive and unproductive labor. There has been little agreement, however, on how these types of labor are to be distinguished. Poulantzas (1975), for example, insists upon productive labor being restricted to the production of material commodities, which would restrict the proletariat to the industrial worker; Bullock (1974), by contrast, includes the production of immaterial "commodities" (education, health, etc.) which enter into the value of labor-power in the sphere of productive work. In a somewhat different direction, it has been contended that those who carry out the "global function of capital" by exercising coercion over the labor process, whether in productive or unproductive enterprises comprise the new middle class (Carchedi, 1975). There are other positions too, but common to all these approaches is the problem of defining the relationship of the occupational structure (the division of labor) to the production of surplus value and hence to the relations of production. It is not intended to enter this difficult terrain here. For present purposes Carchedi's view is adopted. The new middle class comprise all those agents who, within both industrial production and in the tertiary sector of the economy, exercise supervisory and coercive functions (the global function of capital) over agents engaged in the labor process. That is to say, the new middle class comprises those agents who, while they are separated from the means of production or merchant captial, nonetheless carry out the function of extracting surplus value or surplus labor from those engaged in the labor process.

In the case of South Africa, the number of blacks entering surpervisory/coercive roles within the circuit of industrial capital has shown little increase. Within the tertiary sector both the rate of increase and the absolute number of blacks in such roles appears to have been much more pronounced. It is, however, much easier to obtain statistics of total African employment in the tertiary sector by comparison with statistics of Africans in supervisory/coercive roles. In fact, since World War II there has been a vast expansion of the number of Africans employed as wage and salary workers outside of industrial production—in commerce, in education and health and in various state departments—and it is to these categories of workers that the statistics provided below largely relate. It must be stressed that to a considerable extent these employees are engaged in the low wage/salary, low skill jobs within the enterprises and are exploited in the sense that they give up surplus labor; but this is by no means completely so and an increasing number carry out managerial/administrative functions of a supervisory and coercive character. Insofar as it is possible, these different categories will be identified below.

The traditional petit-bourgeoisie is defined simply as including small-scale producers where the owner of the means of production is also the direct producer; owners of small-scale business, particularly, in the retail trade; and the self-employed (e.g., professionals, etc.).

Table I. African Employment in Some Occupational Groups

Year	Professional A Technical & Related		Administrative B Executive & Managerial		Clerical C		Salesworker D		Service, Sport E & Recreation		TOTAL A + B + C + D + E	
	African	all groups Total	African	all groups Total	African	all groups Total	African	all groups Total	African	all groups Total	African	all groups Total
1921	9,756				1,634		13,424					
1936	13,810		975		21,166		3,984					
1946	24,411	109,056	2,647	75,477	28,043	188,407	6,955	68,073	588,845	721,685	650,901	1,162,698
1951	29,455	136,020	5,105	95,611	13,297	219,846	11,110	92,731	639,978	789,880	698,945	1,334,083
1960	48,847	205,520	5,716	68,418	19,267	312,890	28,894	159,782	711,156	902,354	813,520	1,648,964
1970	93,300	330,060	3,400	75,880	96,280	579,090	110,880	329,740	1,011,940	1,226,890	1,315,800	2,581,660

Note: The occupations included with each category is as follows:
Professiona, technical and related worker
Architects; quantity-surveyor; civil, mechanical, electrical, mine, chemical engineers; land surveyor; surveying technican; chemist, physicist, geologist and other physical scientist; veterinarian, biologist, agronomist and related scientist; medical and related professions; professor, teacher and instructor; religious worker; jurists (advocates, magistrates, attorneys); artist, writer and related creative artist (actors, musicans, drawers, etc); draughtsmen and other technicians; other professional, technical and related worker (accountant, actuary, economist, librarian, translator, designer, etc.).
Administrative, executive and managerial worker
Forestry and fishing (excluding farmer and farm managers); mining and quarrying; manufacturing, contruction, gas, water and sanitary services; wholesale and retail trade; financial institutions and insurance; real estate (developing, operating and agency); transport, storage and communications; catering and accommodation services; business services; other service industries; director of companies; public adminstrative official (legislative, elected; and administrative, appointed).
Clerical worker
Accountant; cashier, typist, office-machine operator; clerk, receptionist, clerical worker, etc.
Salesworker
Working proprietor, wholesale and retail trade—insurance and estate salesman, stockbroker, salesman of securities and services, auctioneer; manufacturer's agent; commercial trader; salesman, shop assistant; related worker; floorwalker, canvasser, newsvendor, petrol filling station attendent.
Service, sports and recreation worker
Policeman, guard, firefighter, etc.; caretaker, cleaner, housekeeper, cook, nurse (children's), maitre d'hotel; waiter, wine steward; barber, hairdresser; launderer, dry cleaner, etc.; photographer and camera worker; undertaker, embalmer, entertainment, recreation and other sportsworker (acrobat, trainer, etc.); other service worker: political party organizer, hospital orderly, etc.; unemployed.
Source: Adapted from the 1970, 1936 and 1921 Census Reports.

The division between the petit-bourgeoisie in the white areas and those in the Bantustans must be stressed because the political structure of the Bantustan places the latter in a quite different position, as I will show below, by contrast with the former.

1. The New Petit-Bourgeoisie

The expansion of capitalist production and, in particular, the development of monopoly capitalism in the South African social formation has been accompanied by an increase in large-scale industrial, administrative and financial enterprises and a concomitant expansion of all the sectors of the economy including the so-called tertiary sector. This has produced, of course, important changes in the division of labor. These changes are shown in Table 1, which incudes the total of all races employed in the categories shown and the number of Africans in those categroies between 1946 and 1970 in South Africa as a whole.

From Table 1, the following information can be derived: First, the proportion which Africans constituted of the total employed in all the occupation categories shown in the table, varied as follows:

Table 1.1 Africans as a Percentage of Total Employment in Occupation Categories A, B, C and D

Year	Africans as Percentage of Total
1946	56
1951	52
1960	49
1970	51

It is worth mentioning here that the decline shown in the figures for 1951 and 1960 coincides with the period in which, as I pointed out in the Introduction, the state was taking measures to foster the entry of Afrikaners into the relevant occupations.

Second, whereas the rate by which African employment increased was below the rate of increase of the total work force employed in these occupation groups in the periods 1946–1951 and 1951–1960, in the period 1960–1970, African employment increased faster than the total:

Table 1.2 Percentage increase in Employment in the Categories A, B, C and D

Period	Percentage Increase in African employment	Percentage Increase in Total employment
1946–51	7.4	14.7
1951–60	10.4	23.6
1960–70	61.9	56.5

It is hardly necessary to emphasize the enormous overall increase in the African new middle class between 1960 and 1970.

The difficulty with this picture, however, is that it does not differentiate the levels of employment; and this may be of particular importance in the clerical, sales and service worker categories. *Indeed, for the most part, African employment in these categories does not consist, as the 1960 Census report put it, of workers "whose primary functions are to plan, organize, direct and coordinate the activities of private or public undertakings and organizations."* It would be important to examine more closely the employment pattern of Africans in these categories. However, the official statistics are extremely incomplete and all that can be done here is to indicate the nature of the problem. Table 2 provides a good example of the assymetrical distribution of Africans in two sectors of commerce:

Table 2. African Employment in Commerce (Wholesale and Retail Trade)

Year	Executive, Clerical & Administrative Staff		Shop and Sales Assistants		Other Employees		Total	
	African	Total	African	Total	African	Total	African	Total
1946–47	134	40,517	3,578	56,483	87,508	116,282	91,230	213,282
1952	293	49,622	6,371	62,712	104,331	140,210	111,015	252,744
1960–61	1,106	55,843	12,602	86,378	112,084	157,274	125,792	299,495
1966–67							168,600	419,700
1968–69							181,700	432,800

Source: Adapted from the *South African Statistics, 1970*

Despite these difficulties, however, the trend seems to be clear—a rapid growth at all levels of Africans in occupations which have come to be regarded as new middle class. As far as commerce and business employment is concerned, the picture is perhaps reinforced by the following table:

Table 3. African Employment in Commerce and Business (Showing also Percentage Wage Increases)

		1969	1970	1971	1972	1973	1974	1975
Wholesale Trade	No.	76,700	79,200	80,000	81,700	82,300	83,700	85,400
	A		182,300		2.1	0.7	1.7	1.3
	B				7.4	8.6	12.7	1.4
Retail Trade	No.	103,000	107,100	108,400	111,600	113,300	116,500	117,200
	A				2.9	0.5	2.7	1.0
	B				7.0	13.0	11.5	10.3
Banking Institution	No.	4,566	5,016	5,218	5,383	5,917	6,340	6,388
	A					10.9	5.9	6.1
	B					23.9	23.9	29.4
Building Societies	No.	1,398	1,402	1,466	1,606	1,719	1,863	1,944
	A				9.4	9.3	4.8	7.7
	B				12.0	15.2	18.4	20.0
Insurance	No.			3,509	3,987	4,218	4,440	4,636
	A				15.8	2.3	4.1	6.6
	B				10.0	16.9	23.3	25.2
Licensed Accommodation	No.	26,000	26,000	30,000	32,300	32,700	34,100	35,000
	A						2.8	2.6
	B						5.3	

A = Percentage increase of number over previous year.
B = Percentage increase of wages over previous year.

Source: Compiled from *Quarterly Bulletin of Statistics*

These trends are also apparent in other sectors of employment. Thus, the number of African teachers, in South Africa (excluding the Homelands) has risen as follows:

Table 4. African Schoolteachers (Excluding the Homelands)

Year	No. of African Teachers
1959	25,800
1963	29,496
1968	37,963
1970	45,366
1971	47,145
1972	53,246
1973	57,433
1974	61,976

Source: Compiled from issues of *Annual Survey of Race Relations*

And the trend, although at a much lower numerical level, is similar in respect to senior educational posts.

Table 5. Senior Positions in Schools

	1968	1970	1971	1974	1975
Inspectors of Schools	50	65	93	101	99
Assistant Inspectors	178	293	323	336	332
School Principals	7,430	9,597	10747	11326	11819
Other Senior Capacities	164	277	287	314	296

Source: Compiled from issues of *Annual Survey of Race Relations*

In the Universities, the number of African lecturers and professors although extremely small, has doubled between 1968 and 1975 (47 to 90), but the important increase is in the number of African students. Table 6 shows the African student population.

Table 6. African University Students
(Including Correspondence Students)

Year	No. of African Students
1951–52	811
1957	2,151
1960	1,901
1965	2,413
1968	3,836
1971	5,407
1974	7,845

Source: Compiled from issues of *Annual Survey of Race Relations*

The single partial exception to the trends I have been describing is in the public service (outside of the Bantustans) where African employment has tended, after rising to a peak in 1966, to thereafter decline:

Table 7. African Employment in Central, Provincial and Local Government

Year	No. of Africans Employed
1960	258,164
1963	291,277
1967	353,590
1969	350,718
1972	317,386
1975	333,486

Source: Compiled from issues of the *South African Statistics*

Again, of course, these figures must be taken to include a large number of laborers. Thus, for exmaple, it seems to be clear that only a small proportion of public service employees outside the Bantustans are on fixed establishment posts.

I want to complete this rough statistical picture by bringing together, scanty as they are, some data concerning the Bantustans. The importance of this is that it is particularly in these so-called homelands that the specific political thrust of the African petit-bourgeoisie must be seen.

It was shown in Table 1 that 1,315,800 Africans were in occupations in 1970 which in some sense can be considered to be part of the new middle class. The division of the population in these occupations in the white areas by contrast with the homelands is shown in Table 8.

Table 8. Africans in Certain Occupations in White Areas and in the Bantustan, 1970.

Occupational Category	No. of Africans	
	White Areas	Bantustans
Professional and Technical	45,200	48,100
Administrative, Executive and Managerial	800	2,600
Clerical	78,080	18,200
Saleworkers	70,700	40,180
Service, Sports and Recreation	885,780	109,080
Total	1,080,460	235,340

Source: Compiled from various sources.

Apart from these figures and apart from the public services departments in the Bantustan, the information is extremely sparse. We can add to the above in regard to specific occupations two further points: First, the number of African teachers in the Bantustan rose from 19,668 in 1958 to 34,570 in 1973 (of the latter 8,313 were in the Transkei). Second, as Lipton (1972) has pointed out, the effect of the central governments' spending in the Bantustans (leaving aside for the present expenditure by the Development Corporations) has been to create a preponderance of government jobs:

> Of R200 million spent on the Bantustans during the 1960's, one third went on building of commuter townships, 27 percent on health, hospitals and social services. This large public works program has created a number of jobs. The rest of the money has gone on administrative jobs; therefore, most jobs are in government service—e.g., in the Transkei, 60 percent. (Lipton, 1972.)

This is to some extent reflected in the rise in the number of civil service posts occupied by Africans in the Transkei partly as a result of the process of Africanization and partly as a result of the increase in civil service jobs. Thus, for example, in the Transkei, of the 2,476 posts in the civil service in 1963, 76 percent were occupied by Africans; by 1973, there were 4,383 posts and 92.4 percent of these were filled by Africans. On a smaller scale and the same trend has occurred in the other homelands. Table 9, on page 160, provides the figures for all of the Bantustan over a three-year period.

The totals for each of the years shown was:

1969: 4,249
1970: 6,885
1971: 6,087

In addition to the above there are some 2,000 chiefs and headmen who perform administrative functions in the Bantustan. Given the importance of the chiefs in the political systems of the Bantustans (they are ex-officio members of the legislative assemblies) it is of interest to note that four colleges for the sons of chiefs have been established since 1960. At present there are approximately 100 students at these colleges.

2. The African Traditional Petit-Bourgeoisie

An account of the size and growth of the traditional petit-bourgeoisie can be given much more briefly for two reasons. First, the sources of information are, on the whole, even poorer than in the case of the new middle class; and second, the economic activities of the traditional petit-bourgeoisie are, more or less, narrowly confined to a single sphere—small-scale trading. It would seem that there is virtually no small-scale production outside of agriculture.

Table 9. Number of African Civil Servants in the Bantustans

Homeland	Year	No. of Africans	Percent of Total Employed in Civil Service
TRANSKEI	1969	2,877	90.3
	1970	3,191	91.5
	1971	3,581	92.8
CISKEI	1969	427	67.9
	1970	508	71.4
	1971	605	74.3
BASOTHO QWAQWA	1969	48	85.8
	1970	48	88.5
	1971	126	90.0
BOPHUTHATSWANA	1969	461	63.7
	1970	501	62.9
	1971	583	69.2
LEBOWA	1969	258	58.1
	1970	1,479	86.1
	1971	645	76.2
VENDA	1969	13	22.4
	1970	970	94.1
	1971	282	76.0
GAZANKULU	1969	115	70.6
	1970	188	70.1
	1971	265	73.4

Source: From Horrell (1973), p. 254

Within the white areas, African businesses are restricted to the segregated African townships. For these areas as a whole, the only information it has been possible to obtain at the time of writing related to 1962. In that year there were 7,850 African businesses in the African townships and these consisted mainly of butchers, greengrocers, grocers, wood and coal merchants and restaurants. Hart (1972) has brought together a little more information for Johannesburg townships. She provides the Table 10.

Some idea of the possible extent of African traders share (outside of the Bantustans) of trade by 1974 was given by the *Financial Mail* (March 1, 1974). The journal suggested that of the R720 m per year spent on consumer goods other than clothes and furniture by Africans, 50 percent is spent in white-owned outlets. White outlets account for 80 percent of African purchase of clothes and furniture. (No figure was given for sales by Asian traders.)

Insofar as the Bantustans are concerned, there are total figures of African businessmen available up to 1963, but thereafter the only published figures appear to relate to new undertakings set up with loans from the various state corporations. Hart (1972) provides Table 11.

If we add to these figures the statistics issued by the Bantu Investment Corporation (BIC) and the Xhosa Development Corporation (XDC), it is possible to arrive at an extremely rough total figure. The BIC made 1,166 loans for new businesses between 1959 and 1973, the overwhelmingly major proportion having been granted after 1963. The XDC made 837 loans between 1966 and 1974. We can conclude that about 1,900 new businesses (mainly trading and service businesses) were launched between 1963 and 1974. However, this figure does not take into account business (for example, bank, finance and insurance companies and other businesses) not financed through the corporations. There is no available information on the number of such businesses. Despite all these difficulities, it would perhaps not be too wildly inaccurate to suggest a figure (including hawkers and speculators) of about 8,500 and 9,000 small businessmen in the Bantustans in 1974.

IV THE CONDITIONS OF DEVELOPMENT OF THE AFRICAN PETIT-BOURGEOISIE

It is quite apparent from the previous section that there has been a considerable increase in the size of the African petit-bourgeoisie.

What this account has not shown is the extremely important fact that Africans, within this class and its various fractions, are nearly always economically and in all other ways in a weaker position than their white counterparts. Thus, for example, in the different sectors of the new middle class, Africans receive lower salaries than whites, are in less skilled posts and lower on the hierarchy of authority. Again, in business Africans operate for the most part on a very small scale, are short of capital and credit and so on. Indeed, as I suggested earlier, much of the existing analysis of South Africa focuses on the inferior position of Africans as compared to whites in the class structure (e.g., Slovo, 1976).

While it would be quite wrong to neglect these features of the class structure, the preoccupation with these class differentials has led to a neglect of the conditions of development or change within the class structure. This, of course, is also the

Table 10. Rates of Growth of Business in Johannesburg Township, 1938–1969

(a) Including hawkers and speculators

	No.	Overall Rate of Growth	Average Rate of Growth per annum
1938	192	327.08%	19%
1955	820	105.24%	35%
1958	1,683		

(b) Excluding hawkers and speculators

	No.	Overall Rate of Growth	Average Rate of Growth per annum
1959	1,137		
1969	1,460	28.41%	2.4%

Note: Horrell gives 5,080 for 1952 and 6,477 for 1959, but these presumably include "hawkers and speculators."

Source: Hart, 1972, p. 116.

Table 11. Rates of Growth of African Businesses in the Reserves, 1936–1963

(a) Including hawkers and speculators

	No.	Overall Rate of Growth	Average Rate of Growth per annum
1936	556	148.2%	14.2%
1946	1,350	186.7%	32.1%
1952	3,871	55.8%	9.3%
1958	6,032		

(b) Excluding hawkers and speculators

	No.	Overall Rate of Growth	Average Rate of Growth per annum
1936	226	243.4%	24.3%
1946	838	182.3%	30.4%
1952	2,366	63.7%	10.6%
1958	3,875	18.0%	3.4%
1963	4,576		

Source: Hart, 1972, p. 112.

implication of my remarks in the Introduction. In this section, then, I want to suggest, in a highly tentative way, some of the conditions which have affected the economic situation and political allegiances of the African petit-bourgeoisie in the period stretching roughly from the mid 1960's to the present.

(a) The New Middle Class

It is clear that the fundamental condition of expansion of the new middle class was the expanded reproduction of capitalist production and its transition to the stage of monopoly capitalism in South Africa. This transition and the accompanying intensification of capital in production was stimulated by the World War II and continued with increasing momentum (and some interruption in 1960) into and throughout the 1960's. One effect produced by these changes was a transformation of the division of labor which put in issue, in new ways, the allocation of members of different racial groups to places in that division. (See Legassick, 1974a and 1974b.) This issue, which was particularly important in the 1948 election affected the division of labor both within industrial production and also the tertiary sector—that is, the sector of the new middle class. In the Introduction I referred to the State's intervention, on behalf of Afrikaners, in the process of allocation of agents into the new middle class. That intervention has, however, become modified.

In explaining that modification, it is necessary to refer to the continued extended reproduction of capital intensive production which has had, as one of its consequences, a relative decline in the ratio of labor-power to capital in production and, as already indicated, a relative increase in the tertiary sector occupations. The pattern of job allocation shows (a) both a relative decline of whites in the industrial work force and that they are predominantly clustered in the higher paid, high skilled jobs; and (b) that in the tertiary sector whites are concentrated in the higher paid, higher status, jobs, although Afrikaners, on the whole, occupay lower level jobs than English-speaking employees (see Van der Merwe, *et al.*, 1974). But the expansion of the tertiary sector has meant preeminently the expansion of the lower level jobs and it is precisely these jobs, for the most part, which have become available for Africans in conditions in which there has been both full employment of whites and, at the same time, considerable shortages of labor. The flow of Africans into these jobs has, from time to time, met with opposition from various white trade unions and also from certain factions within the ruling party. However, this notwithstanding and despite the powers of job reservation, on the whole, the state has not impeded the entry of Africans into the jobs in question.

The expanded reproduction of capitalist production has had other repercussive effects, two of which I want to refer to here. The changes in the division of labor already described and, in addition, the trend away from simple, unskilled work to the more complex semiskilled work in the factories, set up new demands for changes in the education of the work force. Clearly, in the tertiary sector (particularly in the service and sales categories, as well as others) a reasonable degree of competence in speaking the official language was a requisite; and, in other sectors (clerical, not to speak of administrative and managerial), competence in writing was necessary. Similarly since semiskilled industrial work normally requires some instruction on the job and communication in doing the work, some degree of literacy is essential.

Indeed, there was a massive expansion of primary school education (the unexpected effects of which were seen in the leading role and extensive participation of school pupils in the recent—June 1976—urban strikes, riots and demonstrations) and some expansion in both secondary school and university education for Africans beginning in the mid 1950's. One important effect of this expansion was the increase in the number of teachers, which I indicated above, and the creation of a whole series of connected administrative and organizational jobs.

The other point I want to touch upon concerns the separate development policies of the government that relate precisely to a particular conjuncture in which the expanded reproduction of monopoly capital in a specific phase of its development is a crucial condition. One spin-off of that policy has been the trend toward Africanization of new middle class occupations in the African townships inside the white areas and, above all, of the high level posts in the civil service of the Bantustans and also the assumption of managerial and similar jobs in the private sector within the Bantustans.

Thus, to sum up it can be said that certain conditions favorable to the entry of Africans into new middle class occupations emerged in the South Africa. That intrusion has, however, been limited by the virtual monopoly which whites hold over the upper regions of these occupations; and to a predominant extent Africans occupy the lower level jobs, that in those jobs devoid of managerial, coordinating and coercive functions, and in which the employee is unequivocally subject to an exploitative relationship—either as a productive wage-laborer giving up surplus value or as an unproductive wageearner giving up surplus labor. At the same time there has emerged a relatively small stratum of administrators, managers and executives.

(b) The Traditional Petit-Bourgeoisie

In this section I will deal first with the traditional petit-bourgeoisie in the white areas and then with its position in the Bantustan.

Since the early 1960's the State has introduced increasingly restrictive regulations governing African business outside of the Bantustans. The rationale for these restrictions has been the official policy that trading cannot be regarded as a "primary" right; it is merely a temporary opportunity and a means of obtaining experience for future trading in the Homelands. By 1973, the main regulations in force provided as follows:

(1) No African may occupy more than one business building. The building, after 1963, could not be erected by the businessman. He could only occupy one of the limited number of council erected buildings which, in the case of shops, could not exceed $2.3m^2$. There can be no freehold rights in fixed property.
(2) Africans cannot form partnerships or companies or run wholesale businesses.
(3) African traders may sell only "daily essential necessities" such as groceries and this excludes services such as petrol stations and dry cleaners.
(4) Trading permits expire annually and are only renewed by the Bantu Affairs Administration Board if the applicant for renewal is regarded as "a fit and proper person."

The effect of these regulations upon African businessmen is obvious—the smallness of the shops restricts the amount of stocks traders can carry; the absence of freehold rights precludes the possibilitiy of raising capital or of obtaining credit; the "one-man-one-business" regulation precludes the development of chain stores; the prohibition of partnerships or companies also limits growth possibilities; the exclusion from wholesale business ensures dependence on merchant capital and exclusion from expansion.

In discussing the conditions of development of the traditional petit-bourgeoisie in the Bantustans, three overlapping aspects must be considered—economic measures taken by the state which have had the effect of expanding that class, the political structures of the Bantustans and the economic relationship of other classes and class fractions to the African traditional petit-bourgeoisie. The point about these factors is that they establish the conditions which, *in the absence of a powerful national liberation movement,* render the petit-bourgeoisie utterly dependent upon the capitalist class and the State.

At the economic level, the State's intervention relates, first, to competition from white traders and second, to the function of providing capital. In regard to the former, the State has acted against the once powerful group of White Traders (to the point of their virtual elimination) in two different ways. First, in granting trading sites, the balance has shifted sharply in favor of Africans over the past ten to fifteen years.

Table 12. Grant of Trading Sites in the Reserves/Bantustans

	Total No. of Trading Sites Granted	Percentage Granted to Africans	Percentage Granted to Non-Africans
To 1948	5,063	59	41
1949–60	1,348	94	6
1961–62	274	99	1

Source: Hart, 1972.

Second, and more importantly, the corporations set up by the State (and financed partly by State funds and partly by deposits made by Africans, particularly the Bantustan legislative assemblies) have used their funds to purchase white businesses. By 1974, in the Transkei, the XDC had purchased 525 white-owned retail trading stations and 20 hotels. Of the trading stations, 350 had been purchased by Africans by 1973; the remainder were still in the possession of the XDC and were operating under African managers. Elsewhere in the Homelands, the BIC had purchased 139 white businesses by 1973 and sold 121 of these to Africans.

The method by which the Corporations made capital available to African businessmen was by means of loans. Between 1966 and 1975, the XDC granted 949 loans, amounting to R7.5 million, for retail, wholesale, catering and accommodation, transport, communication and storage businesses. The loans granted by the BIC between 1959 and 1973 amounted to R9.9 million. Of this amount, more than 85 percent were for trading establishments, 12½ percent for services concerns and about 2 percent for light manufacturing.

The operation of the Corporations, however, is rather more complicated than appears from this brief account. Thus Rogers (1976, p. 68) refers to a statement of the Managing Director of the BIC reported in the *Rand Daily Mail* (September 7, 1974) in whch he stated that between 1959 and 1974 the BIC had provided loans as follows:

African-owned enterprises: R14 million
Corporation-owned enterprises: R20 million
White-owned enterprises: R43 million.

Furthermore, according to Rogers (1976, p. 68), whites are granted loans (presumably for industrial enterprises) on better terms than those granted to Africans. (Indeed, for this very reason, African businessmen in the Venda Bantustan recently started their own business to finance the establishment of African businesses.) By mid 1974, 116 South African firms and 11 foreign firms had established enterprises in the Bantustans as agents of the BIC and XDC. These firms employed about 13,500 Africans and the capital involved amounted to R31,088,000.

Both the BIC and XDC were conducting business on a large scale according to Horrell (1974, pp. 210–214). The BIC reported in 1974 that it was involved in a large number of commercial undertakings—savings banks, wholesalers, retailers, storage, holiday resorts and so on; and, in addition, held a R700,000 investment in transport services. The XDC controlled 144 retail undertakings; and in addition, made a profit of R7,588,987 from its wholesale business in 1972–1973.

Thus, although the picture is far from clear, there seems little doubt that African commerical businesses are expanding and developing, but the corporations, in particular through wholesale business, appear to command considerable power in the commercial sector. At the same time, developments in the industrial sector are monopolized by capital foreign to the Bantustans. What this points to is development of small African business plus dependence.

In one sense the state corporations can be seen as a fraction of large-scale merchant capital exercising dominance over small traders. At the same time, the development of small trade appears to be opening up the possibility both of joint (black/white) investment in enterprises and of black traders obtaining access to capital loans and assistance from the private sector in South Africa. As yet neither of the processes appears to be far advanced, but in recent years it has been made clear by the South African Government and by the Bantustans that capital both through the corporations and "private funds donated direct to homeland leaders (i.e. not through their treasuries)" and therefore "not subject to the controls and audits associated with homeland government treasury funds" (Horrell, 1975, p. 147) was welcome. One important example of capital advancement for small trade from the private sector is the financial assistance given by the petrol and oil companies to African garage proprietors. What is clear is that, for the present, black commercial interests in the Bantustans are almost wholly dependent for capital and credit upon central State or white private capital. Perhaps nothing demonstrates the present dominance of the state corporations in this respect more than the fact "that African deposits in BIC savings banks have exceeded the loans provided to Africans by a considerable margin" (Rogers, 1976, p. 64; and see Horrell, 1973a, p. 40). There is no means available to the African petit-bourgeoisie of concentrating in their hands the small savings of large number of individuals.[3]

Finally, I want to refer briefly to the structure of political dependence of the petit-bourgeoisie. There is, as yet, no adequate analysis which situates the specific character of the Bantustan policy in the context of the phase of capitalist development in which it emerged. Whatever the explanation, however, what is clear is that the erection of the political structure of the Bantustans has extremely important consequences for the position of the African petit-bourgeoisie. Slovo has argued that the Bantustans represent an attempt to externalize the internal colonial relation ". . . in the shape of ethnic states, eventually having all the attributes of *formal* political independence" (Slovo, 1976, p. 137). This, however, misses the point, for although the independence *will* only be formal in the sense that the apparatuses of the Bantustans can only be regarded as specific "local" apparatuses of the central South African state, the crucial consideration is that the Bantustan policy gives to a section of the petit-bourgeoisie control of part, albeit a subordinate part, of the state aparatus.

It is important to stress both these aspects of the Bantustan political structure, since it is this, together with the economic relations of dependence to which I referred above, that determines the class situation of the African petit-bourgeoisie in the Bantustans. Thus, on the one hand, the legislative assemblies and executives with their various administrative departments (including police and army in the

Transkei) and judicial systems were created by the central state. The limits of their powers and operations are circumscribed by the South African state. On the other hand, despite the limited nature of the powers of these subordinate state structures, they are, nonetheless, instruments in the hands of the petit-bourgeoisie which provides some degree of control over productive resources (land and capital) and some means of stabilizing and securing their position. This is shown, on the one side, by the involvement of the Bantustan substates in investment policy, relations with the corporations, negotiations with the central government over the acquisition of land presently occupied by whites, the distribution of such land to Africans, the grant of trading licences and so on. On the other side, these substates are involved in political negotiation with the central government on a variety of issues, notably at present the issue of independence and the problem of the citizenship status of the members of various tribes who live in white South Africa; they exercise legislative functions and exert control over the inhabitants of the Bantustans by means of their own security forces in collaboration with the central state forces and so on.

What we have done in the above discussion is to suggest that there are economic and political structural conditions which provide powerful mechanisms by which the African petit-bourgeoisie in the Bantustans has become linked, in a subordinate and dependent position, to South African capital and the central state, and which, at the same time, provide the conditions for the limited development and reproduction of that class.

V THE POLITICAL POSITION OF THE AFRICAN PETIT-BOURGEOISIE

It is extremely difficult to present a coherent picture of the political position of the African *new middle class* in the urban areas outside the Bantustans. There is no reason to suppose that the different components which go to make up this class constitute a political unity or, indeed, that all of these components constitute a force in the political sense. Given the absence of organized representation of the African new middle class and, therefore, the virtual absence of declared political and ideological positions, their political role must, for the most part, remain obscure.[4] On the whole, this new middle class seems to have been relatively quiescent in the 1960's and in the early 1970's. In the recent urban mass strikes and demonstrations, it had no unified political position; thus, for example, a section of African teachers supported the mass movement, while a further section opposed it. On the other hand, there are suggestions that there was some support for the demonstrations and strikes from among tertiary sector workers.

The African traditional petit-bourgeoisie within the white areas has taken an extremely narrow political stance focused largely on its own economic conditions.

Nothing could be clearer than the racial discrimnatory nature of the restrictions I referred to above on the traders and yet, at least in the last decade or so, the direction of the political line of African petty businessmen seems to have been far removed from any kind of direct challenge to the structure of racial domination (or internal colonialism). The main thrust of their politics has been, on the one hand, to demand the removal of the restrictions imposed upon their trading and business rights *within* the townships. One part of this, it appears, has taken the form of their participation in the Urban Bantu Councils, which incidentally aided the authorities against the demonstrators in the June to September 1976 events. These Councils, established by the State, are of a purely advisory and formal nature functioning within the framework of Apartheid. Another part of their activities has been channeled through the National African Chamber of Commerce, the Johannesburg and District traders association and in the journal *African Businessman,* first published in 1961.

The political position of this petit-bourgeoisie, which I suggest is the outcome of both their (limited) economic development and the absence of a mass base due to the virtual eclipse of the organized liberation movement, can be indicated by some of the statements made by individuals in the recent years.

Addressing the annual conference of the National African Chamber of Commerce in July 1976 (i.e., during the height of the urban struggles), the president called for measures to improve the lot of the black businessman: greater economic rights for Africans in urban areas, lifting of the prevailing restrictions on African businessmen, the planning and building of modern shopping centers and practical and relevant training for black businessmen by semigovernment agencies (*Weekly Star,* July 17, 1976).

Again, in July, 1976, A. Radebe of the National Development and Management Foundation called for better understanding, ''approachability and communication'' between white and black (*Weekly Star,* July 17, 1976).

Finally, a leading African trader, addressing a conference stated:

> If black businessmen can move out of the small general dealers set up into a diversified business area, then the black community will see an emergence of a middle class which will serve as a bulwark against any political uprising in this country. (Horrell, 1976, p. 194.)

Another aspect of the political stance of the African businessmen in white areas has related to the agitation by white concerns (large-scale merchant capital) to be permitted to establish surpermarkets in the African residential areas; with rising African purchasing power, merchant capital has begun to seek to enter into partnership with African businessmen. These moves have been strenously opposed by African traders who insist that the government should maintain its apartheid position on this question.

This line is beginning to receive a response. In 1975, the Minister of Bantu Aministration stated that it was the intention of the government to bring the position of African traders inside the townships, as closely as possible, into line with the procedures followed in the case of white traders in white areas. According to Horrell:

> Traders would . . . be permitted to trade in a larger range of commodities, and also to establish more than one business on the same premises. Partnerships would also be allowed; and where traders had already established a business in a homeland, they would be permitted to retain their existing businesses in the urban residential area indefinitely. The ownership of buildings on leasehold stands for business in African residential areas would now be possible again. . . . (Horrell, 1975, p. 194.)

The white Associated Chamber of Commerce has recently (see *Weekly Star,* November 21, 1976) expressed its strong support for the demands made by African businessmen to remove the restrictions inhibiting their development. This move must be seen as a further step in the process of incorporating African traders and businessmen. The very precariousness of their political position—they have no means of independently organizing a mass base—coupled with the possibilities of rapid economic advancement if restrictions are removed and capital from white sources becomes available, serves to tie them more firmly than ever to established power.

It, of course, does not follow that, in the event of different conditions emerging (for example, the rise of the national liberation movement, economic competition from white traders, etc.), the political position of this fraction of the traditional petit-bourgeoisie will not again alter.

It is, however, the petit-bourgeoisie—both the traditional and, given the administrative/bureaucratic structure, important sections of the new petit-bourgeoisie which is linked to the former—in the Bantustans which is of prime importance. This is so for two reasons. First, because the Bantustans stand at the very center of government policy, they represent the mechanisms for the reproduction and control of the expanding and oversized (from the point of view of capital) reserve army of labor; the establishment and reproduction of the African petit-bourgeoisie is only an effect of this. The second reason is that, given that armed struggle is seen by the liberation movements to be the only possible path toward the transformation of the present structure of South Africa (Slovo, 1976), politics within the Bantustans become of critical political relevance to the national liberation struggle.

I outlined in the previous section the conditions which make the Bantustan petit-bourgeoisie dependent on the state and which, at the same time, give them a vested interest in working the Bantustan system. The way in which the system can be worked will depend, in part, upon the way in which the class or classes in charge of the Bantustan substates relate to the rural masses.

Slovo (1976), as I indicated above, has argued that the petit-bourgeoisie in the Bantustans is incapable of establishing a mass base. There can be no doubt that under the conditions existing in the Bantustans, the plight of the impoverished mass of petty producers can only deteriorate further—the Bantustan governments are not and will not be possessed of the resources needed to better the conditions of the rural producers. While it cannot be assumed that the economic condition of the rural producers will automatically produce a revolutionary movement of the peasantry, nonetheless, the insertion of a revolutionary political presence, whether in the form of guerrilla units or otherwise, may well, given these conditions provoke a rising tide of opposition against the Bantustan regimes. In that event, given the dependence of the petit-bourgeoisie on the central state, it is probable that it will be unable to ally itself with such opposition and turn against the South African state. Therefore, the only alternative will be resort to increased repression with the aid of the South African state (this, indeed, is what Mantanzima has already done in the Transkei) in order to maintain positions already attained.

It has been argued by others,[5] however, that there are two main factions of the petit-bourgeoisie within the Bantustans: one faction (represented mainly by the Transkeian petit-bourgeoisie), which owes its formation to state action and is totally dependent on the central state and thus without any mass base or the possibility of mass support; as against this collaborationist faction there is another faction reflected by the Buthelezi trend, whose *origin* was independent of the central state. This faction has the *possibility* of securing support from the masses, both in the urban areas and the Bantustans, for a policy of reform. So far as the Transkeian petit-bourgeoisie is concerned, the comments made in the previous paragraph apply—it will merely become more repressive. If it is accepted (however problematic it may be) that a section of the petit-bourgeoisie is not so tightly locked into a structure of economic and political dependence as to render it incapable of allying itself with the mass movement, then the question which arises is under what conditions will such an alliance occur?

It has been suggested by O'Meara and Innes (see footnote 5) that there are already in existence the conditions which separate this faction of the petit-bourgeoisie from the state and lead it to seek support from the masses for a limited program of reform.

The first condition is the presence of mass struggle. The worker strikes against the migrant labor system in Namibia in 1972, the massive strike of African workers for higher wages in Durban and elsewhere in 1973 and, above all, the protracted urban struggles between June and September in 1976, signal the renewal of mass struggles and the mass movement which lay more or less dormant between 1963 and 1972.

The second condition, it is argued, is that the Bantustan policy has proved or is beginning to prove itself incapable of satisfying the interests of the petit-bourgeoisie; that is to say, it has reached its limits and can no longer create space for the growth and development of important sections of the African petit-bourgeoisie. Thus the structural conditions for an alliance of the petit-bourgeoisie with the rural masses and urban working class is emerging.

This conclusion is extremely problematical on two grounds. First, while undoubtedly the mass struggles have changed the political complexion of South Africa, these struggles have not yet taken on a form and a peristence which can in any sense be considered as an already present organized power capable of providing the petit-bourgeoisie with a stable base of support. Second, given the role of the state corporations and the supply of foreign capital (which may find additional inducements to go to areas of labor intensive production) referred to above, there seems to be no reason at all to assume that, so far as the petit-bourgeoisie is concerned, the Bantustan policy has reached its limits.

So long as the state continues to secure the position of the African petit-bourgeoisie and provide for its development (even though limited), there seems to be little reason for a shift in the allegiance of this class, *particularly in the absence of an organized and powerful opposition force*. But even if such a force arises, the specific dependence of the petit-bourgeoisie on the state on the basis of its control of the substate apparatus may still limit its response to the use of this as a means of increased repression. Indeed, the rise of the armed struggle may solidify the dependence of the African petit-bourgeoisie and, therefore, its alliance with capital and the state.

The conclusion must be drawn, therefore, that in the *present conjuncture,* at least in the Bantustans where its political position is of much greater importance than in the white urban areas, the African petit-bourgeoisie stands, not merely outside the mainstream of the liberation movement but as a force of reaction.

FOOTNOTES

1. For a theoretical discussion of the concept of internal colonialism and some of the difficulties and obscurities in the notion see, Wolpe (1975). In particular, the argument is advanced in that paper that the existing discussions of internal colonialism tend to obscure both the class structure and the nature of the domination of noncapitalist modes of production by the capitalist modes within the social formation. On this, see also Wolpe (1972). Legassick (1974 and 1974a) also deals with related issues. Slovo (1976) does not directly refer to the above papers, but he appears to attempt a more rigorous theoretical formulation of the internal colonial concept by dealing with the points raised in them. His discussion does not, however, in this respect take the argument much further.

2. Reproduced in Lewin, 1967, p. 55.

3. In this brief discussion of the dependent position of the commerical petit-bourgeoisie, I have not dealt with their relationship to either petty commodity producers or to the small class of larger (perhaps even capitalist) argicultural producers. For a discussion of these classes see O'Meara and Innes (1977). There is no doubt that agricultural producers were an important source of revenue for white traders who, exercising credit controls over producers, were able by means of unequal exchange to accrue large profits. For example, producers, lacking storage facilities, were obliged to sell the whole of their crop to the trader

at low prices only to be obliged to purchase back, at high prices, the same crop for their subsistence at a later date. There seems to be little evidence of the position in the current period.

4. The most articulate public expression in the recent past, of a political/ideological standpoint, has emerged from the black power movement, which appears to have been a movement of students/intellectuals but it would be extremely difficult to connect this movement in any direct way with the new middle class.

5. By Dan O'Meara, Rob Davies and Duncan Innes at a Seminar on the Transkei in which the argument in Innes and O'Meara (1977) were further elaborated. The argument is based largely on analysis of statements by Buthelazi which refer to the masses and their demands. There are, undoubtedly, differences in the political and ideological stances of different fractions of the petit-bourgeoisie and these are reflected in some of the statements made by the leaders. On the other hand, the main burden of the statements reflects the type of involvement and working of the Bantustan structures within the framework of the existing structure in the terms I have suggested in the text.

REFERENCES

African National Congress, ANC, (1969), *Strategy and Tactics of the African National Congress,* adopted by 3rd Consultative Conference of the ANC, Tanzania.

Brandel-Syrier, M. (1971), *Reeftown Elite,* Routledge and Kegan Paul.

Bullock, P. (1974), "Defining Productive Labor for Capital," *Conference of Socialist Economists,* Bulletin, No. 9.

Bureau for Economic Research re Bantu Development (1975), *Bophuthatswana,* Economic Revue, Benbo.

Carchedi, G. (1975), "On the Economic Identification of the New Middle Class," *Economy and Society,* Vol. 4, No. 1.

Hart; G.P. (1972), *Africa Entrepreneurship,* Institute of Social and Economic Research, Rhodes University.

Horowitz, R. (1967), *The Political Economy of South Africa,* Weidenfeld and Nicolson.

Horrell, M. (1973a), *The African Homelands of South Afraica,* S.A. Institute of Race Relations.

Horrell, M. (1973b), *South Africa: Basic Facts and Figures,* S.A. Institute of Race Relations.

Horrell, M. (1974–1975), *A Survey of Race Relation in South Africa,* Annual Survey, South Africa Institute of Race Relations.

Kuper, L. (1965), *An African Bourgeoisie,* Yale University Press.

Legassic, M. (1974a), "South Africa: Capital Accumulation and Violence," *Economy and Society,* Vol. 3, No. 3.

Legassick, M. (1974b), "Legislation, Ideology and Economy in Post-1948 South Africa," *Journal of Southern Africa Studies,* Vol. 1, No. 1.

Lewin, J. (1967), *The Struggle for Racial Equality,* Longmans.

Lipton, M. (1972), "The South African Census and the Bantustan Policy," *The World Today,* Vol. 28, No. 6.

Maasdorp, G. G. (1974), *Economic Development Strategy in the African Homelands,* S.A. Institute of Race Relations.

Malan, T. and Hattingh, P.S. (1975), *Swart Tuislands in Suid-Afrika,* Africa Institute.

Maree, J. and de Vos, P.J. (1975), *Underemployment, Poverty and Migrant Labor in the Transkei and Ciskei,* S.A. Institute of Race Relations.

Moolman, J.H. and Leistner, G.M.E. (1974), *Bophuthatswana,* Africa Institute.

O'Meara, D. and Innes, D. (1977), "Discussion Notes on Class Formation and Ideology in South Africa: The Transkei Region," *Review of African Political Economy*. (Forthcoming.)

Poulantzas, N. (1975), *Classes in Contemporary Capitalism*, New Left Books.

Rogers, B. (1976), *Divide and Rule: South Africa's Bantustans*, International Defence and Aid Fund.

Slovo, J. (1976), "South Africa—No Middle Road," in Davidson, B., Slovo, J. and Wilkinson, A. R. *Southern Africa: The New Politics of Revolution*, Penguin Books.

South African Communist Party, SACP, (1962), *The Road to South African Freedom*, London: Ellis Bowles.

Thompson L. and Butler, J. (1975), *Change in Contemporary South Africa*, University of California Press.

Touissant (1976), "Black Bankers—Friends or Enemies of Liberation?," *Africa Communist*, No. 64, First Quarter.

Van Der Merwe, H. W. *et al.*, (1974), *White South African Elites*, Juta and Company.

Wolpe, H. (1972), "Capitalism and Cheap Labor-power in South Africa: From Segregation to Apartheid," *Economy and Society*, Vol. 1, No. 4.

Wolpe, H. (1975), "The Theory of Internal Colonialism: The South African Case," in Oxaal, I. *et al.* (eds.), *Beyond the Sociology of Development*, London: Routledge and Kegan Paul.

Other References

Department of Information, The Progess of the Bantu Peoples Toward Nationhood."

Department of Information, A State in the Making: Progess in the Transkei.

Fifty Years of South African Statistics, Pretoria: Government Printer.

Financial Mail, 1973–1976.

Quarterly Bulletin of Statistics, Pretoria: Government Printer.

South African Statistics, Pretoria: Government Printer.

"South Africa's Bantustans," *Third World*, Vol. 2, No. 6.

Weekly Star, 1973–1976.

TRANSNATIONALS AND CHEAP LABOR IN THE PERIPHERY

Raúl Trajtenberg, LATIN AMERICAN INSTITUTE OF TRANSNATIONAL STUDIES

As the big corporations began to consolidate their power in the capitalist system at the turn of the century, the expansion to the periphery followed a very clear pattern, closely associated with the predominant international division of labor: specialization of dependent countries on primary production determined the activities of emerging transnationals in that region. At the same time their own strategy of oligopolistic control of markets forced them to expand abroad in order to develop cheap and secure sources of raw materials. This case of expansion dominated the first half of the century and, although declining afterward, still explains today more than a third of foreign direct investment in the periphery.

A second very important situation rose when some underdeveloped countries set their course on an import-substituting type of industrialization under the cover of the twenty years of relative weakness of the central system from 1930 onward. The resulting adaptation that the international division of labor had to undergo would not leave out the big corporations that were becoming increasingly transnational. Even if present from the very early stage of this process, a wave of acquisition of local firms, and of new investment beginning at the end of the fifties, consolidated their dominance of the key industrial sectors producing for the local market in underdeveloped countries.

A complex set of factors explain their quick expansion into the semi-industrialized periphery, ranging from the general external intercapitalist competition raised by European and Japanese revival, to protectionist barriers originated in various class alliances and political regimes in certain countries. As a result, this second type of expansion became the leading one, explaining in the early seventies about half the foreign direct investment in the periphery.

During the 1960's a third type of capital penetration of peripheral countries began to grow, which was of a very different character from the other two. Transnational enterprises started operations in certain countries for the manufacture of goods for export in order to benefit from the particularly favorable conditions offered by highly productive but low-cost labor.

The leading characteristic of the present case is not simply the availability of cheap labor and its utilization by the transnationals. Low wages are a universal feature of peripheral countries and any direct foreign investment automatically benefits from low-cost labor. What characterizes this form of internationalization is that the possibility of using cheap labor becomes the decisive factor and determines its basic character. Thus, a worker employed in the extraction or processing of natural resources is also low-cost labor and the transnational has an obvious interest in earning the resulting additional profits; yet, the primary motive for the foreign investment was to secure the resources in question and the resultant monopoly income. Similarly, in the semi-industrialized countries wages are low enough for certain goods produced by subsidiaries for local consumption to generate additional earnings; yet, the primary aim of direct foreign investment in this case is defense or penetration of protected markets and the monopoly income provided by the defensive barriers, rather than any super profits(which would be sought for anyway). In the type of investment discussed in this paper the motivating factor is the low wages themselves, and it is these that determine the strategy of the transnational enterprise. The additional earnings obtained may be retained in the transnational, or they may be wholly or partly dispersed, if there is sufficient competition in the industry, by being transferred to the consumer (mainly in the developed country), as happens when technical innovations become widely adopted.

The main interest of this internationalization model is that it offers a new insight into the role of the periphery in the evolution of capitalism at the center. The incursion of the transnationals in this model implies in some sections of industry a partial reversal of the prevailing pattern of technological change, with consequent effects on class relationships in the central economies. It is no longer a matter of seeking to reconcile a rising trend in wages with labor-saving technological change by simultaneously increasing labor efficiency in routine repetitive tasks and substituting mechanized or automated operations for those at present done manually or mentally. Nor is it the usual case where wage increases are forestalled by lowering the price of consumer goods, through technological innovation or the action of favorable national and international relative prices, etc.

The new type, on the contrary, means a rediscovery of labor that can be used in a way that the modern evolution of capitalism has made impossible at the center. Thus, the approach will be from the opposite direction, i.e., by isolating the highly labor-intensive processes and transferring them to areas where labor can be used with no less intensity. The effect is equivalent to what would happen in the central country if hours and speed of work could be increased and, particularly, wages reduced. There is some analogy with the conditions prevailing in the early decades of the Industrial Revolution, when intensive accumulation coincided with extensive pauperization.

This analogy must not of course be pushed too far. Workers in the countries receiving this type of investment earn more than they would have earned, *ceteris paribus,* in their ordinary occupations. But the phenomenon must be judged in its true dimension, which is the worldwide scale of transnational planning and the deliberate intention of replacing one labor force by another cheaper one.

In the past industrialized countries were able to draw on these vast reserves of labor power for their own growth, through huge imports of unskilled labor. One of the main effects of this mass immigration has been to reduce labor costs in the central economies by depressing wage levels or at least slowing their rise. At the same time a low-cost segment was appended to the labor force by discriminatory practices against immigrants with regard to access to employment, working conditions and employment stability. Although the recent depression has demonstrated the extraordinary anticyclical effectiveness of such marginal labor for the central economies, the system has had definite limitations owing to the social and political imbalances created, overcrowding of the environment by excessive industrial concentrations, and, more fundamentally, the fact that the way in which the labor market is organized is resistant to excessive market segmentation of the labor force within the developed economies. The type of internationalization discussed in this paper implies precisely a movement in the opposite direction, with the decisive advantage that it completely dissociates home country and receiving country labor markets so that the differences in the wages paid by the same capitalist unit are as great as possible. Thus seen, little of the humanitarian touch with which Western ideology disguises this shift remains. "Taking the work to the workers" is simply a more productive and less troublemaking way of exploiting the labor force in the periphery.

Confirmation that the new trend among the transnationals is closely related to the decline in high levels of immigration to the developed countries (or more industrialized parts of them) is provided by two facts. First, according to ILO (1976b, Chapter 8), the most intense labor migration has occurred in Europe (according to ILO figures there were six million migrant workers in 1974, three-quarters of which lived in France and West Germany) and it is precisely the European transnationals that have been most reluctant—although not totally adverse—to embark on direct investment taking advantage of cheap labor (Franko, 1975, pp. 7–10). On the other hand, the Mexican border industrialization program, which is designed to take advantage of Mexico's cheap labor by installing assembly plants south of the Rio Grande, was started and expanded rapidly at a time when the migration of Mexican *braceros* to the United States was interrupted.

It is clear therefore that the new element is not the existence of wage differences and their exploitation in primary sector productions in underdeveloped countries and marginally in the industrial sector in developed countries. It is the new ability of the big corporations to reorganize production in a way that takes advantage of them.* The arrival of the transnationals at the stage of maturity has opened the way for such reorganization. But, as we shall see later, this strategy is severely limited by various constraints.

The very interesting implications of this expansion pattern concern not only the way it affects capital-labor class relations: also intercapitalist relations are seriously modified, in particular those which happen through frontiers. In fact, any pattern of internationalization that implies direct control by the central classes over productive capital in the periphery usually leads to a weakening of local bourgeoisies, however they react: they tend to vanish when absorbed into the managerial structure of the transnational, they become blurred in identity through forced joint ventures, they are chased into the circulation sphere and accessory industrial sectors, etc. In the present case, as a consequence of the strict vertical integration, which means not only centralized control but even a material absorption into a certain production process, the weakening of local capital (or the prevention of its growth) is much stronger.

The most extreme situation, even if improbable, has conceptual consequences in changing the overall pattern of relations between center and periphery. In our view, the concept of dependence, a crucial organizing conceptual category, belongs to the sphere of ownership relations at the level of intercapitalist relations—i.e., not the most general level. This means that the degree and form of dependence will be no other than the degree and form of subordination of local capitalist classes to the central ones in their joint codetermination over the labor force of the periphery (Vigorito, 1971). If local industrial capital happens to be directly replaced by central capital, the relevant concepts of analysis revert to the main capital-labor relation, a direct relation through frontiers (central capital/peripheric labor), with no mediation by local capital. At the highest degree of dependence, the concept becomes nonoperative.

1. ACCUMULATION FOR CHEAP LABOR IN THE PERIPHERY

If one disregards the innumerable minor differences and combinations, two main variants appear according to the way in which transnationals make use of cheap labor in the underdeveloped countries. The first and most important is the establishment of plants in certain countries to manufacture goods which represent merely one stage in the vertically integrated production line that is internationally controlled by the firm (Michalet, 1976, pp. 23–29). This stage is typically one that involves intensive use of unskilled labor and very limited investment in fixed assets. It generally relates to the assembly of parts imported by the firm from plants in other countries under its control, or the production of articles of a simple type. The end-product is exported to other plants owned by the firm, usually in the home country. From the transnational's point of view, it represents a relocation of a given stage of production inside its worldwide internal flow of goods. From the point of view of the receiving country, it is the insertion of a production sector ranging from almost total insulation from the rest of the economy (when nearly all inputs are imported and the production is exported) to relatively weak integration in that economy (where there is a system of local subcontracting for some of the inputs).

The effect of this variant is visible statistically in terms of subsidiaries created, direct foreign investment, and increase in manufactured exports.

This form of internationalization is particularly frequent in some areas of the metal industries, such as the assembly of machines and electronic equipment, but is also common in the manufacture of photographic equipment, readymade clothing, and the finishing and packaging of various articles. The product may be an intermediate or a final good.

The other major variant is where the transnational organizes production in underdeveloped countries by small local firms or craftsmen, generally of labor-intensive consumer goods for which mechanization is difficult. In this case, part or all the inputs may be imported or some raw materials obtained locally.[1] The final product is generally, but not necessarily, exported to the home country of the transnational or to other industrialized countries under its brand name or trade mark. The transnational may merely act as a marketing agent, but generally does more: it may establish a production program based on advance purchases, standardize product specifications, promote a degree of uniformity and quality control, and provide needed finance for independent producers. This pattern is frequently found in textiles, clothing, toy-making, some kinds of electrical appliances, etc.[2] Some writers (e.g., Hone, 1974) consider this form of internationalization to be of major importance in explaining the explosion of manufacturing for export in some countries of South-East Asia.

The effect of this second variant is only visible statistically in the development of exports of certain manufactured goods by some countries. It does not necessarily involve the creation of manufacturing subsidiaries or direct foreign investment. It does not even require the intervention of any manufacturing corporation—purely commercial corporations or international trading firms may establish the link between the underdeveloped country's products and the industry and consumption in the developed countries. All these forms may coexist.

In reality, owing to the influence of many factors, the range of variants is extremely wide. Some direct investment may be combined with subcontracting to local firms or craftsmen, and manufacturing may be combined with marketing and financial responsibilities. Where direct foreign investment occurs, the structure of ownership may take very different forms, including both outright ownership and the whole gamut of joint ventures. The latter may involve purely formal arrangements for participation by local capital (corresponding to the first variant) or minority shareholding by the transnational to provide access to brand names, trade marks and marketing channels (comparable with the second variant). In South Korea, for example, the percentage of joint ventures is overwhelming (93 percent in manufacturing) and covers practically all types of direct foreign investment (Jo, 1976, pp. 17–21).

The picture is sometimes complicated by the fact that host country governments may require a given quota of local purchases as a stimulus to industrialization. These policies sometimes produce the desired effect of increased use of local inputs. In other cases the transnationals maintain their policies of importing inputs but buy local articles in addition, completely alien to their line of production, in order to comply with the quota, and then resell them (Michalet, 1975, p. 29). Nevertheless, whatever the precise arrangements, the transnationals retain full control of their production and marketing in the underdeveloped countries.[3]

The great variety of situations and the fact that this is a recent phenomenon create serious problems for any evaluation of the significance and direction of this type of expansion by transnationals. Obviously, not all direct foreign investment is based solely on the utilization of cheap labor, even in the countries with which it is most typically associated. Sometimes part of the investment is attributable to the presence of natural resources exploited by foreign enterprises. Sometimes it is attributable to the existence of an internal market that is attractive for investment of the import-substitution type or has already attracted such investment. In any case a growth of internal markets to some extent follows the entry of the transnationals, whatever the motive for entry. In South Korea for example, 58 percent of all direct foreign investment up to 1968 was for the internal market, and 41 percent of it was of the type discussed in this paper. The latter percentage rose to 86 percent during the period 1969–1974, but this did not prevent 16 percent of the total investment in 1974 from being directed to securing internal markets (Jo, 1976, pp. 11–13).

Furthermore, the existence of the second variant mentioned leads logically to the conclusion that some types of international activities may become very substantial without being necessarily associated with direct foreign investment, or may correlate poorly with changes in the latter. The figures for exports of manufactured goods give a rough idea of both variants together, but the exporting activities of local firms acting independently are also included in the figures. It is not therefore surprising that discussion of this subject is plagued by uncertainties.

A few overall figures will give an idea of the steep increase in this type of expansion, showing at the same time that its incidence is still marginal compared with total foreign investment. The indirect character of this indicator must be kept in mind.

If we take South Korea, Hong Kong, Singapore and Taiwan, which are the Asian countries generally regarded as typical examples, total net assets coming from the DAC countries (OECD data, 1972 and 1975) rose from 696 million dollars in 1967 to 2,550 million in 1973, representing an increase in these countries' share in the Asian total from 13.9 percent to 24.2 percent, and an increase in their share in the total for all underdeveloped countries from 2.0 percent to 4.4 percent, with increasing participation in manufacturing activities. The value of exports to developed countries from the first three countries mentioned increased tenfold in ten years, reaching 4,060 million dollars in 1972 (UNCTAD, 1975, p. 17). And their exports doubled in the two following years.[4]

The other prototype case is the Mexican "in-bond" assembly industry (*industria maquiladora*). Bernal Sahagún (1976, p. 182) quotes official sources showing that 429 enterprises with total assets of 63 million dollars were located on the Mexican border in 1974 and engaged in activities covered by the present discussion, plus a further 26 enterprises well inside Mexico. Half of the plants were making electrical or electronic equipment and one quarter were in the footwear and clothing branches (Bernal Sahagún, 1976, p. 184). The whole industry had grown up in the preceding decade. According to UNCTAD figures (1975, p. 17), Mexican exports rose at an average rate of 16.9 percent over the period 1962–1972, though only part of this can be attributed to the cheap labor form of internationalization. (It must be remembered that Mexico is basically a case of penetration by the transnationals in association with an import substitution process and that some types of exports by those transnationals are a marginal consequence.)

Evidence from another angle is provided by the statistics of the U.S. Tariff Commission (1970) on imports of goods assembled abroad by subsidiaries covered by exemptions from the customs tariffs. These also show a steep rise: between 1966 and 1970 imports under section 807.00 from underdeveloped countries rose from 61 million dollars to 500 million, of which 42 percent pertains to Mexico, 24 percent to Hong Kong and 17 percent to Taiwan.

Certain country studies provide some details on the impact of the expansion. For South Korea, Jo (1976, p 4 ff) gives a total of 723 million dollars for 949 direct foreign investment projects approved between 1962 and 1974. The speed of the increase was tremendous. The annual average rose from 6 million dollars over the period 1962–1966 to 36 million in 1967–1971 and then to 172 million in 1972–1974 (the last three-year period representing 74 percent of the cumulative total up to 1974). This acceleration coincides with the recent predominance of the foreign investment directed to cheap labor. At the same time it coincides with a shift in the country of origin: at the beginning of the period the bulk of the investment was American (82 percent up to 1968); at the end of 1974, the cumulative total represented 65 percent for Japan and 28 percent for the United States. Seventy-five percent of this direct foreign investment was in manufacturing, half being distributed over textiles, clothing, electrical equipment and electronics. For Hong Kong, the government estimated a total of 161 enterprises in 1970—half of them divided about equally between electronics and clothing—with total fixed assets of 400 million dollars in manufacturing, almost all invested since 1960. Approximately 50 percent came from the United States and 25 percent from Japan. (Hong Kong Commerce and Industry Department, 1971). For Taiwan, the United Nations (1971, p. 33) indicate a total investment in manufacturing of 270 million dollars over the period 1952–1969, with 60 percent coming from the United States and 21 percent from Japan. For Singapore, IBRD data (1973, p. 6) give a total of 1,800 million dollars of gross fixed assets in manufacturing in 1972, of which one third came from the United States, another third from the Netherlands and United Kingdom together, and 6 percent from Japan.

The cases mentioned above are those which are best known, but the pattern of expansion in pursuit of low wages can be seen in other areas and countries as well, with a rising trend in some of them. For example, van Houten (1973) indicates that there were about twenty assembly enterprises in Jamaica at the beginning of the present decade, exporting 15 million dollars' worth annually. In Haiti also, there were assembly plants which increased exports of manufactures to developed countries from 6.2 million dollars in 1962 to 33.1 million in 1972 and employed a fifth of the urban workers.[5] North Africa performs a similar geographic and economic function vis-à-vis Europe. Recent information (*Le Monde,* August 13, 1976) reports the establishment of 135 enterprises in Tunisia of a similar type.

In spite of its relatively more rapid rate of growth in recent years, this expansion of transnationals' activity is still relatively marginal, and the basic question (discussed later) as to whether it can be expected to develop so much as to become a pivot for a new international division of labor is still open. For example, total American investment in the manufacturing sector of underdeveloped countries rose from 3,525 million dollars in 1966 to 11,147 million in 1975 (Whichard and Friedlin, 1976, p. 46), which is an annual increase of 13.6 percent. For the DAC countries together, total net assets in the underdeveloped countries rose from 33,100 million dollars at the end of 1967[6] to 58,200 million at the end of 1973 (OECD, 1972 and 1975). In view of this, there is no doubt that internationalization in pursuit of low-cost labor is still quite marginal in comparison with the mass of expansion directed toward control of import-substitution processes. If measures are taken in terms of the mass of labor employed, hence value created in the periphery, the importance of the case under discussion would be somewhat higher: primary production and import-subtituting industrialization are of course less labor-intensive than cheap labor-oriented expansion. However, by and large this cheap labor case would still be a minor one.

The present limited character of the new form can be seen also from an analysis of statistics on the transnationals according to their chief markets. According to Franko (1975, p. 8), only 95 out of 1,664 subsidiaries of European transnationals studied (or 5.7 percent) reported exports as their principal market in 1971. The proportion was slightly higher in the case of British transnationals (118 subsidiaries out of 1,962 or 6 percent), but substantially higher in the Japanese (92 out of 435 or 21.1 percent). Apart from the last case, it is clear that the new type of expansion was quite limited, particularly if only subsidiaries mainly exporting from underdeveloped countries are counted (24 British and 29 other European). Vaupel and Curhan (1974, p. 376) estimate that in 1967 only 5.7 percent of American and 7.5 percent of European and Japanese manufacturing subsidiaries had exports as their main market, though the figure was 27 percent for the Japanese if only investment in South-East Asia is considered. Similarly, Belli and Maley (1974, pp. 28–29) indicated that only 10 percent of the sales of American manufacturing subsidiaries in underdeveloped countries went to export markets in 1967–1972 (20–25 percent for subsidiaries in Asia and the Pacific).

The fact that the new type of expansion is only at an early stage is also shown by its concentration in very few receiving countries and the limited trade flows created with the metropolitan countries. For example, UNCTAD data (1975) indicate the following industry groups as having a sizeable and increasing share of manufactured exports of the underdeveloped countries: clothing (2,005 million dollars or 20 percent of the total in 1972, average annual growth of 24 percent over the preceding 10 years); metal products, electrical and transport equipment (1,610 million dollars or 16 percent of the total in 1972, annual average growth 33 percent); miscellaneous industries, i.e., toys, tape recorders, furs, travel goods, plastic materials, etc. (950 million dollars or 9 percent of the total in 1972, annual average growth 23 percent). The high concentration will be noted in these three groups, which are closely bound up with the type of expansion of the transnationals under discussion. As regards clothing, half of the total consisted of exports from Hong Kong. For metal products and electrical and transport equipment, half was made up of United States imports from Hong Kong, Mexico and Singapore. In the ''Miscellaneous'' group, over one third were exports from Hong Kong to the United States.

The following pages will analyze the factors conditioning the viability of cheap-labor oriented expansion and explain why and how this new form has developed. In the conventional literature on the subject the discussion is dominated by the considerations of the material conditions that permit this situation to arise and develop. Thus, technology restrictions, transport costs, infrastructural facilities and the like get the best part of the attention. However, in this case, as in any other where significant changes on the pattern of development are involved, attention should be brought also, and mainly, to the analysis of the class fractions affected by these changes—i.e., how their interests are affected and what power would they have to stimulate, deter or alter this pattern of expansion.

2. FACTORS CONDITIONING THE ACCUMULATION

The decisive element in the cheap labor form of penetration is certainly the increased profit-making capacity obtainable by paying lower wages to workers with a comparable level of productivity—or where the difference between wage levels is in any case greater than that between productivity levels.

Basically this increased rate of profit is produced by an increased rate of surplus value. While there is some production of absolute surplus value since workers have a longer working day, the main thrust is in a peculiar form of production of relative surplus value—shifting production geographically in order to replace one labor force by another with lower value.

The point, however, is not merely higher production of surpluses at the subsidiary; surpluses must also show an improvement at the level of the transnational as a whole, where other factors come into the calculation. The enterprise must also be able to retain the new surpluses as corporate profit, without having them taxed away or withheld in the country of origin or destination, or taken over by other capitalist groups.

With these elements in mind, we shall review a series of questions that are basic to the production and appropriation of increased surplus.

Low wages

The difference in wages at an equivalent level of productivity is the fundamental factor in producing additional surpluses. That the differences are very large is confirmed by the United States Tariff Commission (1970, p. 170). In the case of Mexico, average hourly wages for similar jobs were five times lower in 1969 than in the United States. More extreme were some countries in South-East Asia where average wages were ten times lower (or up to twenty times in an exceptional case such as Taiwan) than the corresponding American wages. The Central American and Caribbean countries occupied an intermediate position.

Other estimates on the whole confirm this. Baerresen (1971, p. 24) made a calculation of wages and fringe benefits in 1969 and concluded that, compared with average wages in the United States, South Korea paid 4 percent, Taiwan 7 percent, Hong Kong 14 percent and Mexico between 13 and 22 percent, while average wages in Japan were one-third of American.

These comparisons must not be treated in purely static terms. Real wages in the countries affected by this type of expansion have evolved differently. On the one hand, in Singapore, wages fell considerably—by 20 percent—from 1965 to 1974.[7] On the other hand, in South Korea, the very low wages at the beginning doubled during the same period.[8] In Taiwan and Hong Kong they increased by about 20 percent.[9] In Mexico during the same time, while the national level of real wages rose by 44 percent[10], in the border zone nominal wages—or wages in dollars at the stable rate of exchange—more than doubled.[11]

As real wages also moved very differently during the period in the countries of origin (5 percent in the United States[12] and 100 percent in Japan[13]) the variation in relative wage costs is more difficult to calculate and the different ways in which the exchange rate moved in relation to domestic prices must also be taken into account. In other words, leaving aside for the moment variations in the price of the product, what matters for the enterprises is the movement of nominal wages in the countries of origin and destination and the effective rate of exchange (including tariffs, subsidies, etc.) between the two currencies. There may be situations—for example, during this ten-year period in Singapore—when a combination of inflation with currency revaluation may lead to both a fall in real wages and increased labor cost for the transnationals.

One must bear in mind, however, that the main concern in the estimation of profitability is the absolute difference in wages, so that a relatively steep rise in real wages may occur in the underdeveloped countries while the absolute differences continue to grow. Thus, the doubling of wages on the Mexican border, as long as the rate of exchange stayed constant, had a greater impact on the calculation of costs for the transnationals than the doubling of wages in South Korea. The same can be said of the big devaluation of the Mexican peso at the end of 1976, which swung results in the opposite direction.

The differences between countries in average wages do not strictly represent the alternative wages cost for the transnationals. Various studies show that the firms pay somewhat higher wages than local firms, though this is truer for American and European transnationals and for more skilled types of worker.[14] Whatever the reason for the higher rates (interfirm competition for the best labor, discouragement of labor conflict, etc.) the higher pay only represents a small part of the difference between local wages and wages in the country of origin, so that the inducement is still operative. In Haiti, for example, the statutory minimum daily wage in 1971 was US$ 1.00 (applying only in modern industry) and the assembly plants paid US$ 1.60 per day (van Houten, 1973, p. 22). With a corresponding wage of US$ 25 in the United States, this left the difference practically intact. The increase of the statutory miminum wage to US$ 1.30 from 1974 (*La Documentation Française,* 1975, p. 56) did not alter the situation.

In view of this, the attraction of the expansion model that we are discussing obviously lies in the possibility of installing production plants in places where the structure of the work force implies incomes associated with local subsistence levels rather than with wages in the country of origin (as would be the case if foreign personnel had to be employed). Indeed, the inducement of lower wages directly influences not only the choice of country for relocation but also the type of processes to be transferred to the periphery.[15]

Peripheral countries as an external reserve army of labor

The reason for the much lower wages paid by subsidiaries than in the countries of origin is no secret. One of the basic characteristics of the underdeveloped economies is the existence of low-income levels among the majority of the population (regardless of the level of incomes in the upper classes, though generally accompanied by a low average per capita income for the country as a whole). This statement is almost tautological since the conventional definition of underdevelopment rests on it.

The structural conditions of underdevelopment often lead at the same time to a high level of unemployment and underemployment, providing a reserve of actually available labor (or labor potentially available with minor incentives and no transformation of the basic structure of the economy). This second aspect is important for the continuance of the initial incentive to invest. Otherwise, increased demand for labor (from foreign investment) might quickly disturb the wage level inducement. This point is of particular significance in this form of internationalization owing to the noticeable amount of direct employment created, unlike the other types of penetration by transnationals where only a very small part of the labor force is affected.

South Korea had extensive reserves of underemployed and unemployed manpower (the visible unemployment rate was 8 percent in the mid 1960's, falling to 3 percent in 1974 and then rising to 6 percent at the end of last year).[16] In Singapore it fell similarly between 1965 and 1973.[17] In Hong Kong, controlled emigration from the People's Republic of China provides the pool needed to stabilize the labor market. In Mexico, widespread underemployment, the steep rise in the border population due to migration and the 200,000 *braceros* who lost their employment in the United States provided the needed labor supply.[18] In the Caribbean there is also a large reserve of potentially available labor. On the other hand, in small economies such as Singapore, the concentration of investments may eventually exhaust the reserve, and lead to labor shortages which may force a change in technological and production choices.

It is useful then to think the role of peripheral countries in the development of central capitalism partly as providing a vast reserve army of labor. The case under discussion, if allowed to develop extensively, would mean delocalization, not only of some stages of production, but of a substantial part of the functions perfomed by the reserve army of labor. This means not only the subsitution of migrant workers into the center, as mentioned earlier, but also part of the need for a local unoccupied labor force in developed countries. Undoubtedly the proper reserve army in the center would certainly not disappear completely (as the stability of their wages depends upon it). On the contrary, the flow of runaway firms would in any case assure its continuous existence. But from the point of view of the functioning of the system as a whole more and more of the usefulness for capitalist accumulation of pressure downways in unskilled labor wages, and more and more of the cyclical adjustment process could be transferred to the periphery.

A thorough understanding of this question would require a detailed study of the manner in which labor reserves in the center and periphery operate, and would exceed the limits of this article. It might be interesting to recall, however, that as with other questions mentioned above concerning technology, dependence relations, etc., this model seems to reestablish, for central accumulation, some of the characteristics of early capitalism. For instance the influx of migrant workers into Europe was only a partial substitute for the exhausted reserves of labor that previously came from surplus population in non- or semi-capitalistic sectors. Even if more flexible than the former rural-to-urban migration inside a country (since migrants could be chased out cyclically more easily than national urban excess population could be made to move back to the rural areas), the constitution of a new reserve army of labor through this cheap labor expansion abroad partly substitutes for the need for this mass of migrants. But not only that. For instance, the system of subcontracting, characteristic of the second variant mentioned above, provides a reserve as flexible as the one required by early accumulation in the center. Thus, the shifting toward subcontracting, with no change in activity of artisans, becomes the moving frontiers of the capitalist industrial sector and, at the same time, the central economies in a wider sense.

Weak labor force, weak nations

The existence of surplus labor in the receiving countries becomes then a distinctive general characteristic of the model under discussion. But the point should not be stretched too far. Unemployment does not produce automatically low wages, just as full employment does not lead inevitably to high wages. The problem cannot be merely stated in terms of an expansion model with unlimited supply of workers and low wages. On the one hand, the situation of employment in the most frequent receiving countries has not been that exceptional (and much less so after affiliates increasingly sponged out part of the prevailing unemployment). On the other hand, even in the midst of widespread unemployment, a partial process of industrialization, such as is involved here, quickly leads to the formation of a separate industrial labor market with a labor union-organized supply. The counterweight of a potential labor supply still rooted in other sectors of the economy is then not enough to keep wages at a subsistence level. Hence, while a combination of low wages with a similar level of productivity is a basic condition for this type of investment, an absence or low level of unionization automatically becomes a parallel political condition.

Although the statistics on the percentage of unionized workers and frequency of labor disputes are very incomplete, those that exist confirm that this condition is operational.

In Hong Kong, for example, Riedel (1974, p. 77) indicates that the total number of unionized workers in the economy fell from 177,000 in 1960 to 143,000 in 1969. The Registrar of Trade Unions gives a unionization rate for 1966 that is equivalent to only 6.5 percent of the half million workers recorded in the manufacturing sector in that year. For the Northern Border of Mexico, Baerresen (1971, pp. 40–43) provides a picture of weak and fragmentary unionization at the end of the 1960's—in some cases without any union at all or with a union openly manipulated by the foreign companies. The trade union situation has changed in recent years, however, thereby making the area less attractive for foreign capital (NACLA, 1975). In the Caribbean, the relative preference for Haiti where "the Government offers total industrial peace to investors (unions having ceased to exist ten years ago)"[19] contrasts with the absence of interest in Trinidad and Tobago in spite of their incipient industrial development, due (among other things) to the high percentage of unionization and the resultant rise in wages.

As regards labor disputes, the available ILO figures (1975, p. 794 ff) provide a striking demonstration of the passiveness induced or forced upon the working class in the countries receiving this type of internationalization. If the number of workers involved in labor disputes is compared with the total employed population of the country, the percentages in South Korea are 0.15 for the three years 1965–1967, 0.18 for 1968–1970 and only 0.002 for 1971–1973. Other less complete figures provided by the ILO give an average of 0.29 percent for Singapore for 1969–1974 and 0.006 percent for Taiwan in 1965–1969. The comparable figures for the United States and Japan in the same decade are in the region of 3 or 4 percent. Semi-industrialized countries such as Argentina also had rates of 3 to 4 percent during periods of relative political and economic liberalization (such as during the civilian governments from 1963 to 1966 and from 1973 to 1974); the rate fell considerably, to 0.05 percent in 1967–1970, which coincided with stricter curbs on unions, and incidentally with a favorable attitude of the Government toward foreign capital investment.

Apart from enabling low wages to be imposed, an absence of labor disputes obviously provides economies in hours and materials lost, which may be considerable in countries where industrial action is frequent.

The weakness of industrial labor on the wages front in these cases has a number of causes. One is that it is faced with firms having a quasi-monopoly in the labor market, vastly greater financial power experience, and one particular advantage: extreme mobility of being able to transfer investments to another country owing to the limited amount of fixed assets required for the kind of production under discussion.

The NACLA study (1975, p. 16 ff) on the Mexican border industrialization program refers to a number of labor disputes that led to closure of plant. It concludes that growing union activity and the resultant wage increases may put an end to the program. The American Chamber of Commerce gave the same warning, accusing the local unions of "killing the goose that lays the golden eggs." After firing 3,000 workers at the end of 1974 as a result of labor disputes in Mexicali, a spokesman for Mattel (the main producer of toys in the United States) said that wages had reached parity with other parts of the world, so that the firm could move to other locations and had now decided to close the plant for good. Cases are also known in Asia of firms transferring their plants more than once.

Thus, the normal assymetric nature of labor markets in capitalist countries becomes exposed in its nakedness. At the same time, state policy in the receiving countries adds to the power of the transnationals by strict curbs on any forms of union organization and mobilization likely to affect wage levels, and hence the profitability, of the transnationals. There are plenty of occasions on which their interests may coincide with those local groups in control of the machinery of government. Moreover, the receiving country suffers from an innate weakness in this investment model. This is because the flexibility and maneuvrability of the transnationals applies not only to labor but also to states. Investments in assembly operations can be dismantled as easily and cheaply as they can be installed. There are no intangibles that tie up capital from direct foreign investment such as the cost involved in prospecting for natural resources (Vaitsos, 1974, p. 341). The operations of subsidiaries have so many links with the rest of the transnational and so few with the rest of the local economy that risks such as the threat of nationalization cease to operate. In addition, reserves of labor are nonnegotiable in monopoly conditions on the world market and cannot be used by receiving countries in an attempt to offset their weakness.

In sum, the receiving countries are left with few options other than that of deciding to admit or exclude this type of foreign capital penetration. Once it is accepted, an active policy of regressive income distribution becomes essential for its efficient functioning.[20]

High productivity

The large differences shown in the wage statistics already quoted relate to workers of comparable productivity and are therefore reflected in unit labor costs of production (and profit levels). This is naturally a vital point. The United States Tariff Commission (1970, p. 171) states that "the productivity of workers in foreign establishments assembling or processing products of United States origin generally approximates that of workers of the same job classifications in the United States."

In other cases the level of productivity of local labor in the commonest types of work may be considerably higher. Baerresen (1971, p. 33) indicates that in Mexico the productivity levels are highest for routine, simple, nondecision-making types of work. In a plant packaging metal links, for example, the workers' productivity was 40 percent higher than in the United States for similar operations. In the electronics firms labor productivity in simple, repetitive jobs (e.g., winding coils) is 10 to 25 percent higher than in plants in the United States, and from zero to 30 percent in sewing operations. He adds that in South Korea the productivity of local workers in routine operations is 20 to 40 percent higher even than that of the Mexicans. The level of productivity falls as the jobs involve a larger element of personal decision and in supervisory jobs and those organized in groups.

There are several further reasons why labor productivity can be maintained at such a high level. From the point of view of the quality of labor, only very low skill levels are required and there are no problems in obtaining this type of labor locally using very short job training programs. This can be seen, for example, from Schreiber (1970, pp. 69–70) on Taiwan, who indicates that most of the workers in the enterprises questioned only needed manual skill. Moreover, the weakness and dependence of labor on this type of employment, and the use of methods involving interworker rivalry, etc. makes it easier to fix hours and intensity of work in excess of those in the country of origin. The available figures on the subject only give a faint reflection of the reality. Even so, ILO statistics (1975, pp. 491–492) show that—taking the combined averaged hours of the United States and Japan in 1970–1975 (41.4 per week)—the average day in Singapore was 18 percent longer, and 24 percent longer in South Korea. It may be accepted then that an important inducement for the transnationals to expand this way has been also the possibility to increase gains by means of absolute surplus value creation.

A few cases give an indication of the particular type of employment relations implicit in this model: along the Mexican border about 90 percent of the work force consisted of single women aged between 16 and 24 years (Bernal Sahagún, 1976, p. 189). This enables enterprises to make substantial savings in labor and/or equipment costs by intensified utilization of the work force. Baerresen (1971, p. 33) states, for example, that electronics firms engage young women workers who can perform without aids the delicate assembly operations for which it is normally necessary to provide microscopes and magnifying glasses for (older) women workers in the United States.

As a direct consequence of high productivity combined with cheap labor, unit labor cost is much lower. In metal products the subsidiaries of American transnationals have an average unit labor cost which represents only 14 percent of the cost in the country of origin (20 percent in Mexico, 8 percent in South-East Asia). For other articles in the list of commonest goods, the cost is an average 27 percent (United States Tariff Commission, 1970, pp. 171–173).

Low capital intensity

Nor are there any factors in relation to machinery or equipment that counterbalance these savings, say, by increasing costs through diseconomies of scale. The processes that are transferred are usually of a type that can be divided up and for which the optimum scale is fairly small. This is clear from the figures of fixed assets per worker. According to Bernal Sahagún (1976, pp. 183–184) the average in the Mexican assembly industry in 1974 was US$ 840 per worker, ranging from US$ 690 in electronics to US$ 2,800 in miscellaneous manufactures. Jo (1976, pp. 30–34) gives interesting data for South Korea. In 1974 the coefficient of capital per worker in foreign export-oriented industry was half the coefficient in industries serving the domestic market and did not differ significantly from local industry as regards degree of mechanization. Helleiner (1973, p. 31) quotes a figure of US$ 1,500 of capital per worker in the export processing zones of Taiwan. Moreover, one fact mentioned by Helleiner should be noted. Some of the branches in which the pattern of international relocation has expanded, for example the machine/tools industry, were already ones that were based on extensive subcontracting in the country of origin. It follows that these must be industries where the advantages of decentralization for the production of specialized parts in small firms exceeded those of centralized production, at least in some areas of production. Substantial wage differences were therefore enough to make this form of internationalization attractive. However, to avoid any misleading generalization, we must remember that only a relatively small number of processes and/or products meet the minimum technical requirements for efficient decentralization.

The counterbalancing factors are not limited to possible economies of scale. All the different types of external economics may be factors limiting this type of relocation, but they tend to be partially neutralized where the subsidiaries are crowded together as in some customs-free zones.

Distance, management, risks

The factors that have been commented up to now deal mainly with the production of surplus at the level of the subsidiary. Of course, this is only one side of the main question: transnationals plan their operations on a global scale, hence what matters is production of surplus for the whole of the firm. Some new factors have to be included into the picture, the principal ones being restrictions raised by long distances that usually exist between different parts of the whole global unit, the need for a very sophisticated control machinery to keep them all together, the types of risk involved in this kind of operation.

As the new locations of production are generally a great distance away, transport costs both ways become a factor seriously limiting the kind of goods suitable for a transfer of production. These will inevitably be products with a relatively high value per unit of weight or volume, and production will be restricted to areas where rapid and regular transport facilities, easy communications and other infrastructure services are available to the foreign firms.

This requirement provides a partial explanation of the choice of products. Helleiner (1973, pp. 36–37) points out that watches and precious metals involve an average transport cost representing only 1 percent of their value; tools and machine parts, 2 percent; photographic equipment and agricultural machinery, 3 percent; and office machines, 4 percent; as contrasted with a general average of 9 or

10 percent (and cases with 30 or 40 percent such as aircraft and leisure boats).

This restriction also explains why the relocation areas are as near as possible to the home center of the transnational (Mexican border and Caribbean for the United States, South Korea for Japan) or else are based on islands or ports on major shipping routes (Singapore, Hong Kong, Taiwan). The ultimate example of avoiding the incidence of transport costs in the relocation of production—and thereby achieving maximum expansion of types of production that are economically viable from this point of view—is the creation of "twin plants," i.e., enterprises with plants on both sides of the Mexico-United States border, in order to move out as many of the labor-intensive operations as possible.

One obvious prerequisite for the new type of internationalization is the enormous development in the techniques of geographically dispersed management that has accompanied it. If the transnationals had not been able to direct and control the management of their plants in all four corners of the world, the hoped-for savings in costs would have been counterbalanced by delays, a fall-off in standards of quality and uniformity, breakdowns in supply, etc. Hence, the present case is of particular interest as a demonstration of the remarkable ability of modern corporations to internationalize production. One of the main features is the ability to separate the stages in certain types of production that it would be impossible or uneconomic to transfer wholly to the underdeveloped countries, and disperse them geographically while maintaining strick central control of the whole process. This makes it possible, for example, in conjunction with the economies of scale already mentioned, to achieve an optimum geographic distribution of operations. It applies not only to production processes with varying degrees of labor or capital intensiveness but also to R and D and centralized conduct of trading and financial accounts, which tend to be retained in the country of origin.

Nevertheless, the fact that the transnationals have this ability should not encourage quick generalizations. Many of the enterprises do not consider the safeguards adequate to ensure a regular supply. Moreover, the other restraining factors noted are substantial. And it is far from certain that the transnationals themselves are interested in developing such transfer to the periphery on a wide scale unless forced to do so, or that forces are operating that are strong enough to oblige them to continue on this course.

Another risk factor, which is not related to production and management technique, but to political uncertainties, is also undergoing a change. Expropriation has traditionally loomed large in discussions on the profitability of foreign direct investment, though there have been few empirical studies of it. However, a good deal of this alleged risk factor has been an attempt to justify the large profit margins of the transnationals rather than an objective element in calculating the degree of profitability to be expected. Thus, even if the capital values declared by the enterprises are accepted, Williams (1975) shows that the statistical occurrence of local appropriation of the capital invested in manufacturing is small, and has been declining for the whole economy during the last two decades. This point could be further cleared up if calculations could take account of the capital actually invested that had been fully amortized during the first years of the investment. Anyway, a discussion of this sort mainly concerns the more traditional forms of foreign investment (extractive industries, securing a share of the process of industrialization of the import-substitution type). In the present type the risks are practically nonexistent because of the intangible nature of the transnational's contribution, its mobility and the absence of alternative for the receiving country.

Policies of the home and host countries

Discussion of the determinants of this new type of expansion would not be complete if it were circumscribed by the increased production of surplus value. The question of appropriation is the essential one since, depending on the attitude and power of the parties involved, surplus appropriated in the transnational—hence profit—would be higher or lower. The key parties involved that could have a stake on this surplus would be the state in the receiving and home countries. National bourgeoisies are too weak to represent a serious threat in the distribution process: a minority share on it seems enough. So taxation systems as well as any indirect transfer mechanism becomes an important element to take into consideration.

We have already mentioned the reasons why the receiving countries submit to the restraints of this type of foreign investment, and are in such a weak stance vis-à-vis the transnationals that they are generally in no position to insist on their share of the surpluses generated. Some observers (Helleiner, 1976) are more optimistic, believing that the receiving countries have some room for maneuvre because of the presence of smaller firms, companies with purely commercial interests and local diversification strategy. However, it is difficult to feel that, in a model of the present kind where all factors tend to weaken the receiving country and to strengthen the transnationals, any significant strategy for local appropriation of the values produced in its territory is likely to occur. The overwhelming economic and technological power of the transnationals compared with the size of these countries, their control of the marketing machinery (which plays a crucial role here) and the mobility already noted do not encourage optimism, especially when any bargaining policy there may be is managed by governments traditionally subject to external influence.

In any case the experience of the past decade is clear enough as regards the distribution of the surpluses generated. Apart from analyzing the statistics (the data are on the whole not likely to be very useful on this aspect), it is important to study the laws and regulations on foreign capital in the countries where this form of investment is predominant. A mere listing of provisions reveals how extremely liberal the governments are, driven on most probably by competition for the favors of the transnationals: extensive or total exemptions from import and export duties, unlimited licenses to import equipment and intermediate products, extensive facilities for transferring profits in various forms, etc. are the keynote.[21] An estimate of the cost of the infrastructure made available to the transnationals by governments would probably suggest in some cases that there had even been a reverse flow that increased the incomes of the transnationals. Further, the question of education expenses should be taken into account. The type of industrial work necessary for assembly, finishing, and related tasks requires something more than raw unskilled labor: some elementary education and training is necessary for the labor force to be prepared for this kind of work. The basic education receiving countries normally provide to their population implies an important public expenditure freely granted to investing firms. When these are transnationals, this can be understood as a disguised transfer abroad.

No less important in this expansion model is the attitude of the state in the industrialized countries of origin. In the variant involving relocation of processes vertically integrated in the transnationals, the companies export the necessary inputs from the home country and reimport the assembled product. Usually this operation is profitable only if the home country government agrees to charge import duty only on the value added abroad and not on the gross value.

The well-known case of sections 806.30 and 807.00 of the United States customs tariff, already mentioned, is the most important and its provisions were the starting point for the great expansion of the transnational assembly industry abroad. The Tariff Commission's 1970 report, mentioned earlier, shows a growth from US$ 60 million to US$ 500 million in the initial period 1966–1970 in imports coming from the underdeveloped countries and covered by section 807.00. During the next three years these imports increased by over 35 percent annually.

The extent to which this type of investment depends on the goodwill of the government of the country of origin is illustrated in the study by Baerresen (1971, p. 62). He estimated that, if the privilege of the two sections of the tariff was canceled, the Mexican border industrialization program would be reduced by 75 percent (including nearly the whole clothing industry and over half of the electronics industry). Not all this international production would disappear completely: part would be transferred to Asia if it was not further penalized by increased duties or import quotas.

The very exceptional and thus fragile nature of this system of relocation is even more obvious if one compares it with the tariff and nontariff barriers, either imposed or voluntarily accepted, which increasingly prevent importation of high-labor intensity articles from less developed countries.[22]

The same situation happens in other developed countries. In Hong Kong's case, for example, its Department of Commerce believes the preferential system over the markets of the United Kingdom, and other Commonwealth territories, to be one of the reasons for the success of industrialization. However, European transnationals have considerably less propensity to embark in cheap labor-oriented ventures than their US counterparts.

In sum, through legislation and customs policies, the attitude of the country of origin has a determinant importance on the profitability of transnationals in this kind of operations. Nevertheless, this is only one aspect of the overall weight the policies of home countries have on the viability of this expansion model.

3. IMPLIED MODEL OF DEVELOPMENT

The case that we have been studying is of wider concern than its quantitative significance in overall direct foreign investment in the underdeveloped countries suggests. The growing attention that it has received is not entirely due to its newness but also to ideological and political reasons. Even some of the most conventionally oriented currents of thinking on development are coming to accept that, in spite of neoclassical economic theory, specialization in primary production for international trade does not create conditions for sustained development in the peripheral economies. On the other hand, the import-substitution model of industrialization has been under attack by the same theory, both because of the endogenous limitations that seemed to arise in the long run and because of its inconsistency with assumed international optima for resource allocation. Hence, industrial development strategies oriented to foreign markets have in recent years become increasingly fashionable.

In such circumstances the increasing importance of the transnationals and their insertion through manufactured goods exporting models looked like the miracle that would deliver the underdeveloped countries from their age-old curse. It seemed at first glance that all the requirements would be met. The underdeveloped nations would establish industries in growth sectors in their countries, and make them efficient enough to participate in the world trade in manufactured goods, without having to go through the lengthy learning process for new industries or having to support the cost of creating a technological infrastructure. They could count on the help of the most effective agent—i.e., the transnationals themselves—for overcoming any protectionist barriers erected by developed countries and could also avoid the heavy cost of marketing. In the process the underdeveloped countries would contribute their most abundant resource, and the overall system would ensure ever-greater integration in the world economy. More employment would be created in underdeveloped countries and (hence) better income distribution would be achieved. While it is true that there are innumerable shades of opinion on the subject, many end up by taking it for granted that a spread of the new type of economic internationalization in one or other of its variants is both feasible and desirable. The reasoning might be convincing *if* it were accepted that the underdeveloped countries have no other way of developing except by exporting manufactured goods to developed countries, and that this type of vertically integrated exporting has a chance of overcoming the protectionist barriers shielding the developed countries' markets.

However, things look quite different if conventional myths on development and the international capitalist order are left aside, in particular the postulate of the need for less developed countries to integrate to the industrialized economies at any cost.

The growth model oriented toward making use of the abundant cheap labor, which enjoys so much official support at present, is the successor of (or may be combined with) the model that held the field for a century, namely exploitation of natural resources for which the periphery was supposed to have the comparative advantage. It is interesting to compare certain aspects of the two models.

There is of course a major difference which is used as the basis of the whole argument—i.e., the fact that this mode of expansion of the transnationals involves a rapid growth of direct employment and payrolls in the recipient economy. In Singapore the firms with partly foreign capital employed on average 60 percent of the industrial labor force in 1971 (The Colombo Plan, 1973, pp. 202–203). In spite of the dissimilarity of the sources of information for the earlier years, the contribution to industrial employment was obviously very large and increasing in this economy with a large manufacturing sector (31.8 percent of total employment in 1971, according to ILO, 1975, p. 318). In Hong Kong the direct effect has been considerably smaller, with foreign firms providing only 10.8 percent of industrial employment in 1971.[23] South Korea had a similar figure (11.6 percent) in 1974[24], with a manufacturing sector representing 17.4 percent of total employment.[25] The direct employment created by foreign firms rose steeply from 1970 to 1972 (from 3 to 10 percent of total industrial employment) and then levelled out. The total effect is obviously larger if one includes the employment created by the subcontracting system, on which there is little systematic information. In any case, the direct effects on employment are certainly much greater in this model of foreign investment than in the other forms of transnational expansion, and the same applies naturally to the total wages distributed. The reasons obviously lie in the particular character of the expansion. But this brings us to the end of the main positive differences; in other respects the effects are similar or sometimes less favorable. It will help if we take the comparative analysis a stage further.

Specialization in the primary sector has been much criticized for a number of reasons by economists concerned with development in the Third World. One is its low growth potential: foreign establishments have traditionally restricted themselves to extracting mineral resources or growing agricultural crops and exporting them in a form as near to the raw state as possible with existing locational constraints. Specialization by making use of cheap labor cannot be said to be anything different. The type of manufacturing mainly concerned with processing imported inputs and reexporting them is inevitably isolated from the rest of the economy. In the variants involving the use of local raw materials or wider subcontracting, there are probably greater growth effects through the creation of some intermediate demand, and a somewhat wider spread of incomes and technology. The scope of the growth effects will however be limited except in cases where an unusual concentration of transnationals in relation to the size of the country creates special conditions.

In 1969, 57 percent of the value of American imports from underdeveloped countries under section 807.00 consisted of inputs previously exported from the United States (reaching nearly 70 percent in Mexico and South Korea).[26] The largest part of the remainder consisted of wages paid, and only a small fraction were local materials used. As this model develops and links with the recipient economy increase, the percentage tends to decline. In 1973 reimports from underdeveloped countries were 43 percent of the value imported under these rules—though this was still double the percentage for imports from other developed countries (especially Japan and Canada) under the same rules. The Japanese transnationals buy on average 45 percent of their intermediate goods in Japan. This figure relates to transnationals of all types; in the more typical sectors under discussion, such as electronics and precision instruments, the percentage is as high as 70 percent.[27]

The primary sector export model is also considered harmful because of the extreme instability that it imposes on the economies concerned, since the developed countries, through the monopoly structures of world markets controlled by them, have no difficulty in passing on to the underdeveloped countries the full impact of their trade cycles, in magnified form. But the vulnerability of the latter in matters of prices and production is even more glaring when investments to make use of low-cost labor predominante. Here it is not merely a question of shrinking demand for the primary products of the peripheral countries (with a consequent collapse of prices) when a depression looms up. In the cases considered, the transnationals have the option, which may become a political necessity because of pressure inside the home country, of transferring the whole production to the country of origin. Although facts are still very recent, there are already some indications of such a trend in behaviour during the latest depression. For example, Bernal Sahagún (1976, p. 190) estimates that during the first half of 1975 alone the aggregate value of production in the assembly plants in Mexico fell by 23 percent, and employmet by one-third (26,000 persons laid off).

Another aspect to which the literature on development has devoted much attention is the transfer of the benefits of technological progress. It has repeatedly been pointed out that the primary exporter model has been unsuitable because of the tendency for prices of primary production to decline relatively to those of manufacturing, with a consequent continuous transfer of incomes from the periphery to the center. In the low-cost labor model the problems are certainly greater. It is not only the question of who benefits from technological progress: the whole issue of participation in the surplus produced in the subsidiary will depend basically on the level and movement of terms of trade, since production is wide open at both ends to external trade. But the price relationship will be of a very special kind: both the prices of inputs and the export prices will be the transnational's own accounting prices, fixed according to its capital accumulation requirements, and any control of these prices by the receiving countries is hardly possible. Scarce natural resources are negotiable in terms of a bilateral monopoly, especially if the underdeveloped country still has some scope for political action vis-à-vis the transnationals. This cannot be done with reserve labor: the fact that it is so plentiful leaves the countries with no bargaining power, at least within the framework imposed by this type of internationalization.

Thus, the transnationals will produce large surpluses that will not only be automatically appropriated by them practically in full but will not even be reflected in the company's accounts owing to their control of the significant variables. The considerably smaller share of the surpluses received by the host countries is perhaps the most important drawback of this model, as compared with the primary exporter model.

In short, the penetration of certain peripheral economies by transnationals in search of low-cost labor has features similar to those of a substantial surrender of sovereignty over part or the whole of the nation's territory, with effects reminiscent of the traditional enclaves of extractive industry. There is a subtle difference between them. The traditional form produces something approaching a transfer of *land* along with the labor living there. The more recent trend is toward a transfer of the *labor* along with the land underneath them. The combination of circumstances that we have mentioned make it unlikely that this model of worldwide expansion by transnationals will turn into a process of sustained accumulation for the receiving countries.[28]

4. PROSPECTS

Much of the recent writing on this new form of internationalization assumes that it will continue to expand, and some writers make it the kingbolt for the changes in international economic relations that are the subject of so much debate at present. This vision is in part kept alive by the conviction shared by many critics of and apologists for the present international order that this form is the one that fits in best with the strategy of the big corporations which are increasingly absorbing the international flow of trade and capital. Certainly, it is also kept alive by the ideological pressure in the field of economics, aimed at justifying a renewal and strengthening of the mechanisms for international domination at present controlled mainly by the transnationals.

The fact that we are dealing with a very new phenomenon on which the information is very incomplete and which cannot yet be seen in its historical perspective should make us extremely cautious. Even if it is accepted that continued expansion of central capitalism could provide a further strong impulsion to fuller utilization of the reserve labor in the underdeveloped countries, attention is drawn in the remainder of this paper to the factors that limit any extrapolation of the recent trends and counteract the pressure to expand in accordance with the model that we have been discussing.

In several countries taken as examples we have seen a staggering rate of growth in exports of manufactured goods, bringing with it a considerable growth of employment and of the economy as a whole. Nevertheless, it is extremely doubtful whether this experience can be extrapolated.

In the first place, the period of expansion of the type under discussion has coincided with a period of substantial growth in the central economies and in international trade. This growth has been smoothly transmitted to the receiving countries for this type of investment, precisely because of the characteristic of this model, open to integration with the central economies. Most analysts agree that it will be difficult to reach such a speed of expansion again. Just as rapid growth is transmitted with a multiplier effect, any stagnation or slowdown will have automatic and magnified effects on this mode of internationalization.

There is a close connection between this and the kind of opposition that this form of expansion has aroused in the home countries themselves. The effect of the transnationals on the home country is a highly topical issue, and the opposition to the enterprises comes from various (and sometimes opposite) directions. Now the issue as to whether the expansion model based on cheap labor involves an "export of jobs" is the one that has generated the strongest opposition, mainly centered in the big American labor unions. We will not go into the details of this debate as to the positive or negative direct and indirect effects on employment in the home country. But it is important to remember that more is involved than the overall effect on the home economies: even if the jobs eliminated as a result of foreign investment are offset by new job creation, the labor organizations would tend to object since union power is reduced by any fall in employment in the industries or occupations in which they have a stake (Cox, 1976). The position of the AFL-CIO, which is that it does not oppose international development but insists that fair competition rules be respected, leads in practice to direct opposition to the type of foreign investment characteristic of the model under discussion here. To imagine that the assembly operations could be carried out abroad while respecting United States labor standards and wage levels would be a contradiction in terms.

The bitter fight regarding protectionism or trade liberalization clauses is a direct result. The labor organizations in the United States were from the beginning opposed to the exceptions allowing products assembled abroad to be reimported under tax exemptions, and the report of the Tariff Commission, to which reference has already been made, was in fact one of the results of union and political pressure. The pressure was renewed during the drafting of the Trade Act of 1974, and it can be said that its effectiveness in maintaining protectionist barriers in favor of American industry is still very great (Sepúlveda, 1976). To be sure, they were not able to prevent the system of assembly abroad from expanding. But this coincided with a period of accelerated growth of the home economy, and the combination of growth with relocation did not create too many problems. It is less certain that the resistance can be easily overcome in a period such as the one that is probably approaching.

In any case, the prospects for importing labor-intensive final products are being increasingly eroded, and not only by union pressure. Helleiner (1976, pp. 199–200) thinks that the coalition of local industrial interests in the developed countries (unions, employers and politicians), usually in marginal areas and covering less-privileged groups of workers, represents a political force that will be difficult to overcome, even for transnationals interested in economic rationalization where it is to their advantage. As regards the variant that is linked with vertical integration inside the transnational, it is more difficult to see at what point expansion would begin to compromise the present economic and political balance in the developed countries. But this point is almost certainly closer than would be consistent with really widespread adoption of the system.

Second, the experiment has so far been extremely limited as regards the kind of country in which it has occurred. The two best-known cases are Hong Kong and Singapore. These are two city-states with a combined area of no more than 1,700 square kilometers[29] and a combined population of 6.3 million in 1973 (i.e., hardly 0.3 percent of the total population of the underdeveloped countries).[30] They have been the recipients of a major flow of foreign capital, mainly for export industries: the net foreign assets of the DAC countries in 1973 were US$ 1,460 million,[31] equivalent to US$ 299.9 per inhabitant. The opening-up of developed country markets to the manufactures of the two countries through the intermediary of the transnationals has been no less significant: together they exported in 1973 goods worth US$ 5,302—equivalent to US$ 181.6 per inhabitant.[32]

It would be out of question for the underdeveloped countries as a group to take (even implicitly) these two countries as a "development model." To see why, one need only take one of the large countries with concentrations of reserve labor (since the point is labor exploitation). India, for example, with 574 million inhabitants in 1973[33] had only US$ 1,780 million of net foreign assets[34] and US$ 1,493 million of manufactured exports[35] (or US$ 3.1 and 2.6 per inhabitant). The application to India of the coefficients for Hong Kong and Singapore would imply five times as many net foreign assets in India as the total for manufacturing in *all* underdeveloped countries in 1973, and twenty times the total manufactured exports of all the underdeveloped countries in 1973.

South Korea and Taiwan are also small countries, though larger and more integrated economically than the first two. Here the coefficients are lower: an average of US$ 22.6 of net foreign assets per inhabitant and US$ 95.8 of manufactured exports per inhabitant. But even here, application of the coefficients to India would give equally improbable figures.

That mass mobilization of capital resources on this scale is possible in the long term cannot be denied. Nor is it impossible that the developed countries should open up their markets to mass imports of manufactured goods from the underdeveloped countries, as would be needed for even a modest extension of this model. But these are not lines of thought that can be accepted, since they are in flat contradiction to the inherently dependent pattern of relationships in the current structure of international relations. There are no serious grounds for accepting the hypothesis of such changes in isolation from other equally radical changes in economic and political systems.

On the other hand, it is easy to see why this kind of model is so attractive for the formulation of capitalist development strategies for small countries with few natural resources, and where few growth effects can be expected from the spontaneous or induced growth of the internal market. In some cases it is even assumed that external dependence is a phenomenon inevitably associated with the small size of the economy; with such an approach it is not surprising that the discussion becomes diverted to the marginal aspects of the form taken by the cruder mechanisms of subordination and possible palliatives, leaving the main questions out of account.

Third, the model has limitation of various kinds that arise out of the way in which it came into being and that have been discussed in some detail in the earlier sections of this paper. Even as regards the choice of product the restrictions cannot easily be overcome. The products chosen are ones where, at certain stages of the production process, there is a need for intensive use of unskilled labor, where little investment in fixed assets is required, where the production stage is relatively independent of the earlier and later stages, and where the physical nature of the intermediate products are such that this stage can be moved to places far away from the central production area without excessive cost.

A special form of market structure and ownership is also needed. The production of the goods (and the intermediate stages) must be largely under the control of the transnationals, which alone are able to internationalize production in this way; but at the same time, in spite of the extremely concentrated and oligopolistic structure of the markets dominated by the transnationals, there must be a sufficiently large competitive inducement to adopt this type of arrangement for reducing costs.

The limiting conditions as regards technical aspects, ownership and market structure are not the only ones. Our earlier analysis of the conditions showed that the countries must fulfil certain requirements as regards economic structure and political model, if they are to receive such investments. Only a combination of factors can provide an attractive, stable basis for such operations, namely a large supply of labor suitable for industrial work, low wages, communication facilities and other infrastructure required for industry, and a regime which is willing and able to maintain and increase the advantages for the transnationals through a policy of curbs on labor unions and of wide concessions to foreign capital. Only exceptionally can some countries, such as Mexico, with a different general attitude toward foreign capital, offset this disadvantage to the transnationals of the United States by immediate geographical proximity and a system of privileges within well-defined limits.

A discussion of the political implications of a spread of this form of internationalization to a large number of underdeveloped countries would go beyond the limits set for this paper. It is clear that the unevenness and turns and twists in the political evolution of the countries of the Third World have created a variety of situations in which the conditions for such expansion exist, where governments are extremely keen to attract such forms of foreign capital and where the opposition is weak and disorganized. Nevertheless, there is reason to think that growing difficulties of an internal character also lie ahead for any wide spread of this model. The long-term trend in the underdeveloped countries is toward nationalistic assertion, growing state intervention over the economic system and increasing reaction against the low standard of living of the masses, all of which runs counter to the principles of this model of internationalization.

FOOTNOTES

*The present period will certainly produce interesting evidence in the dispute on the flexibility of technological progress and its relation to the structure of ownership, since the transnationals will show whether or not they are capable of developing a new technology adapted to fuller use of the labor reserve in the underdeveloped countries. Up to now it has been a matter of changes in the location of production rather than of production technology, but the time elapsed has been too brief to make any judgement possible.

1. Keith Griffin has rightly pointed out to the present writer that an extreme example of utilization of local resources is in the manufacture of wigs from natural hair, where the raw material is also provided by the work force.

2. See Watanabe (1972), pp. 433–434, for an analysis of this type of relationship, which he terms "international commercial subcontracting."

3. Although both variants basically imply an expansion of exports of manufactured goods, this does not mean that the expansion only arises as a result of this type of internationalization. Some semi-industrialized countries have rapidly increased their exports of manufactured goods to developed countries. For example, Brazil with a cumulative annual rate of 23 percent from 1962 to 1972, and Mexico with a rate of 16.9 percent (UNCTAD, 1975, p. 17). While this has some features in common with the cases under discussion in this paper, it must be placed in a totally different context, i.e., the fruition and successful international appropriation of an import-substitution industrialization process accompanied by strong pressure from the host country to limit imbalance in external accounts. In any case, the presence of the transnationals in the countries mentioned is due to entirely different motives—the basic one being to secure a local market that is relatively insulated from the international market, plus the expansion of manufactures as a marginal by-product (Sabolo and Trajtenberg, 1975).

4. IBRD (1975), Annex Table 3.3: Hong Kong Census and Statistics Department (1976, p. 19); Singapore Department of Statistics (1976), p. 34.
5. UNCTAD (1975), p. 17; and *La Documentation Française* (1975).
6. Of which a third is in the manufacturing sector.
7. Estimated from United Nations data (1975, p. 387) and ILO data (1975, pp. 609 and 749).
8. Estimated from IBRD data (1975), Annex Table 8.1.
9. Taiwan Directorate-General of Budget, Accounting and Statistics (1975), pp. 176–181; United Nations (1975), p. 122; and Hong Kong Census and Statistics Department (1976), p. 9.
10. IBRD (1976), Annex Table 8.10.
11. Bernal Sahagún (1976), p. 187.
12. United States Department of Labor (1976), p. 102.
13. Japan Institute of Labor (1974); and ILO (1975), pp. 609 and 749.
14. See ILO (1976a, pp. 27–35); Sabolo and Trajtenberg, with Sajhau (1976), pp. 41–46.
15. Of course the linkage with wage differences is not purely mechanical and automatic. On the one hand, there are a number of other important factors (which we will consider later) affecting the internationalization strategy. On the other hand, variations in relative wage costs are more likely to affect new channels of expansion (new plants or expansion of existing subsidiaries) than the transfer of operations already started in the host country. This is due—even when the fixed capital involved is quite small—to reluctance caused by the need for establishing new political and commercial contacts, acquiring local knowledge, etc. In addition, the standard of comparison when deciding on changes in the strategy will lie between alternative receiving countries rather than with the country of origin.
16. United Nations (1975), pp. 222–223; and ILO (1975), p. 437.
17. IBRD (1975), Annex Table 2.
18. Bernal Sahagún (1976), p. 179.
19. *La Documentation Française* (1975), p. 56.
20. The fact that these regimes may be expected to be stable is particularly attractive to foreign capital. Obviously the transnationals are less concerned with stability in general than with a durable policy favoring their interests. Nevertheless, it is important that there should be unvarying rules of behaviour. For example, Watanabe (1972, p. 427) quotes European and Japanese enterprises concerned with this type of investment (in Hong Kong) as saying that political stability is the main factor to be considered in investment decisions.
21. See United States Tariff Commission (1970); United Nations (1976); Schreiber (1970), p. 29 ff; Bernal Sahagún (1976), p. 177 ff.
22. Quoted by Watanabe (1972), pp. 444, 445, 469.
23. Hong Kong Commerce and Industry Department.
24. Jo (1976), p. 22.
25. ILO (1975), p. 367.
26. United States Tariff Commission (1970), Table A-76.
27. Yoshino (1974).
28. See also the comments of Vaitsos (1975), p. 36 ff on this.
29. *Far Eastern Economic Review* (1975), pp. 169 and 271.
30. United Nations (1975), pp. 112 and 374.
31. OECD (1975), p. 5.
32. Hong Kong Census and Statistics Department (1976); and Singapore Department of Statistics (1976).

33. United Nations (1975), p. 126.
34. OECD (1975), p. 5.
35. UNCTAD (1976), p. 164.

REFERENCES

Baerresen, Donald W. (1971), *The Border Industrialization Program of Mexico,* Lexington, Mass.: Heath.

Belli, R. D. and Maley Jr., L.C. (August, 1974), "Sales by Majority-owned Foreign Affiliates of U.S. Companies, 1966–72," *Survey of Current Business,* Vol. 54, No. 8, Part II.

Bernal Sahagún, V. M., in Collaboration with Gutiérrez Arriola A. and Olmedo Carranza, B. (July, 1976), "*The Impact of Multinational Corporations on Employment and Income: The Case in Mexico,*" WEP 2–28 / Working Paper 13, ILO, Geneva.

The Colombo Plan (1973), *The Special Topic: Joint Ventures,* Washington.

Cox, Robert W. (January, 1976), "Labor and the Multinationals," *Foreign Affairs.*

La Documentation Française (May, 1975), "Problèmes d' Amérique Latine", Notes et Etudes Documentaires No. 4190–4191, Paris.

Far Eastern Economic Review (December, 1975), *Asia 1975 Yearbook,* Hong Kong.

Franko, L. G. (October, 1975), "Multinational Enterprise, the International Division of Labor in Manufactures and the Developing Countries," WEP 2–28 / Working Paper 4, ILO, Geneva.

Helleiner, G. K. (March, 1973), "Manufactured Exports from Less-Developed Countries and Multinational Firms," *The Economic Journal.*

———. (June, 1976), "Multinational Corporations, Manufactured Exports and Employment in Less Developed Countries," in *Tripartite World Conference on Employment Income Distribution and Social Progress and the International Division of Labor,* Background Papers, Vol. II, ILO, Geneva.

Hone, Angus (February, 1974), "Multinational Corporations and Multinational Buying Groups: Their Impact on the Growth of Asia's Exports of Manufactures—Myths and Realities," *World Development.*

Hong Kong Census and Statistics Department (February 1976), *Hong Kong Monthly Digest of Statistics,* Hong Kong.

Hong Kong Commerce and Industry Department (1971), *Foreign Investment in Hong Kong's Industry,* Hong Kong. (Mimeo).

———. *A Report on the Progress of Foreign Investment in Hong Kong's Industry Since the 1970 Survey,* Hong Kong. (Mimeo.)

van Houten, Jan F. (June 1973), "Assembly Industries in the Caribbean," *Finance and Development,* Vol. 10, No. 2.

IBRD (1973), *Current Economic Position and Prospects of Singapore,* Washington.

———. (May, 1975), *Current Economic Position and Prospects of the Republic of Korea,* Washington.

———. (March, 1976), *An Updating Report on the Economy of Mexico,* Washington.

ILO (1975), *Yearbook of Labor Statistics, 1975,* Geneva.

———. (1976a), *Wages and Working Conditions in Multinational Enterprises,* Geneva.

———. (1976b), *Employment, Growth and Basic Needs, A One-World Problem,* Geneva.

Japan Institute of Labor (1974), *Japan Labor Statistics.*

Jo, S. H. (July 1976), *The Impact of Multinational Firms on Employment and Incomes—The Case Study of South Korea,* WEP 2–28 / Working Paper 12, ILO, Geneva.

Michalet, Charles-Albert (November, 1975), *Transfert technologique par les firmes multinationales et capacité d'absorption des pays en voie de développement,* OECD. (Mimeo.)
———. (November, 1976), *The Multinational Companies and the New International Division of Labor,* WEP 2–28 / Working Paper 5, ILO, Geneva.
NACLA (July-August, 1975), *Latin American and Empire Report,* Vol. IX, No. 5.
OECD (1972), *Les actifs correspondant aux investissements directs du secteur privé des pays du C.A.D. dans les pays en voie de développement. Etat à la fin de 1967,* OECD, Paris.
———. (1975), *Investissements par le secteur privé des pays membres du C.A.D. dans les pays en voie de développement, Etat des actifs à la fin de 1973,* OECD, Paris. (Mimeo.)
Riedel, James (1974), *The Industrialization of Hong Kong,* Tubingen: J.C.B. Mohr.
Sabolo, Yves and Trajtenberg, Raúl (February, 1975), *The Impact of Multinational Firms on Employment and Incomes in the Developing Countries—Methodological Note,* WEP 2–28 / Working Paper 1, ILO, Geneva.
Sabolo, Yves and Trajtenberg, Raúl, in collaboration with Sajhau, J. P. (January, 1976), "The Impact of Transnational Enterprises on Employment in the Developing Countries—Preliminary Results" WEP 2–28 / Working Paper 6, ILO, Geneva.
Schreiber, Jordan (1970), *U.S. Corporate Investment in Taiwan,* Cambridge, Mass.
Sepúlveda, César (January–February, 1976), "La Nueva Ley de Comercio Exterior de los Estados Unidos y los países en desarrollo," *El Trimestre Económico,* Vol. XLIII(1), No. 169.
Singapore Department of Statistics (April, 1976), *Monthly Digest of Statistics,* Vol. 15, No. 4.
Taiwan Directorate General of Budget, Accounting and Statistics (1975), *Statistical Yearbook of the Republic of China,* Taipei.
UNCTAD (1975), *Trade in Manufactures of Developing Countries and Territories, 1973 Review,* New York: United Nations.
———. (1976), *Handbook of International Trade and Development Statistics,* New York: United Nations.
United Nations (1971), *Economic Survey of Asia and the Far East, 1970,* Bangkok.
———. (1975), *Statistical Yearbook for Asia and the Pacific, 1974,* Bangkok: United Nations.
———. (1976). *National Legislation and Regulations Relating to Transnational Corporations,* Report of the Secretariat presented to the 2nd Session of the Commission on Transnational Enterprises, Lima.
United States Department of Labor (January, 1976), *Monthly Labor Review,* Washington.
United States Tariff Commission (September, 1970), *Economic Factors Affecting the Use of Items 807.00 and 806.30 of the Tariff Schedules of the U.S.,* Washington.
Vaitsos, C. V. (1974), "Employment Effects of the Foreign Direct Investments in Developing Countries," in Edwards, E. O., ed., *Employment in Developing Nations.*"
———. (1975), *Power, Knowledge and Development Policy: Relations between Transnational Enterprises and Developing Countries,*" Mexico: Centro de Investigación y Docencia Económica. (Mimeo.)
Vaupel, J. W. and Curhan, J. P. (1974), *The World's Multinational Enterprises; A Sourcebook of Tables Based on a Study of the Largest U.S. and Non-U.S. Manufacturing Corporations,*" Geneva: Center for Education in International Management.
Vigorito, R. (1971), "Contribución a la teoría de la producción y la distribución." (*Unpublished manuscripts.*)

Watanabe, S. (May, 1972), ''International Subcontracting, Employment and Skill Promotion,'' *International Labor Review,* pp. 425–451.

Whichard, O. G. and Freidlin, J. N. (August, 1976), ''U.S. Direct Investment Abroad in 1975,'' *Survey of Current Business.*

Williams, K. L. (July, 1975), ''The Extent and Significance of the Nationalization of Foreign-owned Assets in Developing Countries, 1956–1972,'' *Oxford Economic Papers,* New Series, Vol. 27, No. 2.

Yoshino, M. Y. (Fall, 1974), ''The Multinational Spread of Japanese Manufacturing Investment since World War II,'' *Business History Review,* Special Issue: ''Multinational Enterprise.''

PROLETARIAT DICTATORSHIP AND THE DEVELOPMENT OF PRODUCTIVE FORCES IN CHINA

Ng Gek-Boo, GENEVA, SWITZERLAND

INTRODUCTION

Ever since human society was divided into classes, the ruling classes have used the state machinery to suppress their antagonistic classes in order to uphold their dominant position. A socialist society is not an exception. The dictatorship of the proletariat is essentially the class struggle waged by the class representative of socialism in a capitalist society, the proletariat, against the bourgeoisie after the proletariat has seized political power and the bourgeoisie has been defeated but not yet destroyed (see Lenin, 1918).

In this paper we attempt to show how the proletariat dictatorship is carried out in the Chinese context with respect to the economic base and the realm of superstructure. Our purpose is to illustrate the thesis that in a socialist society the continual revolution in both the relations of production and the superstructure under the dictatorship of the proletariat is of paramount importance for the development of the productive forces, which has in turn further consolidated the dictatorship of the proletariat.

The paper is divided into five sections. Section 1 provides a brief account on the need for proletariat dictatorship during the period of socialism. The dictatorship of the proletariat in the economic base and the realm of superstructure is discussed in Sections 2 and 3 respectively. Section 4 explains how the revolution in economic base and superstructure has contributed to the development of productive forces. The final section, Section 5, sets forth some concluding remarks in regard to the elements of Chinese proletariat dictatorship.

1. NEED FOR PROLETARIAT DICTATORSHIP DURING THE PERIOD OF SOCIALISM

The Communist Party of China (CPC) adopted a new constitution at its Tenth National Congress held in August, 1973. In this constitution "the establishment of the dictatorship of the proletariat over the bourgeoisie" is viewed as the basic program of the Party. At the end of 1974, Mao called upon the Chinese people to study "Why did Lenin speak of exercising dictatorship over the bourgeoisie?" In the new constitution of the People's Republic of China, adopted in January, 1975, the need for proletariat dictatorship is further reaffirmed.

Why is it necessary for proletariat dictatorship in a socialist state where the proletariat has taken political power? The answer lies in the fact that the socialist society emerges from the capitalist society. As a negation of the old society it is "thus in every respect, economically, morally and intellectually, still stamped with the birthmarks of the old society" (Marx, 1875, p. 12).

First of all, there are classes and class struggle in a socialist society. The overthrown landlords and capitalists would not have dried out automatically even after the expropriation of their private ownership of the means of production. Yet the resistance of the former ruling class has increased tremendously not only because of their defeat and their subjective desire for survival, but also because of their international connections and the strength of international capital (see Lenin 1918, 1919, 1920). China is not an exception. Numerous attempts were made by the exploiting class to deflect the new regime and to restore the previous owenership system during the period of rehabilitation (1950–1952), while the socialist ownership remained relatively weak in industry and the small but individual farming system prevailed in the countryside. As a result of suppression of landlords and the collectivization of agriculture, and the socialization of industry and commerce, large-scale resistance of the counterrevolutionaries was gradually cleared out (Mao, 1957, p. 115). But class struggle remained very acute in some areas, and was expressed in such new forms as the 1957 attacks of the bourgeois Rightists within the Communist Party on the policy of supressing counterrevolutionaries (Mao, 1957; Robinson, 1969).

Second, there are bourgeois rights in a socialist society. On the one hand, the present system of ownership still consists of the two kinds of socialist public ownership—namely, ownership by the whole people, and collective ownership (Chang, 1975, p. 6).[1] Moreover, there are also private plots and family sidelines[2] in the vast rural areas where the law of value still has a certain role to play. Given these defects of the ownership system and the stage of the development of the productive forces, it is still necessary to have the exchange of commodities by means of money between the two kinds of socialist ownership, as well as within the two kinds of ownership themselves. This simply implies that money can legally be turned into commodities, and, in some cases, illegally turned into capital for the purposes of speculation and exploitation. (*Hong-qi,* Nos. 5 and 8, 1975, and No. 1, 1976.)

On the other hand, income distribution in a socialist society is still dominated by the principle "to each according to his work," This principal is realized mainly through the operation of the eight-grade wage system in industry and the workpoint system[3] in agriculture. In fact this principle of distribution is still a bourgeois right because "equal right is an unequal right for unequal labor" (Marx, 1875, p. 16). As Marx explains:

> . . . the equality consists in the fact that measurement is made with an equal standard, labor. But one man is superior to another physically or mentally and so supplies more labor in the same time, or can work for a longer time. . . . Further, one worker is married, another not; one has more children than another, and so on and so forth. Thus, with an equal performance of labor, and hence an equal share in social consumption fund, one will in fact receive more than another, one will be richer than another, and so on. To avoid all these defects, right instead of being equal would have to be unequal. (Marx, 1875, pp. 16–17.)

Thus inequalities between social groups and between individuals are inevitable in a socialist society.

Third, the three great differences, namely, the differences between workers and peasants, between town and countryside, and between mental and manual labor, still exist under socialism. In the old society, the state apparatus and the ruling class were concentrated in towns, while the oppressed class was mainly struggling in the countryside. Also, there was a process of separation between handicrafts and agriculture and, consequently, a separation between manufacturing and agriculture, and therefore between workers and peasants. And there was, and is, (see Braverman, 1974) a separation between manual and mental labor. Apparently the existence of these differences reflects not only the positions of different social groups in production and their mutual relations, but also the defects of the socialist system from which the restoration of capitalism can still take place; the difference between town and countryside, for instance, can well become the basis of collusion between the urban and the rural capitalist forces, especially in the suburban areas. The abolition of these differences, as a necessary condition for the complete abolition of classes, has become a crucial task in a socialist society (see Lenin, 1919).

Fourth, with a predominantly agricultural economy inherited from a semifeudal and semicolonial society, the problem of small production (especially among the peasantry) is particularly serious in China. "Small production engenders capitalism and the bourgeoisie continuously, daily, hourly, spontaneously and on a mass scale," and it can be an economic basis for the preservation and restoration of capitalism in a socialist state (Lenin, 1920, p. 6). This is indicated not only by the polarization of rural population[4] and the emergence of new rich peasants[5] immediately after land reform, but also by the recent reappearance of the practice of san-zi-yi-bao,[6] which was introduced in the early 1960's but was severely criticized later (*People's Daily,* January 3, 1976). Above all, the habitual, spontaneous forces toward capitalism among the well-to-do middle peasants after the collectivization of agriculture have remained fairly serious in rural China (Hua, 1975, p. 7).

In addition to the above-mentioned birthmarks of the old society, the influence from the ideology and culture of the exploiting class does not disappear immediately according to the change in the system of ownership. The remolding of the petit bourgeoisie (especially among the intellectuals) and the establishment of the proletarian and revolutionary outlook among the working class are also very strenuous tasks. All these suggest that any socialist society is in fact a bourgeois state without the bourgeoisie (see Lenin, 1917).

Despite the change in the system of ownership, it is quite clear that the extension and intensification of the bourgeois rights and the further widening of the three great differences can well lead to the emergence of a new bourgeoisie and threaten the dictatorship of the proletariat. Yet these defects are inevitable in a socialist society and they cannot be eliminated within a short period of time. Socialism has therefore become a transitional period between capitalism and communism. During this transitional period proletariat dictatorship is absolutely essential for restricting and reducing the bourgeois rights and for revolutionizing the realm of superstructure so as to create the conditions in which capitalism can neither survive nor restore.

But what is the major target of proletariat dictatorship in a socialist society when the counterrevolutionaries have been suppressed? Here in lies Mao's remarkable contribution to Marxist theory by advancing the thesis that the bourgeoisie is right in the Communist Party itself. Why? Apparently there are such social bases as class struggle and forces of habit of small production, and such economic bases as the three great differences for capitalist restoration in all organization, including the Communist Party. What is equally important, however, is the fact that the Communist Party is the ruling party; it has supreme power in all affairs, especially since the accomplishment of the socialist transformation of the national economy. Not only is party policy of paramount importance in guiding decision-making of the administration at all levels, but also party cadres have become authoritative in all administrative units such as ministries, factories and communes. This administrative structure may engender a bourgeoisie within the Party, and become a source of capitalist restoration, as pointed out by Mao in the May 16, 1966 Circular of the Centre Committee of the CPC: "These representatives of the bourgeoisie who have sneaked into the Party, the government, the army and various spheres of culture are a bunch of counter-revolutionary revisionists. Once conditions are ripe, they will sieze political power and turn the dictatorship of the proletariat into a dictatorship of the bourgeoisie" (Peking Review, No. 21, 1976, p. 7).

On the other hand, the class struggle in a socialist society will inevitably affect policy formulation. Given the ruling position of the Communist Party, it is quite clear that only the Communist Party can formulate policy; and only the Party authority can change its own policy and materialize such change. The dissolution of 15,000 cooperatives (comprising 400,000 peasant households) in 1955 in Chekiang Province by the Party authority through a single action was only one typical example for illustration (Mao, 1955, p. 9). Regular ideological rectification of the party members is, therefore, stressed, and the significance of the Cultural Revolution in depriving the power of those bourgeois elements of the Party has been reaffirmed.

An immediate implication of the preceding discussion is that there are contradictions between the socialist economic base and the superstructure, both of which are still far from perfect during the period of socialism. These contradictions, however, can be resolved only by deepening the continual revolution under the dictatorship of the proletariat (*The Constitution,* 1975, p. 8).

2. DEVELOPMENT OF SOCIALIST ECONOMIC BASE

The development of the socialist economic base for the consolidation of the dictatorship of the proletariat has been a major task of the CPC since 1949. This task includes the transformation of the system of the ownership of the means of production, the change of the social relations corresponding to the capitalist relations of production, and the realization of the socialist principle of distribution.

The transformation of the system of ownership[7]

After the land reform in 1952, the economy consisted of five kinds of ownership; namely, by the state, by the cooperatives, joint state-private, by capitalists, and by individuals (mostly peasants and handicraftsmen). The national economy was dominated by the ownership of capitalists and individuals whose joint proportion in gross value of output was as high as 78.7 percent (*Ten Great Years*, p. 32). This proportion, however, declined to only 2.9 percent in 1957 as a result of agricultural collectivization and the socialist transformation of industry and commerce.

The socialist transformation of the system of ownership in the agricultural sector is of vital importance for the success of developing a socialist economic base; for nearly 90 percent of the population were inhabitants in the rural areas. The inital task of the CPC was to carry out land reform for achieving the objective of "land to the tillers" so that the social basis of feudalism in rural areas could be substantially weakened. This was essentially the redistribution of the land and other means of production from the landlords and rich peasants to the middle peasants and the poor and lower-middle peasants who accounted for 90 percent of rural population but owned only 30 percent of land. The change in the system of land ownership was a crucial factor for the CPC to win the overwhelming support from the peasantry who benefited from the revolution.

The socialist transformation of agriculture, however, was far from complete in the early 1950's, as Mao describes:

> . . . the spontaneous forces of capitalism have been steadily growing in the countryside in recent years, with new rich peasants springing up everywhere and many well-to-do middle peasants striving to become rich peasants. On the other hand, many poor peasants are still living in poverty for lack of sufficient means of production, with some in debt and others selling or renting out their land. If this tendency goes unchecked, the polarization in the countryside will be aggravated day by day. Those peasants who lose their land and those who remain in poverty will complain that we are doing nothing to save them from ruin or to help them overcome their difficulties. Nor will the well-to-do middle peasants who are heading in the capitalist direction be pleased with us, for we shall never be able to satisfy their demands unless we intend to take the capitalist road. Can the worker-peasant alliance continue to stand firm in these circumstances? Obviously not. (Mao, 1955, pp. 26–27.)

The small farm system, moreover, had failed to grow adequately to keep pace with the rapid progress of the industrial sector. Mao, therefore, proposes to expedite the process of collectivization with a view to eliminating the rich-peasant economy as well as to expanding farm production. (*Ibid.*)

The socialist transformation of agriculture was carried out step by step so that the peasants could gradually adopt a new mode of life (*Ibid.*). The movement of agricultural producers' mutual-aid teams[8] during 1953–1954, for example, was followed by the cooperative movement during 1955–1957, and the setting up of the commune system in 1958.[9] The accomplishment of agricultural collectivization was accompanied by the completion in the main of the socialist transformation of industry and commerce. The continued revolution in the system of ownership eventually brought about the predominace of the ownership by the whole people in industry and commerce and collective ownership in agriculture, as shown in Table 1.

The present ownership pattern implies that the strenuous task of socialist revolution in the system of ownership has yet to be completed. A fundamental weakness of the ownership system is that peasants who collectively own the means of production, still have certain freedom in arranging the production of their own units. The predominance of collective ownership in agriculture has, therefore, made it difficult for the coordination of production planning between agriculture and industry. Moreover, inequalities between peasants and workers, and between

Table 1. Ownership Pattern by Industry, 1974 (%)

	Gross value of output		
Kinds of ownership	Agriculture	Industry	Commerce: volume of retail sales
Ownership by the whole people	10.0	86.0	92.5
Collective Ownership	90.0	14.0	7.3
Individual Ownership	*	*	0.2
Total	100.0	100.0	100.0

Source: Chang (1975), p. 6.
*negligible

peasants associated with collective units varying in resource endowment are inevitable. Explicitly this ownership system reflects the contradictions between workers and peasants as well as among the peasants themselves. Hence it is of vital importance for transforming the collective ownership of agriculture into the ownership by the whole people. Under a unified ownership by the whole people, a nationwide common-wage system can be introduced and the differences between town and countryside and between peasants and workers considerably reduced. Of course, the final objective is the transition from socialism to communism in which both the issues of the system of ownership and of distribution are no longer in existence.

The success of the transition from the present system of ownership to the one kind of socialist ownership by the whole people depends very much on whether the vast majority of the masses can benefit economically from such a transition. Only then will the overwhelming support of the masses be expected. Two complementary factors have thus become very important: (1) the magnitude of inequality between peasants and workers, and among peasants themselves; and (2) the strength of the sector under the ownership by the whole people. The smaller the difference between peasants and workers and the stronger the position of the sector under the ownership by the whole people, the greater will be the success of such transition. If the magnitude of the inequality is insignificant, less strength will be required for the sector under the ownership by the whole people in fulfilling the conditions of benefiting the masses materially. Of course, if the political consciousness of the masses is raised to such a level that they are prepared to sacrifice in the short-run for gaining in the long-run from the revolution in the system of ownership and the resultant development of productive forces, it is still possible that the transition of ownership will take place successfully when both the conditions of transition are not sufficiently mature. This principle also applies to the transition of ownership within the collective economy from the level of production team to the level of production brigade and communes.

The transition of ownership, therefore, consists of two processes. The first process is to accelerate agricultural development (especially agricultural mechanization and rural industrialization), and to reduce the productivity gap between agriculture and industry. Undoubtedly, industrialization is crucial for strengthening the position of the sector under the ownership by the whole people in accelerating the process of ownership transition. The second process is to reduce ineqalities between collectives and to raise the level of collectivity in rural areas.[10] Here we shall focus on the first process and discuss the second process later.

The sectoral relation between industry and agriculture reflects the relation between workers and peasants in society. In capitalist-society, failure to ensure the proportionate development of various economic sectors can easily lead to soaring prices and production crisis. In China, the CPC adopted the policy slogan "taking agriculture as the foundation and industry as the leading factor," in January, 1961, for both economic and political reasons. Economically, industrialization is an unattainable goal when the agricultural sector remains backward and fails to provide industry with a steadily growing domestic market, manpower, food and raw materials and surplus. The industrial sector, on the other hand, plays its leading role by providing the agricultural sector with various inputs for mechanization and modernizaton. Also, the development of light industry creates demand for farm products, as well as generating surplus for the development of heavy industry, which holds the key to industrialization and the modernization of national defense.[11] Politically, this policy will enchance the worker-peasant alliance because it ensures the supply of manufactured goods to rural areas so that the peasants also benefit from the process of industrialization. Meanwhile, the introduction of this policy helps the nation to uphold the principle of self-reliance and political independence, since the economy does not have to depend on foreign trade as the sources of primary raw materials and the markets of manufacturing industries.

This stress on agricultural development has led to the launching of a nationwide program of industrial support to agriculture, in which the urban modern industries are urged to supply adequate but cheaper and better consumption and capital goods to rural areas. It aslo includes the extensive development of rural small-scale industries, which is part of the policy of "walking on two legs."[12] On the other hand, the price of agricultural and sideline products has been raised steadily by the state, and the price of manufactured goods has been cut. This has resulted in the improvement of the domestic terms of trade by 45 percent in favor of agriculture during 1950–1975 (*Peking Review*, No. 37, 1975). Moreover, agricultural tax is fixed, and its share in the value of total farm output has declined steadily since 1952.

Apparently the introduction of all these policy measures aim at erasing the birthmarks of the old society, especially the three great differences. Has the State played a role in the transformation of the system of ownership? Surely the confiscation of bureaucrat capital and land reform in the early 1950's are the examples. Yet the state machinery has been used extensively for transforming the private ownership into state ownership in the industrial sector, and accelerating the process of collectivization in agriculture. The variation of interest rates shown in Table 2 is an example. In addition, the control of foreign trade and wholesale trade by the state and the introduction of legislative measures such as the planned purchase and supply of food-grain have undoubtedly contributed to the disintegration of the capitalist forces in both urban and rural areas. But it is also very clear that the transformation of the system of ownership has in turn further consolidated the worker-peasant alliance and the dictatorhsip of the proletariat.

Table 2. Monthly Interest Rates of Loans Provided by the State in October 1955 (%)

Industry	
State	0.48
State-private joint venture	0.69
Private	0.99
Commerce	
State and cooperatives	0.60
Joint-venture	0.81
Private	1.35
Agriculture	
Cooperative fund of poor peasants*	0.40
Cooperatives	0.60
Individuals	0.90

Source: Hsi (1962), pp. 211–212.

*The loan is provided for the poor peasants having difficulties in paying their shares in the cooperative fund.

Social Relations

The mutual relations between different social groups in production is an important element of the relations of production in socialist society. After the socialist transformation of the system of ownership has been accomplished, management has become a key issue in consolidating the socialist economic base (see Mao,

1974). A main purpose of revolution in the management of factories and communes is, of course, to establish the social relations corresponding to socialism.

The major task of revolutionizing factory management is to abolish the absolute authority of the managerial staff and to reduce the privileges of experts and technicians (see Bettelheim, 1974). The measures introduced for improving the relations between different social groups in factories can be summed up by the "An-kang Charter" issued in 1960.[13] New institutional arrangements in the Charter include the participation of workers in management and the participation of cadres in manual labor, the change of irrational codes and conventions, and the combination of workers, cadres and technicians in management and research. In addition, more and more workers have been promoted to become leading cadres of factories since 1966.[14]

Peasants also participate actively in the management of people's communes. Generally speaking, key posts in communes are held by poor and lower-middle peasants who are not only the majority of rural population, but also the most reliable ally of workers in the countryside and the major force of revolution in the Chinese context. (See Mao, 1956; Hua, 1975; and *The Constitution,* 1975.) In addition to production, poor and lower-middle peasants also participate in and control the management of supply and marketing cooperatives.[15] This aims at ensuring the interests of the masses during the development process of the collective economy.

There are two noticeable features of management in both factories and communes. First, the principle of a three-in-one combination of the old, the middle-aged and the young is introduced. This is viewed as a necessary measure for bringing up revolutionary successors. Next, mass supervision is emphasized. Financial transactions and accounts in rural collectives, for instance, have to be rendered to the masses for examination and comments.

In view of promoting the relation between cadres and the masses, the need for cadres at all levels to participate in collective productive labor is institutionalized (see *The Constitution*, p. 19). The number of working days for local cadres to participate in collective farming, for example, has been fixed at 100, 200 and 300 respectively at the country, the commune and the production brigade and team levels. As compared with 60 working days for cadres at the commune level to participate in collective farming in the mid 1960's, the figure of the early 1970's is much higher (see Ng, 1976b, p. 44). Moreover, a rotation system for leading party cadres to participate regularly in collective farming is being popularized in rural China (see *People's Daily*, June 26, 1976). All these may be seen as measures for restricting bourgeois rights, avoiding social stratification and solving local problems on the spot.

Party cadres of the state organs participate in collective labor and integrate themselves with the masses through the May 7th Cadres Schools which were first established in Heilungkiang Province in 1968 according to Mao's May 7th directive. In the May 7th Cadres Schools, students engage in farm production and study Marxism simultaneously for a period of six months to one year, and then return to their original units. To prevent the bourgeois life among the leading party cadres, all the students of the schools, regardless of their original position, live together in dormitories and share similar food and working conditions.

Distribution

In socialist society, material supply is still not abundant and the political consciousness of the masses is not adequately high. In order to ensure the development of productive forces during this transition period, the national product has to be distributed to the people according to work. This socialist principle of distribution, however, remains a bourgeois right, as explained in Section 1. It is thus necessary to carry out reforms in the form of distribution in socialist society.

In China an eight-grade wage system is introduced for workers. According to Bettelheim (1974, pp. 15–16), the ratio between the bottom and the top rates of this eight-grade wage system is around 1:3. The average wage rates, however, vary considerably from one factory to another. Generally speaking, workers in heavy industry receive more than those in light industry, while, for similar types of jobs, urban wage rates are always higher than the rural ones. Meanwhile, technicians and managerial staff are paid by a relatively higher wage scale, but the ratio between the average salary of managerial staff and the average pay of workers was reported to be less than 2:1 in most cases, and the highest was 3:1 (Richman, 1969, p. 805).

Income inequality between workers and technicans, between workers and managerial staff, and among workers themselves, therefore, is unavoidable. One of the measures for reducing income inequality among workers is to raise the wage rates of the bottom scales. Nevertheless, income disparity among workers is far less marked than that among peasants; for the similar wage system which is applied in industry owned predominantly by the whole people cannot be applied in the agricultural sector under collective ownership.

In rural areas the issue of distribution is complicated by the system of ownership, especially the three-tier ownership pattern of the people's communes.[16] Inequality exists not only between individual households, but also between collectives of various levels (i.e., communes, production brigades and production teams). Income disparity between members varying in dependency ratio and skill and physical conditions may be quite considerable, even within the same collective unit (Ng, 1976b, p. 3). Yet this disparity is widened by the difference in resource endowment and economic performance between collective units in which the peasants are associated. Given the principle of distribution and the ownership pattern of the commune system, inequality in rural China exists at all dimensions: between the production teams of the same production brigades and the production brigades of the same commune; between the communes within a country; and between collectives across the countryside. Such a situation has become a main concern of the CPC, for it is the economic basis for the emergence of the well-to-do middle peasants in rural areas.

As the widening of income disparity among the peasantry is apparently not conducive to the objective of socialism, some measures have been consistently introduced for reducing it. Administrative and material assistance, for instance, are usually provided by the production brigade or commune to its associated poor production teams, and by the county or the prefecture administration to its associated production brigades and communes. An important step for reducing intracommune inequality is to raise the level of collectivity and to transfer the ownership from the production team to production brigade and commune. On the other hand, the transfer of the collective ownership to the ownership by the whole people has become a vital step for the further reduction of intercommune inequality, mainly because a common wage scheme can be applied in all communes owned by the whole people.

Within a collective unit the workpoint system has also been gradually reformed for reducing inequality between member households. Apart from introducing equal pay for equal work between sexes, the number of grades and the common difference between grades have also been reduced. Meanwhile, the criteria of assessment of workpoints have been changed: politically conscious and hard-working members are awarded with additional number of workpoints (see Ng, 1976b, Section 3.2).

More significantly, the "need" element has been gradually added in income distribution in both factories and communes. In factories, social services such as education, housing and medical care are provided for the workers on a "need" basis. Expenditure on workers' welfare schemes could be as high as 30–40 percent of wage expenditure (see Comrades, 1973). Communes have even started to distribute food-grain to members according to need.[17]

"Distribution according to work" remains the predominant principle of distribution in socialist society. Strictly speaking, this is material incentive. The use of material-incentive schemes, however, is supplemented by the introduction of nonmaterial incentive schemes. Through the lessons of 1958, during which private plots were abolished and the commune was the basic accounting unit, the CPC learned that absolute egalitarianism could not be achieved during the period of socialism. That is, "right can never be higher than the economic structure of society and its cultural development conditioned thereby" (Marx, 1875, p. 17). But this does not prevent the use of nonmaterial incentives for mobilizing the masses. As a matter of fact, both the An-kang Charter and the nationwide campaigns of "learning from Taching" propagate "politics in command" and "the spirit of communism." Explicitly, this indicates the Chinese view that material incentives, no matter how important and necessary they are, should not be the only type of incentives for mobilization during the period of socialism. In other words, nonmaterial incentives should be gradually added, and should become increasingly important as the level of concsiousness of the masses rises. Eventually material incentives will be replaced by nonmaterial incentives—as soon as socialism is replaced by communism.

Finally, the preceding discussion clearly shows the decisive role played by the system of ownership in the relations of production as a whole and in the position of various social groups in production and the form of distribution of product. Rural China is an illustrative example. Although the land reform had contributed to the complete change of the relations between peasants and landlords, and to the improvement of the well-being of the masses, the existence of an individual small farming system had also failed to check against polarization. It is only after collectivization that the vast majority of the peasantry, especially the poor and lower-middle peasants, have improved both socially and economically, as compared with the period under the systems of individual farming and mutual-aid team. (Rich peasants, on the other hand, were no longer rich after collectivization, for they had lost the sources of hired labor and rental income.) Inequality, however, remains under the three-tier ownership pattern of the commune system. The problem of distribution can only be solved after the transfer of collective ownership to the ownership by the whole people. Yet, the mutual relations between people and the form of distribution will affect the system of ownership. Given certain conditions, either may play the decisive role in the relations of production. The aggravation of inequality and the abuse of power by party cadres, for instance, can finally lead to the change in the relations of production and weaken the socialist economic base.

3. REVOLUTION IN THE REALM OF SUPERSTRUCTURE

The realm of superstructure refers to the political and ideological dimensions of class domination, including political and legislative bodies, art, philosophy and religion. Its relation with economic base is one of dialectical unity.[18] Theoretically speaking the economic base is decisive in a sense that the entire superstructure is founded on the economic base; and following the setting up of the socialist economic base, the old superstructure should be changed accordingly. The transformation of the entire superstructure, however, does not always take place satisfactorily after the change in economic base, mainly because the ideological resistance of the capitalist is "the most deep-seated and the strongest." A backward superstructure may still exist after the change of ownership, and this may hinder the consolidation of the new economic base as well as the dictatorship of the proletariat.

In this section we shall discuss how the revolution in the realm of superstructure is taking place in China. But we refer only to some selected issues such as the change in education system and the direction of arts and literature, and the migration of urban educated youth to rural areas.

Education

The Chinese educational system has changed substantially since liberation, especially after the Cultural Revolution. The changes in the educational system include curriculum, teaching method, enrollment system and management. The reform of the education system is carried out in accordance with Mao's instruction that "education must serve proletarian politics and be combined with productive labor," although it should be noted that the reform of educational system is still at an experimental stage and a new educational system has yet to emerge for the future.

First of all, new curricula for schools and colleges are designed for revolutionizing the outlook of students and for meeting the needs of factories and communes for manpower and skills. As a whole the new curricula in both urban and rural schools and colleges emphasize the teaching of such courses as animal husbandry, bookkeeping and veterinary so that education can contribute directly to the growth of productive forces. More significantly, teaching materials were thoroughly revised so as to serve the purpose of transforming the ideology of students and of establishing the proletariat world outlook among the younger generations. Politics, therefore, has become a major subject in schools at all levels.

A very important change of the curricula is the emphasis on the participation of students in industrial and farm production. As a result schools in urban areas are encouraged to set up their own factories and farms, and in rural areas schools have their own farms and experimental plots. College and university students have to participate regularly in production in factories and communes, while some agricultural colleges have moved from towns to rural areas. Clearly an objective of this "open-door education" system it to integrate schools with society, students and teachers with the masses, and to narrow the difference between mental and manual labor.

The changes in curricula and teaching methods were followed by the setting up of a new enrollment system for colleges and universities. Essentially the new enrollment system is a response to Mao's call for following the method of Shanghai Machine Tools Plants in training technicians from among the workers. Under this system secondary school graduates can only be enrolled after they have acquired a few years practical experience and have been recommended by the masses and the local party committee. The students, therefore, are politically reliable, and they are also more likely to return to work in their original units after graduation.

The new system has also promoted new links between schools and factories and rural collective units.[19] Owing to these links, graduates become useful to the society and are welcomed by the masses. In rural areas, for example, most graduates have become instructors of the political and cultural evening schools, agro-technicians, mechanics and electricians, barefoot doctors, and veterinarians. Thus education has in fact become an effective instrument for both the development of productive forces and the consolidation of the dictatorship of the proletariat.

Logically, the control of management of schools and colleges by the working class has become vital for the proletariat revolution in education. While workers participate in running schools and universities in urban areas, poor and lower-middle peasants have been assigned to the management committee of schools and colleges.

Last, the education of the peasantry is considered by Mao as a serious problem and a fundamental task of the CPC (see Mao, 1949 and 1956). This is due to the existence of the influence of the centuries-old feudalism and of the spontaneous forces of small production. In rural China a political education network has been set up for propagating socialism and criticizing capitalism. This theoretical, tutorial network consists of stations at the commune level, teams at the production brigade level and tutors at the production team level. In many areas there are class education exhibition rooms for explaining to the younger generations about the past.

Arts and Literature

Like education, arts and literature, as part of the superstructure, had lagged behind the change in the economic base. Mao himself was very much concerned about the backwardness of the nation's arts and literature. After liberation he went further to set up the criteria for judging the nature of arts and literature, such as whether they help to accelerate socialist transformation of the national economy and to consolidate the people's democratic dictatorship and the leadership of the communist party (Mao, 1957, pp. 119–120). By the end of 1963 the situation got worse, and Mao bitterly complained that arts had become a serious problem and "had fell to the edge of revisionism." He even referred to the Ministry of Culture as the "Ministry of Emperors, Kings, Generals, and Ministers, the Ministry of Talents and Beauties, and the Ministry of Foreign Mummies" (*Peking Review*, No. 28, 1976).

The backwardness of arts and literature in socialist China was indicated by their lack of criticizing the legacies of the Confucian school of thought and their divorce from the masses. Confucians despised productive labor and the masses, advocated male chauvinism and the restoration of the old political order and proposed elite management and urban-rural separation.[20] The influence of these legacies had no doubt been very unfavorable to the movement of urban educated youth to rural areas, the reform of education system, and the setting up of a commune system and the new system of factory management. The Confucian legacies, however, had never been criticized on a mass scale until the early 1970's when the Lin-Piao affair was linked.

On the other hand, arts and literature, under the influence of Confucianism and revisionism, did not serve the common masses. Neither did they propagate socialism and the new socialist institutional settings such as barefoot doctors and workers' participation in management.

All this was naturally found incompatible with socialist development. The superstructure, therefore, had even played a disruptive role in the development of a new socialist economic base. It is thus not surprising that arts and literature had become a main target of the Cultural Revolution. The Chinese case is perhaps a good example of the arduousness of the task of revolutionizing the superstructure after the socialist economic base has been founded.

Migration of Urban Educated Youth to Rural Areas

In 1966 the CPC started to initiate the urban educated youth to migrate to rural areas. The number of migrants reached 12 million during the period 1966–1975, partly as a result of the change in education system. The main purpose, however, is to provide an opportunity for the young school-leavers to be reeducated by the poor and lower-middle peasants about the hardships and sufferings of the old society. In addition, as all these migrated youth are engaged in collective farming and part of them will settle down in the countryside, this measure is clearly of farreaching significance for narrowing the three great differences, particularly the one between mental and manual labor.

In short, the revolution in the realm of superstructure seems much more complicated than that in the relations of production. Furthermore, the change in the outlook of the peasantry and the younger generation, and the development of new arts and literature, require a long period of time.

4. GRASP REVOLUTION, PROMOTE PRODUCTION: THE GROWTH OF PRODUCTIVE FORCES

Within a short period of three years after liberation, China managed to restore industrial and agricultural production. By 1952, both grain and cotton output had surpassed the preliberation peak (*Ten Great Years*). The rapid growth of productive forces in China since 1949 is well-known; some self-explanatory evidence is provided in Table 3 below. The infant mortality dropped from 200 per thousand in 1949 to around 25 per thousand in 1973. By 1975, China had achieved a five-year universal education program. Meanwhile, a network consisting of hospitals in counties, clinics in communes, health stations in production brigades and health aids in production teams, has been set up in rural areas.

How does the revolution in both the relations of production and the superstructure contribute to the rapid growth of productive forces? Let us begin with the

Table 3. Major Indicators of the Growth of Productive Forces

	1949	*1957*	*1974*
Population ('000)	548,770	656,630	800,000
Grain output (million tons)	110	185	275
Per capita grain output (Kg)	200	282	344
Steel output ('000 tons)	158	5,350	23,000*

Source: Ng (1976a), Table 1.
*Referring to 1972.

change in the system of ownership. The socialist transformation of industry and commerce and the collectivization of agriculture have facilitated national development planning, because the relations between the two kinds of socialist public ownership are no doubt relatively much more coherent than that between the state sector and the private sector of the early 1950's. This system of ownership makes it possible that the development of industry and agriculture (or alternatively, the growth of the two kinds of ownerhsip) complement and promote each other within a self-reliant, integrated economic framework.

The correct handling of the relations between industry and agriculture under socialism, of course, is of paramount importance for the rapid expansion of the economy. Apparently the predominance of the sector under the ownership by the whole people in the economy is a necessary condition for the introduction of various policy measures for accelerating agricultural development as well as for improving the livelihood of the peasantry. The achievement of self-sufficiency in food-grain in the traditionally low-yield and grain-deficient areas like Hopei, Honan and Shantung Provinces, for example, was very much attributed to the policy of industrial support to agriculture and "walking on two legs." Indeed, it is amazing to see how a province like Hopei is able to direct its industrial sector to produce diesel engines and water pumps for meeting the urgent needs of the agricultural sector. Of course, the whole program of industrial support to agriculture is first of all based on political rationality rather than profitability.

The success of the policy of walking on two legs is particularly relevant to the ownership system. In China, the coexistence between the small-scale, backward industry and the large-scale, modern industry is possible mainly because the state runs both small and big enterprises. For the state, the losses of the large enterprise resulting from providing technical assistance to its smaller counterpart will be covered by the gains from the small one as a result of technical progress (see Wheelwright and McFarlane, 1970, Chapter 9).

The collectively owned small local enterprises also coexist with, and receive support from, the large ones owned by the whole people. This is partly because they are indispensable for rural industrialization and agricultural mechanization which, as explained earlier, are crucial for ownership transition and for narrowing the three great differences; and partly because, given China's economic setting, the growth of the productive forces in the agricultural sector is vital for achieving national industrialization.

In the agricultural sector, land reform had been a stimulant of farm production simply because the poor and lower-middle peasants were no longer working for landlords and rich peasants. The crucial role of land reform in promoting production was reflected by the rapid expansion of grain and cotton output during the early 1950's (see *Ten Great Years*). After land reform, production keeps on leaping with the revolution in the system of ownership, and the role of the relations of production in the development of productive forces in rural areas remains. The abolition of returns on land during the cooperative movement, for instance, had helped to raise the rate of collective accumulation and to accelerate the growth of the collective economy (see Soo, 1976). Yet some statistical evidence suggests that the rate of collective accumulation was much higher in people's communes than in agricultural producers' cooperatives. Followed by the rise in the level of collectivity, the rate of collective accumulation in the early 1970's was even higher than in the 1960's (see Ng, 1976b, Table 5).

There are a few reasons for the correlation between the growth of collective economy and the changes in the system of ownership. First, the size of private plots and the incomes from family sidelines are very limited under the commune system. Given this ownership system and the resultant change in the form of distribution, peasants can be considerably better off only through working hard for the development of the collective economy. Provided that the livelihood of the masses has been gradually improved year by year, peasants are unlikely to resist a higher rate of collective accumulation. They know how important it is to accumulate more for future progress of the collective as well as for the interests of the individuals. For this reason they are willing to participate in water conservation and soil improvement projects during the slack seasons so as to accelerate collective capital formation. Next, the increase in the scale of collectives also strengthens the financial and manpower positions of the collectives in developing farm infrastructure and rural industries, in resisting natural calamities, and in expediting technical progress.

The subsequent changes in the form of distribution also plays a role in promoting the growth of productive forces. The introduction of the socialist principle of distribution in cooperatives, for instance, was the main reason for the rapid growth of labor forces in the mid 1960's (see Mao, 1956, and Soo, 1976). The realization of the principle of equal pay for equal work between sexes is also vital for mobilizing the female labor force.[21] On the other hand, the adherence to the socialist principle of distribution is also conducive to the development of the productive forces. This is because consumption in a less inegalitarian society is less conspicuous and ostentatious, so that resources can be reserved for productive use.

The superiority of the socialist system over the capitalist system in the development of productive forces is also indicated by the types of altruistic cooperation and the new but creative role played by workers and peasants in China. Under the two kinds of socialist public ownership, the relationship between factories and between collectives is not one between buyers and sellers; it is fairly homogeneous. Close cooperation between factories and between communes is no doubt important for rapid technological formation in China. Illustrative examples cannot be enumerated one by one; however: the remodelling work for Shanghai's 1,000 old boilers in 1969 was completed within 80 days as a result of mobilizing 200,000 people of all trades; The Anshan Iron and Steel Company and the Taching Oilfield have contributed respectively to the development of the nation's steel industry and petroleum industry; and workers' technical innovation was the predominant factor that accounted for the rapid progress of the Farm Machine Workshop of Sinhui County in Kwangtung Province (Ng 1976a, p. 51).

There are similar cases in communes. The enthusiasm of the masses in socialism can be seen from the setting up of a nationwide scientific experimentation network at county, commune, production brigade and production team levels; and the participation of over 10 million peasants in scientific experiments. The peasants have also begun to advance new agro-techniques such as the first variety of short-stalk rice seedlings with soil in Chekiang Province. Rural collectives learn from each other; diffusion of technology is rapid and effective. All these show that "the masses have boundless creative power," and they are the "motive force in the making of world history."

The revolution in the realm of superstructure has also indirectly contributed to the rapid of productive forces. The movement of criticizing Confucian legacies is essential for realizing the principle of equal pay for equal work between sexes, and for restoring the creativity of the masses. Reforms of the education system also facilitate technological formation in both industry and agriculture. The capitalist spontaneous forces in rural areas are being restricted as a result of educating the peasantry. This also promotes the growth of the collective economy. On the other hand, the improvement in the access of peasants to medical and health services, as a result of training barefoot doctors and of the setting up of a cooperative medical scheme, has become an important source of additional labor supply in rural areas (see *People's Daily*, December 24, 1973 and September 16, 1974).

In China the relations of production as a whole are, therefore, in conformity with the development of productive forces. However, as shown in Sections 2 and 3, both the socialist economic base and the superstructure are far from perfect. These imperfections are still in contradictory forms to the development of productive forces, and should be constantly checked. Thus continued revolution under the dictatorship of the proletariat holds the key to the spiral growth of productive forces in socialist society.

Dialectically speaking, the rapid development of productive forces has in turn helped to consolidate the dictatorship of the proletariat in China. As we explained in Section 1, a reason for the existence of bourgeois rights in socialist society is the lack of abundant commodity supply. The increase in material supply resulting from the growth of productive forces has in fact restricted the bourgeois rights of socialist society.

The growth of productive forces also has an impact on superstucture. As pointed out by Mao, "The social and economic physiognomy of China will not undergo a complete change until the socialist transformation of the social and economic system is accomplished and until, in the technical field, machinery is used, wherever possible, in every branch of production and in every place" (Mao, 1955, p. 28).

5. PROLETARIAT DICTATORSHIP: THE CHINESE STYLE

The Chinese proletariat and the peasants under the guidance of proletariat revolutionary theory have seized political power for twenty-seven years, and have gone through a number of revolutionary upheavals since the birth of CPC. At this stage it should not be too difficult to sum up the features of proletariat dictatorship in China.

First of all, the dictatorship of the proletariat in China is characterized by the active participation of the masses. In the process of revolutionizing the relations of production and the superstructure, the masses at the grassroots level have indeed made their very significant contributions. These contributions, moreover, are not limited by their participation in the movements for revolutionary changes; the working class has in fact gone further to gain control over the management of factories, research institutions, communes, hospitals and clinics, schools and colleges, etc. The active participation of the masses verifies that the Chinese revolution is bound to be a proletariat revolution which is a self-conscious movement of the immense majority for their own interest (Marx and Engles, 1848, p. 45).

Subsequently, new forms of mass participation in revolution have emerged, especially since the Cultural Revolution (i.e., open debates, big-character posters, etc.). The right of workers to strike against irrational codes and conventions and the right of the masses to criticize the party cadres and further ensured in the new constitutions of the CPC and the People's Republic. The participation of the masses, however, is also indispensable for the consolidation of the socialist economic base[22] and the development of productive forces.

Second, the Chinese revolution is characterized by its continuity. Taking the post-liberation period as an example: during the period of land reform and economic rehabilitation, the Thoughts Reform Campaign was initiated for the intellectuals in 1950. Subsequently, there were the Three Antis Campaign (against corruption, waste and bureaucracy) and the Five Antis Campaign (against bribery, tax evasion, fraud, theft of government property contracts and stealing economic information for private speculation) directed respectively to party cadres and capitalists. Later on, there were socialist education movements (from the fall of 1962 to the summer of 1966), including the "Four Clean-ups Movement"[23] (see Robinson 1969). This was followed by the Cultural Revolution during 1966–1969. And it has not ended with the achievements of the Cultural Revolution. In the early 1970's there were movements such as the criticism of Lin Piao and Confucius and the study of the theory of proletariat dictatorship.

Third, in each mass campaign targets were clearly set. The isolation of landlords in land reform movement and the concentration on "party persons in authority who are taking the capitalist road" in the Cultural Revolution are examples. At the end of the each campaign the vast majority (i.e., peasants in land reform and party members in Cultural Revolution) were educated and united.[24]

Of course all these movements were the class struggle waged by the proletariat and peasants against the bourgeoisie and landlords. The state has been acting as a repressive organ. Nevertheless the experience suggests that the support and participation of the masses has become increasingly important for the success of all social movements.[25]

The overall objective of the proletariat dictatorship remains unchanged; the ultimate objective is to eliminate classes and bourgeois rights. The historical role of proletariat dictatorship in the transitional period will come to an end as soon as the conditions set out by Marx for communism are fulfilled:

> In a higher phase of communist society, after the enslaving subordination of the individual to the division of labor, and with it also the antithesis between mental and physical labor, has vanished; after labor has become not only a means of life but itself life's prime want; after the productive forces have also increased with the all-round development of the individual, and all the springs of cooperative wealth flow more abundantly—only then can the narrow horizon of bourgeois right be crossed in its entirety and society inscribe on its banners: From each according to his ability, to each according to his needs. (Marx, 1875, p. 17.)

FOOTNOTES

1. In the Chinese context collective ownership denotes the ownership of the means of production by such collective units as communes, production brigades, production teams and urban neighborhood committees. During the period of socialism the collective ownership will be transferred to the ownership by the whole people represented through the state administration.

2. The size of private plots is about 5–7 percent of the cultivable area. On average, the share of private income in total household income is around 10–20 percent. The prior

development and absolute predominance of the collective economy remain. (*The Constitution of the People's Republic of China,* 1975, p. 17.)

3. The workpoint system has two accounting procedures: (1) the calculation of the number of workpoints earned by each member and (2) the determination of the value of daily workpoints. For details, see Ng (1976b).

4. For example, nearly half of the number of poor peasant households were indebted in 1953, and there were transactions of land in many areas. The number of new rich peasants who engaged in usury and speculation had also increased in most areas. See Soo (1976).

5. The terms rich, middle and poor and lower-middle peasants refer to the original class status before land reform. For the definition of these classes in rural China, see Mao (1933). The terms "new rich peasants" and "new middle peasants or well-to-do middle peasants" refer respectively to those who rose to the status of rich and middle peasants as defined.

6. This means "three contracts and one reward"—a policy which was introduced in the early 1960's as material incentives for expanding farm output.

7. China's socialist revolution was carried out in two stages: new democracy and socialism. This is due to the semicolonial and semifeudal character of Chinese society. Given the backwardness of China's economy before 1949, the establishment of an independent democratic society is necessary for the success of socialist revolution. See Mao (1940).

8. An early form of the agricultural producers' mutual-aid teams was the mutal-aid working groups and ploughing teams of the liberated areas during the late 1920's and the 1930's. This was still based on individual ownership, but members helped each other on the principle of voluntary participation and mutual benefits.

9. The cooperative movement was developed by two stages. The agricultural producers' cooperatives were only semisocialist in nature, because members who pooled their land and other major means of production as shares, still retained their private ownership and received dividends from their shares. These were abolished in the advanced agricultural producers' cooperatives, and the principle of distribution according to work has since been observed.

10. The level of collectivity in a people's commune is determined by the share of the commune and brigades in the total fixed assets of the whole commune. The larger the share, the higher is the level of collectivity. The level of collectivity can also be shown by the level of the basic accounting unit in the three-tier commune system.

11. The order of priorities of agriculture, light industry and heavy industry in China's development planning does not mean that the agricultural sector would receive the lion's share of state investment. In fact, the investment in heavy industry has been proportionally greater than that in light industry and agriculture. See Ng (1976a).

12. Apart from the simultaneous development of large-scale and small-scale industries, "walking on two legs" also applies to the use of both modern and indigenous technologies and the establishment of both state and local enterprises.

13. An-kang is the abbreviation of the Anshan Iron and Steel Comapny in Northeast China.

14. During the period 1966–1975, around 100,000 workers were promoted to participate in management in China. (*People's Daily*, February 27, 1976.)

15. Seventy percent of the number of supply and marketing cooperatives, in rural areas, were controlled by the poor and lower-middle peasants. (*Ibid.*)

16. The crux of the matter is that each collective unit exercises its own administrative function and is responsible for its surplus and losses.

17. It should be noted that the policy measures adopted by communes for reducing inequality vary considerably between localities. In Tachai, the famous production brigade of Hsiyang County in Shansi Province, food-grain is distributed to each member completely

according to need. But in other areas only part of the distributed food-grain is shared by members, the rest still distributed according to work. See Ng (1976b).

18. In his speech in November 1958 concerning Stalin's paper on "Economic Problems of Socialism in the USSR" Mao criticized Stalin for not talking about the superstructure and the relation between the superstructure and the economic base. (See Mao, 1974).

19. The Chaoyang Agricultural College of Liaoning Province is a good example for illustrating the links between communes and colleges under the new educational system. The college enrols students recommended by the communes and provides courses required by the communes. Students return to work in their associated communes during the vacations and after graduation. As the system has helped to solve many technical problems, it is welcomed by the peasants. (*Kwangming Daily,* December 12, 1974.)

20. Some of the Confucius legacies can be seen from the following popular quotations:

> those who work with their minds govern, those who work with their hands are governed; those who live in the town are mainly officials and gentlemen; the people mostly live outside the town; and only the highest who are the wise and the lowest who are the stupid cannot be changed. See Yang (1974.).

21. In 1974 the share of women in total number of employees was 40 percent in Peking's scientific and technical units, 35 percent in Shanghai industry and around 40 to 50 percent in rural areas. See Ng (1976a).

22. The period of agricultural collectivization, for example, was intially planned for eighteen years (1949–1967). But it was completed within nine years (1949–1957). Moreover, the term "People's Commune" was also created by the masses after extensive discussions. Naturally the masses are ready to protect and improve the new institution which they have created.

23. This movement was originally initiated for clearing the accounts, stocks, finance and workpoints in rural areas. It was then developed into a national one for the rectification of politics, economy, organization and ideology.

24. According to Mao, China should have more social movements like Cultural Revolution in the future. (*People's Daily* May 16, 1976.)

25. After reviewing the experience of socialist education movement and the Cultural Revolution, Mao came to the conclusion that all the movements prior to the Cultural Revolution did not succeed in changing the outlook of the masses and consolidating the dictatorship of the proletariat, because "we did not find a form, a method, to arouse the broad masses to expose our dark aspect openly, in an all-round way and from below" (*Peking Review,* No. 7, 1976). In view of maintaining this tradition, the "open-door rectification" of party committees at the grassroots level has been repeatedly emphasized.

REFERENCES

Bettelheim, C. (1974), *Cultural Revolution and Industrial Organization in China: Changes in Management and Division of Labor* (translated by Ehrenfeld, Alfred), New York and London: Monthly Review Press.

Braverman, H. (1974), *Labor and Monoploy Capital: The Degradation of Work in the Twentieth Century,* New York: Monthly Review Press.

Burcheet, V. and Rewi, A. (1976), *China: The Quality of Life,* Penguin Books.

Chang, C. C. (1975), *On Excercising All-Round Dictatorhsip over the Bourgeoisie,* Peking: Foreign Language Press.

Comrades of the Shanghai Hutung Shipyards and the Sixth Economic Study Group of Shanghai Municipal May 7th School (1973), *Two Kinds of Society, Two Kinds of Wages* (in Chinese), Shanghai: Renmin-Chuban-She.

The Consitution of the People's Republic of China (1975), Peking: Foreign Language Press.

Hong-qi.

Hsi, T. H. (1962), *An Analysis of China's National Economy During the Period of Transition* (in Chinese), Peking: Renmin-Chuban-She.

Hua, K. F. (1975), *Let the Whole Party Mobilize for a Vast Effort to Develop Agriculture and Build Tachai-type Counties throughout the Country,* Peking: Foreign Language Press.

Kwangming Daily.

Lenin, V.I. (1917), *The State and Revolution: The Marxist Teaching in the State and the Tasks of the Proletariat in the Revolution,* Peking: Foreign Language Press, 1973.

———. (1918), *The Immediate Tasks of the Soviet Government,* Moscow: Progress Publishers, 1970.

———. (1919), *Economics and Politics in the Era of the Dictatorship of the Proletariat,* Peking: Foreign Language Press, 1975.

———. (1920), *Left-wing Communism, An Infantile Disorder,* Peking: Foreign Language Press, 1975.

Mao, Tsetung (1933), "How to Differentiate the Classes in the Rural Areas," in *Selected Works of Mao Tsetung,* Vol. I pp. 137–139, Peking: Foreign Language Press, 1967.

———. (1940), "On New Democracy," *ibid.,* Vol. II, pp. 339–384.

———. (1942), "Talks at the Yenan Forum on Literature and Art," *ibid.,* Vol. III, pp. 69–98.

———. (1949), "On the People's Democratic Dictatorship: in Commemoration of the Twenty-eighth Anniversary of the Communist Party of China," *ibid.*, Vo. IV, pp. 411–424.

———. (1955), *On the Question of Agricultural Cooperation,* Peking: Foreign Language Press.

———. (ed.) (1956), *Socialist Upsurge in China's Countryside,* Peking: Foreign Language Press.

———. (1957), "On the Correct Handling of Contradictions among the People," in Mao Tsetung, (1968), *Four Essays on Philosophy,* Peking: Foreign Language Press.

———. (1974), *Miscellany of Mao Tsetung Thought, 1949–1968,* Hong Kong: Joint Publication Research, Science.

Marx, K. (1875), *Critique of the Gotha Programme,* Peking: Foreign Language Press, 1972.

Marx, K. and Engels, F. (1848), *Manifesto of the Communist Party,* Peking: Foreign Language Press.

Ng, G. B. (1976a), "China's Road to Development, Equality and Full Employment," *Background Paper for World Employment Conference,* International Labor Office, Geneva, unpublished.

———. (1976b), "Rural Inequalities and the Commune System in China," *Working Paper, Rural Employment Policy Research Program,* International Labor Office, Geneva.

Peking Review.

People's Daily.

People's Daily Editorial (1976), "The Great Cultural Revolution will Shine Forever—in Commemoration of the Tenth Anniversary of the May 16, 1966 'Circular' of the Central Committee of the Communist Party of China," *Peking Review,* No. 21.

Richman, B. (1969), *Industrial Society in Communist China,* New York: Random House.

Robinson, J. (1969), *The Cultural Revolution in China,* Pelican Books.

———. (1975), *Economic Management in China,* London: Anglo-Chinese Educational Institute.

Schram, S. (ed.) (1974), *Mao Tsetung Unrehearsed, Talks and Letters: 1956–1971* (translated by Chinnery, John and Tieyun), Penguin Books.

Soo, H. (1976), *The Socialist Road of China's Agriculture* (in Chinese), Peking: Renmin-Chuban-She.

Ten Great Years: Statistics of the Economic and Cultural Achievements of the People's Republic of China, Peking, Introduction by Mah Feng-hwa, Occasional Paper No. 5, Program in East Asian Studies, Western Washington State College.

Wheelwright E. L. and McFarlane, B. (1970), *The Chinese Road to Socialism,* a Pelican book.

Yan Jung-kuo (1974), "Confucius—A Thinker who Stubbornly supports the Slave System," in *Selected Articles of Criticizing Lim Piao and Confucius,* Peking: Foreign Language Press.

Yao, W. Y. (1975), *On the Social Basis of the Lin Piao Anti-Party Clique,* Peking: Foreign Language Press.